COMING HOME TO THE POND

DAVID GARRED

cover design & illustration by daphne dain

BRANTA BOOKS

First Printing June, 2001
Second Printing August, 2001

**NATIONAL LIBRARY OF CANADA
CATALOGUING IN PUBLICATION DATA**

Garred, David, 1929-
   Coming home to the pond

ISBN 0-9688412-0-1

   **1. Canada goose. 2. Garred, David, 1929- --Journeys.
I. Title.**

G465.G37 2001   598.4'178   C2001-900130-4

Printed and bound in Canada by DocuLink International

BRANTA BOOKS
Box 312, 300 Earl Grey Drive
Kanata, Ontario
CANADA, K2T 1C1

613 599 8313
joydavid@istar.ca

For Joyce who, from the
moment she entered my life,
filled it with love, laughter
and compassion.

All in good time
Shall these things come to me
Let's venture out
That we may do and see
Just for ourselves
From hills that we shall climb
What pastures far
May yield, all in good time.

Table of Contents

St. John's Anglican Church, Parish of March.

Chapter One

Coming home to the Pond

"I have some good news and I have some bad news." With these words Dr. Finkelstein certainly caught my attention. Two weeks earlier, I had visited him for the first time. It took only a brief examination before he quickly cut out a dime sized mole on my temple. "The bad news is that the mole was melanoma cancer. The good news is that it was a superficial melanoma 0.50mm in depth. I can say with a high degree of confidence that there is a 99% probability that you will still be around in five years. However you must now set a time with a plastic surgeon to cut out the surrounding skin tissue as early as possible."

He had already tentatively booked me with the surgeon for the following Monday at the Cancer Clinic of the Ottawa Civic Hospital and obviously I was available.

I took the news at face value, calmly. I was more concerned with how my dear wife Joyce would react to this development. What was going on inside her I will really never know. She took it very objectively and immediately reminded me of the dermatologist's positive outlook which she too adopted.

The Civic Hospital is a long established place of healing, renowned for its Heart Institute and other specialties of excellence.

I didn't particularly like the prospect of being a patient at the cancer clinic, and within myself I was somewhat apprehensive as we entered. There is a large waiting room for relatives and patients. New patients undergo the formalities associated with establishing their condition both physical and mental at the time of entry.

Many personal questions are raised, with great emphasis placed on where and to whom the patient can look for physical and moral support. Joyce insisted on being with me throughout all of this.

The plastic surgeon was very good and the procedure took about 30 to 40 minutes. Joyce met me at the reception area where professional and volunteer staff had been most helpful.

As we left, I looked around. There were several people emotionally distressed, whose loved ones had a much more severe problem than mine. It was a wake up call.

The following day the discolouration caused by the trauma of the surgery made me look like a racoon. For the first time, I began to have doubts. I have been blessed with good health all my life — but melanoma — this was a problem bigger than any I had ever faced up to.

I went to my church, St. John's Anglican, where I had been warden to the rector David Clunie for two years. I had come to look upon him as both a friend and a spiritual leader. Together we prayed that this "obstacle" would be overcome. Throughout all of this Joyce was a source of enormous encouragement. But I had nevertheless had a wake up call, and I vowed to do something about it.

My son and daughter are both happily married and between them I now had three grandchildren, each healthy and smart as a whip.

Joyce and I are not wealthy but we are comfortable and have everything we could possibly need to live well.

In Joyce's words said to me on more than one occasion, "We are truly blessed."

The one thing that we had promised ourselves long ago was to use our retirement to travel, and this is what we decided to do.

Early in 1999 we embarked on a year of adventures together travelling to some fabulous countries and exotic places that I, at least, had only read of. That is what this story is about.

When we first began to think about taking a major trip, we debated whether or not it would be better to have firm reservations for hotels. Some friends with whom we talked about this scoffed at the need to reserve, citing the advantages and freedom offered when each day is played by ear.

I was reminded of an incident which happened to a good friend of mine a few years ago, during a period when the company we both worked for had undergone an expansion in capacity and was investigating areas of the market which might be a logical home for it.

The product was liner board used in producing corrugated containers and other industrial applications such as automatic wrapping of newsprint. A sizable market existed for newswrap, but the nature of the industry is such that the mills are where the trees are, and for the most part, are found in remote locations, particularly in eastern Canada, and not all that easy to get at in the case of the island of Newfoundland.

Nevertheless an interesting market existed there and it was decided that we would go after it.

My friend was managing sales of this product at that time and so he called in the fellow who covered the newsprint industry and suggested that a trip to Newfoundland was in order. He pointed out that there was excellent air service into the two principal centres where newsprint was being produced and the trip could be completed in three days. Unfortunately the recipient of the news was aghast at this proposal. He had a hopeless fear of flying. Instead he offered an alternative. He would be willing to drive it — even to the extent of travelling on weekends — as long as he didn't have to fly.

Reluctantly, my friend agreed.

Now getting into Newfoundland under any circumstances including flying can be a bit haphazard because of the weather. Just off the east coast, the cold Labrador current passes close to the warm gulf stream. This can sometimes create weather systems which seem to blanket the area on the east with clouds that rise up almost endlessly above the Avalon Peninsula.

Driving may offer a higher level of certainty but from Montreal it involved 1100 miles to Sydney, Nova Scotia, putting the car on the ocean-going ferry from Sydney across the Gulf of St. Lawrence to Port aux Basques Harbour in Newfoundland, and then getting back on the Trans Canada highway to Cornerbrook and Grand Falls a further 300 miles, the better part of four days. This must then be repeated for the home journey. Allowing a day in each of the two cities being visited, the proposed surface route would therefore take about ten days. One could readily understand the reluctance of my friend to agree readily, considering the more efficient alternative.

Nevertheless he did, out of sympathy for the other fellow's fear of flying. And then he sat back and waited, and waited.

Finally the fellow returned to the office, and my friend, eagerly anticipating several thousand tons of new business, greeted him asking, "How did you make out?" The weary traveller looked at him sheepishly and replied, "He wasn't in."

Needless to say we made firm reservations.

Although we had travelled numerous times to the southern United States mainly to Florida, but also to the Carolinas, the strength of the US dollar against all currency including Canadian was such that we found ourselves looking at other alternatives. We seriously considered Portugal, the Algarve in particular. Then we came across an interesting advertisement on the travel page, which described some very intriguing destinations in the south of France at surprisingly reasonable prices.

We decided to investigate. What we discovered was that we could spend a month on the Côte D'Azur in February or March for as little as 5400F each including air fare. Exotic locations like Menton, Villefranche, Cannes and Cap Esterel, all within first class resort compounds with spectacular locations and views.

The temperature in March would not equal the warmth of Florida but 60 - 70 degrees F. is a far cry from 10 or 20 degrees below freezing which we could expect in Ottawa at that time. The ozone depletion problem had pretty well ruled out sunbathing. Moreover, there was infinitely more to see and do in the south of France than Florida could ever offer.

So we jumped at it. We both spoke acceptable French. We were keenly interested in history and antiquities and being in the land of the French impressionists wasn't exactly a deterrent!

Initially we tried to book one half of the month at Aix-en-Provence but this was oversold early. We firmed up with two weeks at Cannes and the second two weeks at Cap Esterel near St-Raphael.

Further investigation indicated that few long term vacationers rent a car, they buy them! Then sell them back to the auto company on the way out and in so doing save about one-third of rental costs.

We would be spending one month in time share condominiums, so this also meant doing most of our own cooking. This was shaping up as a bit of an adventure!

In preparation for our month in Provence Joyce took great pains to collect healthy appetizing recipes which she carefully packed in her suitcase. Wanting to conform to true Provençal cuisine she assembled small pouches of every conceivable spice that would enable her to serve up these fabulous dishes so that we could really feel that we belonged. There was garlic and ginger, cumin, tarragon, thyme, curry, cinnamon, basil, oregano, black pepper and bay leaf — enough to make your mouth water.

Now, cooking does not come naturally to Joyce, she has to work at it in a very determined way.

She has become quite proficient at baking muffins and prides herself in the fact that they are probably the healthiest that can be made.

Every cooking episode starts about three days ahead of time. The cook book is placed in a counter stand, open at the critical page, as a reminder to her of the task ahead. Finally the day arrives and every conceivable bowl, pot, and mixing dish is brought into play as she converges all weaponry. At last the muffins are ready and they are proudly placed on a cooling rack for all to see.

The used cooking vessels are placed for me to see (and to do something about).

Her approach to baking muffins was not always this professional. Early in her cooking career she bought a commercial muffin mix and began attacking the job. From the safety of the living room I could hear the rattle of talented hands mixing up a storm. Suddenly everything was silent and she emerged from the kitchen with muffin mix up to her elbows. "You're never going to believe this," she said. "The directions on the box said mix by hand and I did."

At one time we owned a delightful vacation home in Quechee, Vermont. Because we were starting from scratch, Joyce saw this as an opportunity to equip the kitchen with the very latest in gadgets, as an incentive to raise the level of her "cuisine" ability.

Some of it got used, but our standard fare because of time constraints was usually a broiled chicken breast along with a baked potato and vegetable done in the microwave. Eventually we sold the property to a lovely couple from Rhode Island. The lady was so impressed by all the kitchen equipment that Joyce's name became almost legendary in Vermont cooking circles.

Coming back to the Provençal recipes. Although the kitchen was tiny, it did afford an opportunity to experiment with the Provençal cuisine. However one tends to forget how good and how cheap French wines are (and their bread). By the time we got into the bread and wine, the recipes became second priority. We did use the thyme in salads and the cinnamon in warm milk but most of the spices made it home on the return flight.

During the days of our courtship she really pulled out all the stops. On one occasion she went to great lengths to prepare Hungarian goulash for me. The only trouble was that in her innocence she put in an entire garlic when the recipe called for a bud. It was ghastly! Nevertheless I put on a brave front and told her it was great. A few years later when we had married, we got into some silly argument over a meaningless issue and I blurted out — "Besides I hate your Hungarian goulash!" It was such a non sequitur that she burst into laughter and that was the end of the argument.

During the same courtship period she served up a delicious home made spaghetti and meat sauce. About two hours later I was doubled over with stomach cramps. "What is it," she asked with much concern. "It's nothing," I replied, "spaghetti always affects me this way," lying gallantly! I had to go home early because of the cramps. Then about midnight she developed them herself. Remembering that she had made the sauce in advance and then stored it overnight in the aluminum pan she had made it in, she thought she had poisoned me. I survived and continue to survive! I've probably become immune.

During the winter we play indoor tennis at West Ottawa Tennis Club which has six excellent clay courts under a bubble. At the end of each season they mix everybody up into teams and we have a round robin based on the Olympics. Last year we played for Mexico. Everyone must contribute a dish to a pot luck buffet.

"What can we possibly make that is Mexican?" Joyce asked. "Just leave it to me," I said, "I'll make a superb Mexican salad," something I had never done before.

My exposure to Mexican food had been limited to the usual fast food varieties plus a brief encounter with a jalapenos pepper on an Iberian flight from Mexico City to Montreal.

I bought the usual varieties of lettuce, topped them up with mustard leaves and added a beautiful selection of peppers of every kind and shape (none of which I tasted beforehand). There were red, yellow, orange and green ones about the size of a large crabapple. The whole thing was dressed up with a souped up vinaigrette to which I added Tabasco sauce and chili peppers.

When the buffet was laid out I stood back waiting for the compliments. The reaction was mixed. When my turn in the buffet came I chose a selection of the mustard leaves and a couple of the colourful peppers. I took one aggressive bite of one of the colourful peppers and was on fire. I could hardly speak. I ran over to the bar and asked for a cold beer which seemed to take ages in coming. But that didn't quench the fire. However, with more beer, it began to ease off.

Later a woman was entering the buffet line. She said "hello!" I said "be careful of that Mexican salad it's extremely hot. I nearly blew my head off with one of those cute little peppers."

"What kind of inconsiderate person would bring a salad like that to a buffet?" She asked incredulously. I just shook my head. "Some swine I suppose."

Chapter Two

France - Cannes

We were due to leave for France on March 5th. The weeks leading up to this date had thrown terrible weather at us, right up until the day before our flight. For a brief 48 hour period the heavens opened up and the skies cleared. Our flight on Air France left one hour late.

During my working career I often flew to many different destinations in North America and the Caribbean. I cannot remember ever having been jammed into such confined seating as on this Air France 747. Arriving at Charles de Gaulle late, it was nip and tuck whether we would be able to make our connection to Nice. Fortunately it too was late so we managed to connect with minutes to spare.

In contrast with the overseas flight, the Nice flight was on an Airbus which was newer and more comfortable than the 747.

On arrival at Nice we bought and took possession of our Peugeot. It was an automatic sub compact which handled very nicely at speeds of up to 100 km after which it began to labour. We drove the 30 miles down the A-8 and arrived at Cannes.

We were immediately impressed with the location and quality of the overall facility of Cannes Villa Francia, which like all Pierre et Vacances destinations is strategically placed to provide superb views of the Mediterranean. However we had arrived at 2 p.m. and our apartment would not be available until 5 p.m. We therefore had 3 hours to kill so we decided to get some basic groceries.

For an Anglophone even our best efforts at conversing in French can be crossed up by our not always perfect pronunciation. For several years Joyce and I lived in Habitat 67 in Montreal which in itself was a wonderful experience.

Every apartment had a large private terrace with built in flower boxes which require watering from time to time. We were discussing, as we often did in those days, how to spell the French equivalent of watering, *"arroser"*. We decided to ask the doorman. Joyce approached him and asked, "Monsieur, arroser - ça prend un ou deux Rs?" "Ça dépend," he replied. "La grandeur du jardin, aussi le temps, chaque exemple est différent." Joyce had made the question sound like *"heures"* instead of *"Rs"*. We found it funnier than he did.

You can take the game a step further using the word *"voler"* to fly. How many *"Ls"* does it take? If you are thinking *"aile"* you'd probably reply two.

French is a very precise language. Between the endless forms of conjugations and assigning masculine and feminine gender to nouns, pronouns, adjectives and verbs, it is extremely difficult to be precise, and sometimes one can make real bloopers in the process.

Back in the 70s when everyone in the Quebec business world was busy taking French lessons, usually paid for by their respective companies, I was in a total immersion program for a week at a time at my company's nature centre at Harrington, Que.

We had been hard at work at various exercises for about four days. The mind tends to become a bit dazzled when we swing into the various tenses, and such was the case when the course leader threw a question at me that I knew the answer to, but could not spit it out. When he gave the answer to me, I recognized it immediately and meant to say in French, *"Je le sais comme le dos de ma main."* Instead I came out with *"Je le sais comme la derrière de maman."* Something quite different.

Would you buy a used car from this man? This was the caption under a photo of Richard Nixon with a five o'clock shadow in an election campaign in the 60s.

By contrast, you would surely have no problem placing your trust in little children competing for your business with a lemonade stand. Or would you?

There were very few residents of Habitat who had young children. Most were adult singles or empty nesters who wanted to live downtown. There were however 3 or 4 families of little children at Habitat and quite a few dogs.

One of the security guards used to love escorting the tiny kids around the complex on Halloween. Everyone dressed up, even the security guard who wore a black mask. The dog also got into the act with a clown's hat tied to his head. You could hear the squeals of delight and the dog barking excitedly as they made their rounds.

Now these little geezers lived a few floors up from us and occasionally we would bump into them on the elevator. Joyce could always get them going by comparing boo-boos — cuts and scrapes, on their knees and elbows, always letting the kids win the game.

One Saturday we had been shopping and returned in mid-day to find these little entrepreneurs had set up a lemonade stand, ten cents a paper cup full. Naturally we always believed in supporting local businesses so we each ordered a cup. We really didn't want a whole cupful but we got it anyway. Joyce couldn't finish hers, so most of it was still in the cup. She looked around for somewhere to dispose of it, when one of the little tykes said I'll take it for you.

He then proceeded to pour the rest of the partly drunk cupful back into the jug for the next customer.

Would you buy a used car from this man? Probably.

⸻

Early in our marriage, Joyce underwent surgery to correct a problem related to clicking in the mandibular joint. This required her to have her jaw wired for six weeks, which restricted her to a liquid diet for the duration.

If you can imagine the situation, Joyce, a lawyer, was unable to communicate verbally, and it became necessary for her to write all conversations at work.

With me, however, there was no such luck. I was expected to carry on normal conversations with someone who could only grunt through her teeth. At first I was accused of not trying to understand her. This degenerated to receiving notes from her — the sum effect was — that I just didn't understand the King's English.

At the time we lived in Habitat 67 on the 7th and 8th floors which meant that we took the elevator both up and down. My office was a ten minute drive away on Dominion Square so I was able to get home at noon to check on her and help her if necessary.

About the third or fourth day into it she began taking walks to strengthen herself, coming back in time for lunch.

Now Montreal and its environs are notorious for having power failures, and this of course is what fate had in mind for Joyce as she entered the elevator after her walk. She was the sole passenger somewhere between the 3rd and 4th floors when the power went out and with it the lights.

There she was alone in the dark, unable to communicate so she did the only thing she could, she began tapping on the door.

There were several security guards on duty at Habitat, and during the day seldom fewer than three. They swung into action.

"Someone is trapped in the lobby 2 elevator," a resident reported. The security guards ran up to the third and fourth floors. "Who is inside — keep calm." Then they repeated it in French. All they got in return was more tapping and a lot of stifled mumbling. "Who are you?" they yelled again. More tapping and mumbling. *"Qui est là?"* they tried again in French. Joyce could hear them outside and kept on tapping and mumbling. "Aah it's some crazy woman in there," said one guard. "She doesn't even speak French or English," added the other. "Must be a foreigner." So they left.

A half hour later in the pitch black Joyce was near hysteria when the power returned and the elevator continued up.

In the meantime having walked up I had arrived home and not knowing what had been going on with Joyce was enjoying a leisurely lunch when I heard a key in the door. I opened it and Joyce collapsed in my arms sobbing and trying unsuccessfully to tell me what had happened. When I couldn't understand her she threw up her hands in disgust and wrote me a note.

Meanwhile, on our way into Villa Francia we had spotted a good looking boulangerie so we headed back to it. Having got this far *tout en français* I decided to go all out.

We had been warned that food prices were extremely high so upon entering the boulangerie I noticed a posted price of 3.60 under the baguettes. I thought this meant 3 point six francs, so I asked for clarification. The pronunciation of franc is quite guttural and sounds very much like cent. So when she replied *"Non Monsieur, c'est trois francs soixante,"* what I heard was 3 cent soixante or 360 francs.

I was stunned. We had just paid 8F a litre for gas but 360F was beyond belief. I went outside in shock. I spoke to an elderly man on a bicycle who had just bought baguettes and I asked him how the ordinary man in the street could possibly survive at these prices. He shrugged and said I might find it for a bit less down the street.

I told Joyce the bad news. Our holiday was on the verge of being ruined. In any event we needed bottled water so we stopped at a gas station and snapped up a 6 pack of 1.5L at 7F each. (I later discovered I could buy them for 4F each.)

I asked the proprietor about bread prices and told him the story. He laughed and said 360F was indeed a lot to pay for bread, and suggested that I try again. When I did, it cost 3.6F. I bought two loaves.

No bread I have eaten anywhere in North America, or for that matter in other countries we have visited which border the Mediterranean, can equal French bread, particularly baguettes. I don't know whether it is the technique, or the type of flour, but French bread takes the prize both for taste and texture.

In North America there are many pretenders but only in small family bakeries can you come close.

There is such a bakery operating in Ottawa and it has to be the best kept secret in town. It is the Portuguese bakery on Nelson St. just off Rideau. If you hadn't been told about it you'd probably pass it by. They bake a number of delicious specialty breads including baguettes, 9 grain bread, corn bread, and flat olive bread. It is highly personalized and if you happen to pick up a loaf not baked the same day you will be redirected to today's baking. If we are entertaining and need something special, we always drive the 12-13 miles into town to be sure we have the best.

━━━━━━━━━━━━━━━━━━━━━

When we finally took possession, our apartment at Villa Francia was so small you would think it was designed for children. The teacups were like play dishes and held about 2 oz. It was very cold outside during the night, in the upper 30's, and two of our radiators weren't working, so we slept with sweaters on.

The beds at all Pierre et Vacances destinations in the south of France are not the luxurious kind we are used to in North America. They are smaller, quite a bit narrower and often futons, so that sleep is a bit harder to come by, particularly if you are a bit that way by nature.

From an early age Joyce had been a very restless sleeper. Even at age three her mother took her to the family physician to try to find out why. Years later she is still trying to find out why.

Early in our marriage I was curious when I saw the eye mask. Then the ear plugs. A cassette recorder became part of our nightly ritual — with some smooth talking psychologist repeating over and over — "your right arm is heavy, your right arm is heavy."

By the end of six months, I had memorized the psychologist's dialogue, but by then even I was having trouble sleeping. The fact that the tape shut off with a loud click just as you were dozing off didn't help.

Every night she sets the alarm for the following morning. One night she mistakenly set it to go off a half hour after she set it. When it did, she leapt out of bed, threw off the eye mask and disgustedly blurted out, "another rotten night's sleep."

We slept in until 9:30, then later in the morning went to downtown Cannes to the Fourville Market for food. Prices at the market were comparable to Canada. There is a shuttle bus between Villa Francia and downtown Cannes which many of the residents used rather than going through the hassle of driving a car. We took the shuttle and met a couple from Nanaimo, Wally and Aileen Scott. They were leaving in a few days but offered to show us how to get to Géant supermarket the following morning. Géant is a cross between Loblaws and Costco, with a very wide selection of most household needs.

The good news was that quite decent table wines were available at about 18F a bottle. We stocked up on provisions and produce of marvellous quality offered at comparable prices to North America. All fruit and vegetables are vastly superior to those available in North America even those grown in the sun belt of Florida.

When we returned to our apartment I measured it just for fun. The bedroom is 8' x 9'. The living room, dining area, kitchen combined is 9' x 13'. Because of the tight fit it was necessary to manoeuvre around two or three doors to get to the bathroom. And yet, with it all, it would be possible with a lot of organization to sleep 4 people! The French always did like things cosy.

After lunch we settled in to watch TV. CNN in English was nothing but politics. There was a German talk show where everybody was arguing. The Italian network offered a game show in which the grand prize was a toaster. Out of 3 French channels we picked up "Murder She Wrote" in French. Jessica had suddenly developed a very sultry voice!

The next day we set off on our first exploration inland to Grasse, the perfume capital of Provence, and also to Gourdon a unique "village perché" set on top of a cliff that drops 1800 feet down to the Loup Valley. The ride up to Gourdon was one of the hairiest we've ever had. Mountain roads with very little between you and a 7 or 800 foot drop off the edge. We both were nervous wrecks when we reached this tiny mountain village which by that point dropped the whole 1800 feet down to the valley. It was quite spectacular.

The château itself was built about 1610. We bought some Provençal lavender sachets from a shop lady who gave us the name of a really good restaurant, reasonable priced, in Nice.

We had brought our lunch which we ate sitting at the edge of the cliff at Gourdon, and then continued on to Grasse, where we went on a tour of the original Fragonard factory and museum.

It takes an average of 1 tonne of flower petals to yield 1 litre of perfume oil. They employ a distillation process much like alcohol production. The distillation kettles are copper and very colourful. We saw several discarded distillation kettles in junkyards on the road. They would make an interesting display properly cleaned up.

En route back to Villa Francia we stopped off at Géant to replenish our supplies.

We spent one half hour in a panic looking for Joyce's wallet which turned up in her purse.

Then another half hour trying to find her luggage key which turned up in her money belt!

We both always choose good hiding places.

At supper we ate lots of fresh fruit, especially oranges, which came from Spain or Malta. They were out of this world! We also noticed a difference in the quality of bran flakes which are called *"pétales"*. They were better than we get at home, so they must have altered the formula.

The following day our destinations were Vence and St-Paul-de-Vence. We were of course in what was at one time a Roman province. Vence developed around the old walled town which was built on the foundations of the Roman town of Vintium. There are two cornerstones in the cathedral dating from 240 A.D. There is a very nice Chagall mosaic in the chapel.

We then moved on to St-Paul-de-Vence which can be seen from the A-8. It is a spectacular old walled "village perché" dating back before the 13th century. It is in wonderful condition, but the old homes inside are now pretty well all stores and restaurants, catering to tourists. We visited the cathedral which has a Tintoretto. Then the old graveyard where we saw the grave of Marc Chagall. There is a museum which has photos of famous visitors including Harry Truman, King Hussein, and numerous other major celebrities.

Just outside the main gate is the *"Colombe d'Or"* a world famous auberge and 4 star restaurant where dinner with wine starts at 400F per person, and where Simone Signoret and Yves Montand honeymooned. There were several long black limousines and police waiting outside, so somebody important was having lunch. I took Joyce's photo just outside the Colombe D'Or gate, looking like she didn't belong there, with her packsack and running shoes.

Everywhere you travel, the road signs which really mean straight ahead, point left or right. Also the autoroute signs which start out saying A-8 suddenly start showing a symbol sign of a boulevard with two lanes and a divider. One innovation on French streets is their stoplights. If you happen to advance too far so that the main lights are out of view overhead, they have mini lights aimed at you from the side which help.

Well I guess I have evened things out. I lost my key to the apartment. We searched everywhere all day yesterday to no avail. But sitting in the car in the sunshine at the dock at Antibes I noticed a glitter down the side of the seat "et voilà - le clef!" It had fallen out of my pocket while I was driving.

Antibes started as a Greek trading post, then a Roman settlement. Later a church was established there. It really came into prominence when the Château Grimaldi was erected there.

Saint-Paul-de-Vence

Fort Carré, Antibes
Napoleon imprisoned 1794

Napoleon added to its fame when he returned from Elba in 1815 and began his famous march north along what is called the Route Napoleon.

The fort where he stayed is close to the parking lot and the basin where the million dollar yachts are moored. We walked about a half mile up to the fort only to find a sign saying closed Thursdays. We returned to the car a bit discouraged and had lunch.

Joyce noticed two men talking beside a small bus. She asked them how we could find the Château Grimaldi and the Église Immaculée Conception. The men said, "just park your car here and we'll take you there for nothing and also pick you up and bring you back. We run every 15 minutes."

We got to see the château and a nice collection of Picasso. He had lived there in 1946.

The church did not open until 3 p.m. and when we got there we found ourselves participating in a funeral. The hearse arrived with a two level compartment. The casket in the lower and flowers in the upper. Sort of riding in an old time train with upper and lower berths.

We hadn't yet got inside the church but the tears of grief of the widow proved too much and we decided to just slip away quietly. As we did a stray dog wandered in on the event and went up to a large display of floral tributes near the door. After a lot of sniffing, he decided not to make a contribution, much to our relief but not his!

The jitney got us back to the car safely and we called it a day.

On the 12th we left at 8:45 to link up with the A-8 to Monaco. It was another gorgeous day, about 70 degrees F. The closer you get to the Italian frontier the more mountainous the terrain becomes. Grenoble is only 150 miles away. There are numerous tunnels carved through the mountains many of which are over a half mile in length. Tunnels do not seem to deter the maniacs behind the wheels. We had to maintain 120km per hour just to stay even. We were being passed by cars doing 140 - 160 km per hour!

When we broke through the mountains to the coastal road we were still up at about 1500 feet as we began our descent into Monaco. There were palatial high rises everywhere, literally carved into the mountains.

At the base, you pass the casino and turn towards the palace, the cathedral and Museum of Oceanography. To access them there is a huge multi-story underground parking facility which brings you to the terrace level where the museum is located. Further up about half a mile you come to the cathedral and palace. On the way you pass beautiful botanical gardens which overlook a cliff and a drop of 3-400 feet to an exclusive harbour area, occupied by some very expensive yachts.

Wealth is evident everywhere. The entire area seems manicured and spotless. They pay for it all with gambling profits. There are lots of German tourists. We walked around the palace and gardens, bought a few souvenirs and then headed out along the coastal road. It is a spectacular drive. Houses perched so precariously and high, that you wonder how they were ever constructed up there.

A few miles west we came upon one of the most pleasant surprises of our holiday. The village perché of Eze. Set on an isolated rock mountain up 1700 feet from the sea, and between the coastal road and the sea, it is magnificent.

Not too far away to the west is another Pierre et Vacances location, Villafranche.

We climbed up to the summit, probably 300 feet above the road. It is absolutely pristine. Every tiny lane is decorated with pebble mosaic sidewalks in floral and geometric designs. Near the top is a hotel and terrace bar overlooking the sea. Rooms go for about $500 US a night. We met a young man there from Montreal who was applying for a job. He was on his second interview.

At the very top there are the ruins of an old château and a tropical garden which wasn't in bloom while we were there. We soaked in the marvellous view, got dizzy looking down and then headed back to the parking lot. Joyce went to the ladies room at the base. There was an attendant dressed in a cashmere sweater. Outdone again!

We continued on, absorbing all the beauty of this special part of the world.

Earlier this week when in St-Paul-de-Vence we wanted to see the highly regarded museum *"Fondation Maeght"*, but couldn't find it. So we set out today to do so.

As is often the case, between the roundabouts and grand prix drivers we ended up lost and found ourselves in Mougins. This was a lucky break because it is one of the loveliest areas in Provence. It also has a 15th century fortified inner town which is beautiful. Set on a small hill it has many of the best restaurants in the area. Picasso lived here for the last 15 years of his life and dozens of celebrities have homes there.

In the centre of the old town is the Église St-Jacques-le-Majeure. When we entered this tiny church, the organist was practising on a huge pipe organ. It was a real treat to sit and listen to fabulous music for 15 or 20 minutes.

Afterward we walked through the narrow lanes of the old village and bought almond croissants at a boulangerie which were delicious. So getting lost sometimes has its benefits.

In the course of our travels we found ourselves lost many times, particularly as we toured the back roads among the hills. If you want to be sure of where you are going, it is critical to know where you are, and there are lessons to be learned from each experience.

When I was new to the paper industry, my boss thought it appropriate for me to join a trade association known as the Printing House Craftsmen. This organization met once a month in the Sheraton Mount Royal Hotel and was open not only to those directly working in the printing trade, but also to associated industries such as paper mills, ink manufacturers, and those who supplied printing presses, from the simple platen variety to highly sophisticated multi colour machines designed for high production plants.

On the evening that I was to be inducted, my boss at the time apologized for his inability to attend, due to a conflicting prior commitment. I approached a co-worker who had belonged to the association for several years and suggested that we go over together. Unfortunately he also had a prior commitment. However he told me that meetings were always held in the Champlain Room of the hotel at 6:30 p.m. and to just go by myself. He said that I'd probably see people I knew there, with whom I could sit at dinner.

I confidently sauntered into the Champlain Room which was already filled with men socializing at a cocktail party prior to dinner. I introduced myself and my Company, picked up a drink and thought there were a surprising number of people related to equipment, but I rationalized that this was part of the business.

I sat down at a table for eight and was a bit puzzled by the amount of technical conversation that passed back and forth around the table. When a topic came up that I knew nothing about, I kept silent. When someone asked for my opinion, I simply said I agreed with the last person, but I was becoming a bit uneasy.

The hotel served up an excellent roast beef dinner and one of the people at my table bought wine for all of us. It was very pleasant.

When the time came for introduction of the guest speaker he turned out to be from Chrysler Corporation speaking on the new high torque engine. I began to panic and turned to my neighbour at the table and asked him what meeting this was. "Why this is the society of automotive engineers," he replied.

At this point I decided that discretion was the better part of valour, and I excused myself.

I had enjoyed several drinks, a great meal and highly sophisticated conversations simply by saying nothing, or agreeing with everything and all the time without knowing where I was!

As it turned out, for that evening only, the printers had been reassigned to another room in the hotel.

It does pay to know not only where you are going, but also where you are!

We did not have too much trouble finding the Musée Fondation Maeght the second time around. In fact we arrived well ahead of time. The property is large and tucked into a well maintained natural setting in a forested area near St-Paul-de-Vence.

The museum gets very high marks for the quality and importance of the works exhibited, but it is relatively small when compared with the monumental museums found in Paris.

We saw many works by Miro, an important Chagall and two very large Riopelles. There were dozens of large contemporary sculptures set among mature pines. A number of classes of schoolchildren were being led through the museum in English. We watched and listened as their leader discussed a number of paintings. We wanted to hear her opinion on a large Riopelle. She gave it muted praise. One painting which we found to be completely lopsided, she praised for balance! As is the case back home, there were many modern or contemporary works that we had difficulty identifying with. Nevertheless it is a wonderful museum, well worth seeking out.

The weather and sunshine continued to be marvellous. It was about 70 degrees F. today, very pleasant to be out among the pines looking at great works of art.

We had noticed that when there is an east wind from industrial Italy 150 - 200 miles away, there is a fairly high level of atmospheric pollution. That plus the fact that every second person had a stinking cigarette in his or her hand.

The women we saw, even at fairly mundane pastimes, put far more importance on dressing up than we do in North America. Many of them seen during the day look like they might be headed for the symphony. High heels always, and scarves as an accessory, which come in all price ranges and can even be bought at newsstands.

On Sunday we headed up into the foothills to St-Cézaire-sur-Siagne, a pretty village set on a hill overlooking the Siagne River which is really more of a mountain stream. The town contains a 13th century "Chapelle du Cimetière" which contains a Roman tomb found nearby. There is a great lookout overlooking the Siagne Valley below.

We met a very nice French couple and took each others' pictures. Then we all went to explore the grotto. The stalactites have a very high iron content and can be played like a xylophone.

The Ides! We had been putting off doing Nice because it is so large and commercial. We found it to be dirty and passé. It was probably something special 100 years ago. The old inner city was a major disappointment reminding me of the souks in Morocco.

The one positive thing we saw was the Matisse Museum, which although small, is excellent — even if you need a tour guide to find it.

The little villages in unique locations are far more fun and worth seeking out.

We did find the Provençal Restaurant recommended to us by the lady in Gourdon. We found it average in quality.

By comparison we found Cannes a much more interesting city and it appears to be generally more prosperous. Nice is just too big and is the 5th largest city in France.

We headed home on the A-8 which is the most expensive toll road in France and hits you for 15F a pop for a fairly short run.

The following day we took it easy, did some shopping and got our first roll of film developed. The pictures turned out fine but the cost for 24-35mm prints was excessive.

Later in the day we drove to downtown Cannes to do some shopping on Rue Antibes, which has the classy stores in Cannes. While in a fairly large lady's shop I noticed alarms ringing. When we walked out the door, a clerk came after us and asked us to return to the store, saying, "I'm not accusing you of anything." Nevertheless she asked us to walk through the electronic sensors, which we did, and of course they were silent. The woman apologised.

I suppose because we were casually dressed, Joyce in jeans and carrying a packsack and me in my sloppy sun hat and wearing running shoes, we looked out of place. Unless you are dressed to kill you are an exception.

————————————————

If clothes make the man then the corollary must also be true.

Several years ago I had gone off on a spur of the moment one week holiday to Nassau. It was the week before Christmas and you could still get a pretty good deal before the high season began.

I was forty six at the time and in pretty good shape but I had decided that for that week I would get away from the dress code that the business world of that time demanded, and go casual.

I had been there for 3 or 4 days when the spirit moved me to walk into town — a distance of about two miles. I was wearing blue jeans, running shoes and a grey turtleneck sweater. I had also been sunbathing all summer long so I had a tan to match the attire.

The Christmas spirit was evident throughout the commercial area. There were decorations in the windows, carols being piped over an outdoor sound system and I was feeling pretty loose.

About one hundred yards ahead I spotted an elderly Bahamian lady all dressed up in her Salvation Army uniform, vigorously ringing the bell and trying to get passers-by focused on the pot hanging from the usual tripod.

I could see her looking at me while I was still some distance from her and concluded that I wasn't going to get past her without putting some folding money in the pot.

"Merry Christmas to you Sir," she greeted me with enthusiasm, "we'd like to invite you to dinner."

I smiled back and thanked her advising that I already had arranged for dinner. I doubled my intended donation. But the next day I put on a clean shirt!

We continued along Antibes Street. A few blocks along I noticed several piles of dog poop, one of which had been stepped on. Sure enough it was me. I then spent the next half hour stepping in puddles, which aroused the curiosity of the natives. This is one of the most disconcerting negatives about France. There is no poop and scoop law nor does anyone have the slightest concern about where and how often their dogs — often large — deposit their compliments. It has become a problem of such proportions that dog owners are now subject to very expensive fines for infractions by their dogs.

When we got back to Villa Francia a woman about 40 and two units up from us was sunning herself. This was the first instance of bare chested sunning that we saw, but it is very common here in high season.

Having toured the better shops, Joyce had decided that the bright floral designs of Provençal fabrics belonged in our kitchen at home. So I could see that we would be spending time in fabric shops.

St. Patrick's Day isn't a big thing in France. The weather forecast indicated thunderstorms to the east and fair weather to the west. So we decided to head down the coast to St-Raphael and Fréjus close to where our next destination is at Cap Esterel.

We took the shore road called *"La Corniche d'Or"* which was spectacular. It reminded me of the rocky coast of Maine except that all of the rocks and mountains are a rusty orange colour. The wind was up so that the breakers were a beautiful creamy white. We stopped several times along the route and soaked it in.

On our way to St-Raphael we passed the Cap Esterel facility and went in to see if we could ensure that we got a better apartment than the one at Cannes. It is enormous. 1450 units, swimming pool, tennis courts, 9 holes of golf and miles of hiking trails. It would probably be a bit cooler as they get both a heavy breeze off the sea as well as the *"mistral"* winds which originate in Siberia.

The area is very upscale, prosperous and dotted with luxurious villas along the coast, much like the big shore homes at Kennebunk.

The city of St-Raphael is lovely. The harbour is stacked elbow to elbow with expensive yachts. The streets are clean and well maintained.

We ate lunch on a park bench in front of the harbour. Then we went into the Église Notre Dame which is on the harbour, and which has some very interesting stations of the cross done in pottery.

There is also a museum of archeology which we would hit next time. We then drove into Fréjus, the town adjoining St. Raphael. It is one of the oldest Roman settlements (49 B.C.). It has many roman structures still intact including the ruins of a massive aqueduct which extends for 25 kilometres.

The Cathédrale St-Léonce et Clôitre is also located there. The baptistry dates back to the 4th century, and the cathedral itself from the 12th century.

As usual, everything closed up for two and a half hours at lunch, so we would have to return to really see it.

We headed back on the Corniche d'Or passing the huge Cross of Lorraine Monument dedicated to the Free French resistance. The weather had steadily improved so on our return we stopped just outside of Cannes at Napouli, a château restored by Henry Clews, an American artist and his wife. It sits right at water's edge in a small cove. There are many interesting objets d'art inside which were collected by Clews.

At that point I began to feel squeamish. By the time we got home I had a fever of 101 degrees and a queezy tummy. Nurse Joyce sprang into action and by morning it was gone. I would have to watch what I ate.

Today is Sarah's birthday, 2 years old. I hope she had a wonderful day.

We had been cleaning up prior to our departure on Saturday. I was taking it easy. Joyce was doing a laundry. While there she met a very nice couple from Niagara on the Lake, Marg and Cliff Smyth. They invited us for drinks the following night. While I was trying to rest in the apartment, painters were outside scraping and sanding the railing upstairs. As I didn't get much rest, I read up on places we hoped to see over the next two weeks, Aix, Arles, Nîmes, Avignon, Pont de Gard, Orange, all of which date B.C., some as early as 5-600 B.C.! The Roman engineering was phenomenal but there was an ample amount of labour with no fringe benefits!

As we were winding down the first half of our tour of Provence, I reflected on some things which are a must. Peanut butter is an invaluable item, easy to bring, easy to store and marvellous on French baguettes. Cans of tuna and salmon are valuable if you have the space. Comparable costs for these are 2 -3 times what we pay back home. This also seems to be true of fresh fish.

About 11 a.m. it warmed up to about 60 degrees F. There had been a mistral overnight. We set out on a walk and got as far as the west end of Cannes *"Croisette"*, the main part of town. We found a post office just in time at 5 minutes to 12. They, like everyone else, close down tight for 2 hours of lunch. The clerk pointed out that if we bought a pack of 10 prestamped envelopes we would save about 5%. In addition, a postcard placed inside would be treated as first class mail and be delivered faster than a simple postcard.

Everywhere we have wandered, we have been impressed by the quality and number of monuments to French patriots who have died for France in many wars. It is very similar to the way the Americans honour their dead and veterans. In each of the many towns we have visited there is always a well maintained cenotaph, sometimes listing only 3 or 4 who have died in the service of France. The Cross of Lorraine on the Corniche d'Or is a great example.

Many towns have streets named after the day of liberation, May 8, 1945. There were many courageous men and women who worked under extreme risk in *"la résistance"* — many who paid the ultimate price. It is ironic that some Canadians look upon Americans as flag waving nationalists. Perhaps they might consider them differently if they could see that countries of Europe such as France display patriotism in much the same way.

Walking back from the post office we bumped into Cliff and Margaret Smyth and continued on up Wester Wymess Road to Villa Francia with them. They had gone shopping in the opposite direction. The climb up the hill made us both perspire and we had to change our shirts when we got back.

It had warmed up to about 65 degrees F. and it was very pleasant sitting in our private garden as I wrote this.

Every few minutes a cheer rose up from just over the hill in front of us. There was a group playing *boules* on a gravel court — a favourite Provençal pastime. A tiny green ball seemed to be the object of their affection. The players use a silver ball about the size of a baseball which they use to try to hit or get close to the green ball. They then judge who is closest. The trouble was, all the balls look the same. Whose is whose! Meanwhile the adoring girlfriends who had brought food and wine for their heroes, smiled approvingly as each ball was thrown. It was a bit like trying to figure out cricket.

At 5 p.m. we were expected at the Smyth's for drinks. Meanwhile we were soaking up the warm sun (with sweaters on).

The painters had now finished working on the unit over us and were now 2 -3 units to the left painting the railings for the gal who sunbathes. For some reason they were taking longer on that unit!

The layout of Villa Francia consists of about 20 blocks of 8 or 10 units both up and down. Some are strategically placed to afford an unobstructed view of the town below and the sea. Within view of our garden is a unit which also appears to have a roof garden. It would already have a great view from the lower floors. If one had managed to book one of the better located units of which I'd estimate two-thirds are, it would be fabulous. As it is we could just make out the sea behind the large trees in front of us. The key seems to be to book a 2 bedroom unit which vastly improves the chances of a great location. This at an additional cost of 1200F a month — well worth it.

The Smyth's apartment was such a unit. Everything was larger and the view was spectacular. The so-called second bedroom was a joke. It was nothing more than a big cupboard with bunk beds and a window. But if that is not a major consideration it is a better deal to go for a 2 bedroom unit.

We spent a very pleasant time with the Smyths. They have seen much of the same country that we have, except that they have done it by train or by bus, both of which provide excellent services. We drank more wine than I intended and Margaret served up "tapenade" a conserve of ripe or green olive combined with anchovies, garlic, and capers. It was delicious.

They pointed out some differences in train travel. Even though you have bought a ticket you must always have it validated before entering a train. Buses do not have toilets. Places which they had visited to date and recommended included Lourmarin, Luberon, Cap Ferrat, Keriolis, le Pont Julien, Sospel.

We exchanged phone numbers and looked forward to seeing each other again.

Moving day! We were supposed to leave the place as we found it. Instead we left it better than we found it.

On checking out we discovered that we had been paying 120f a week for underground parking. However if Villa Francia has advantages one of them is security. It is difficult to enter the property if you don't have access codes to the main doors. I suppose a smart cat burglar could wait till someone opened the garage doors and then sneak in. However I did notice one of the maintenance men walking a very large Alsatian dog who probably works nights.

Having checked out we now had seven and a half hours to kill before we could check in at Cap Esterel. Compounding the problem was the fact that the car was loaded to the gills, so even if we stopped to see something, one of us would have to remain with the car. This following the cardinal rule of never leaving anything that can be seen in the car for fear of theft.

So when we got to Fréjus about 11 a.m. Saturday the Cathédrale St-Léonce was open until 12 noon. Then closed till 4 p.m. We parked in the no charge "clôitre" parking area about 2 blocks from the church. I was assigned the task of casing the joint briefly then returning to the car which Joyce was minding. I completed my task in 15 minutes returning to find Joyce sunning in the parking lot.

I repeated what she needed to know and then sat back and waited. About 12:15 old smiley came sauntering around the corner, bag in hand. She had managed to work in some shopping even as she toured the historic cathedral. She had bought a Provençal design table cloth.

I assumed this task was now complete but she then informed me that it was 100% cotton and that she would also now need Polyester cotton to prevent wrinkling. So the search continues.

We then drove around Fréjus trying to find a brasserie with a parking space near it. Fat chance. We ended-up right on the waterfront in St. Raphael where we had eaten lunch a few days earlier. We grabbed a parking spot. Joyce minded the car and its cargo and I set out to find a brasserie which would make two baguette sandwiches to go.

Unfortunately every restaurant near the waterfront was mid-upper scale. I finally found a brasserie doing a land office business on Promenade Guilbeault. I confidently charged past the waiters to what I thought was the short order counter when one waiter stopped me and asked, *"vous voulez peepee?"* I said no. He repeated, *"Vous voulez peepee?"* I was so flustered I blurted out *"Non je veux acheter deux baguettes pour emporter."* At which point he showed me 3 buns and said this is all we have, you have to find a boulangerie.

Hopelessly outdone, I skulked out and up the street. I finally found a *"traiteur"* who had a good assortment of ready made sandwiches on baguettes. I bought a chicken and tomato one to which she added a little vinaigrette, paid 25 francs and got back to Joyce. We split the sandwich, ate a banana and moved on.

There is a Géant in Fréjus but we couldn't find it. However we had seen a Leclerc sign, another supermarché we knew about, so we headed back near the cutoff for C.R.E.P.S., a youth training camp, and found Leclerc. Joyce minded the car and its contents and I went shopping. Now it's hard enough to shop in your own home town, but this store had toilet tissue behind clothing and facial tissues with medecines. The Kleenex had a menthol scent in it and the local brand had a skin softener in it. On top of that you could only buy midget packs put up 18 to a pack.

In any event, I completed the shopping list and even checked out the difference between beef and horsemeat. Horsemeat is darker. Now fully supplied, we set out for Cap Esterel on a leisurely drive. We had to pull over several times to let the maniacs by.

Almost back to Cap Esterel there is a park built around a rocky beach. It was here that on Aug. 15, 1944 the 36th US infantry division landed with French troops and began the push which took them into Germany and Austria and ultimately the defeat of the Nazi regime. There is a fine but simple memorial which includes an assault barge U.S. 282 from which infantry troops came ashore. It is probably less than 2 miles from where we are staying.

St-Tropez

Chapter Three

Cap Esterel

We took a run at checking in early at 3:30. No such luck. We went through the usual administrative nonsense in the continuing denials of admission until finally at 5 minutes past 5 p.m. I complained that the room had been promised for 5 p.m. A charming receptionist insisted that according to the computer the room was still not ready.

I complained again that it was promised for 5 p.m. She asked me what time it was. I replied that it was 5 minutes past 5 p.m. With a great triumphant smile she said well then it must be ready and gave me the keys!

The wait was worth it. This unit was on the second floor overlooking the sea and was everything we could want. A lovely balcony view. A better layout than Cannes Villa Francia and, just as important, an apparent desire on the part of counter staff to please. We would like this place.

The first day of Spring! It was another sunny day. The sun was trying to break up a cloud system which it usually does by mid-morning.

We had a superb view of the sea to the left and the inner grounds and golf course on the right.

The complex encircles this huge landscaped area with planned walkways and mature trees. On the other side of the apartment village were tennis courts, more golf course, a large outdoor parking lot and an absolutely huge bunker style underground garage which probably holds 5-600 cars.

The golf course was short but sporty. There was an arched entryway coming in to the inner village from the inner garden paths which passed by our unit. Once inside there were dozens of stores and restaurants so that you felt as though you were truly in a village. The services were pretty complete.

As you walk up the village lane from our position you come to a central area where the pools and a huge patio were located. Several restaurants are set up with sidewalk café tables where you can order anything from a dinner to a cup of coffee.

When we looked out to the inner garden area where the paths converged, a very large tomcat seemed to have established his territory. He would lounge around awaiting the challenges presented when the innocent dog walkers got taken by surprise. Then all hell broke loose. The dogs went hysterical at the sight of the cat. The owners fought frantically to restrain the dogs, which by then were barking up a storm. The cat unfazed by it all simply arched his back and waited till it all passed. Then, having reestablished his territory, once again went back to lounging around. The incident was repeated a few times a day and became a sport.

There were a lot of dogs in Cannes. But here it seemed that every second family had brought a dog. There was one dog for every 3 people in the reception line. Tiny handfuls or huge sheepdogs, they were everywhere.

Joyce even saw a group of men playing cards at a bar near the patio and pool. They had drawn up an extra chair and an enormous Alsatian was sitting in it ready to join in the game if invited. Even the dogs had privileges. They were charged 200F a week to stay here.

Across the view over the golf course was a fairly good sized mountain with a lighthouse on top. Immediately south on the other side of it is Dramont Beach where the 1944 landings took place.

Every Sunday morning there was a huge flea market on the beach at Fréjus (an extension of St-Raphael). Joyce had heard about it yesterday and wanted to check out the fabric stalls for more Provençal designs. She ended up buying a watch (which fell apart later) and I picked up oranges and bananas. There were hordes of people milling around, many with their dogs. One elderly gentlemen was carrying a small shopping bag and sticking out of the top was a nose and a pair of tiny ears. I stopped him and asked if I could take its picture. He handed me the basket and said why don't you take the dog. I declined with thanks. A small but interested crowd gathered while I aimed the camera. Everyone seemed to approve. No doubt a baguette would end up in there in due course with the dog.

We moved on to a stall where interesting pastries were being sold. We selected a twisted pastry stick reputed to contain almonds and other interesting goodies. We bought one. It contained nothing but pastry and powdered sugar. Another stall was hawking miracle knives, guaranteed to cut anything for six months. There were many cute household articles made with Provençal designs including tiny sofas with miniature cushions which were facial tissue box covers. Many varieties of animals, cats, ducks etc. which contained lavender. At the south end there was even a sizeable display of beds and mattresses.

We did it all and then went back to our car and ate lunch, being careful each time a local came walking by, to raise the windows. We remembered the horror story of hands reaching into our friends' car to grab a purse. They had to arm wrestle a character in Marseille who had grabbed her purse. She held on and her husband grabbed his motorcycle helmet which came off. At that point he took off and they ended up with the helmet.

Our friends Cliff and Margaret also got pickpocketed. They immediately notified Visa etc., and were able to block off any charges. However the thief managed to rack up $3000.00 in unauthorized charges — all under $200. When they went to the Cannes police it was shortly after 12 noon and they were advised — sorry we're closed for lunch. Come back at 2 p.m. They did. And they were shown a room where the entire walls were lined with stolen purses. While they were there, one officer came in with another 7 or 8 in his arms.

So, we were very cautious about theft — especially in the car.

Driving back to Cap Esterel we stopped once more at Dramont Beach, site of the 1944 landing.

We parked the car near the monument and then walked down to the water's edge — about two hundred yards. Several groups and families were picnicking. Even though the terrain is gravel and the beach itself smooth rock cobble stones, the women were dressed in high heels and tweed jackets, sipping wine and munching on delicacies.

We scrambled down to the water's edge, marvelled at the clarity of the water and took a few photos. I picked up a small smooth grey rock from the landing site to bring back to my daughter who collects rocks of significance.

We returned to Cap Esterel and flaked out. Seven and a half hours of killing time yesterday had caught up with us. It was now completely sunny and 70 degrees F. There were many places in the upper and west Var that we wanted to see. The problem was that they are just beyond a reasonable day's drive and might necessitate an overnight stay to do it efficiently. We decided to test the time and distance from Cap Esterel to determine what was reasonably possible.

Aix was a 2 hour drive from the Cap via the A-8. Getting to Avignon and Orange was another matter. We aimed for Orange and it took us three and a half hours — about 150 miles, not all on the autoroute. We reached the great Antique Theatre about 11:40 a.m. We got inside but at 12 noon everything shut down until 1:30.

A ticket to the Roman Theatre also admitted us to the Orange Museum across the street. However the shut down for lunch made it necessary to kill some time. Although we usually brought lunch, we felt that we should try the local fare.

Immediately facing the theatre is Rue Christie Sud. Just around the corner is a wonderful little patisserie/traiteur called *"Le Caesar"*. It was not busy when we entered just after 12 noon.

Shortly thereafter the noon trade began to arrive and in no time people were lined up in the street waiting to order. The place was run by a very attractive young woman — believe it or not wearing a shapely high fashion black suit. Her helper, who did most of the legwork, was more appropriately dressed in a white chef's outfit, suited to someone loading baguettes in the oven or placing ingredients in a stuffed baguette.

None of the other restaurants or shops were doing nearly as well, so we must have lucked out.

The Romans established a settlement in Orange around 100 BC. The monumental theatre which is in excellent condition is still used for concerts and plays and was completed in 25 BC.

A sizeable and remarkably detailed Arc de Triomphe was also built about the same time. We walked down Victor Hugo to the arch and took a couple of photos. Then we wandered into the place de ville and found an interesting monument to Rambaud II. By this time it was 1:30 and the museum was open.

There were numerous examples of Roman artifacts most of which were damaged. On the second floor there were a number of painted murals depicting life 3-400 years ago and showing the almost feudal nature of life. One other interesting note. There was a small swiftly flowing river running through Orange. In 1924 a major flood hit the town putting most of it under 6-10 ft of water. There was a marker on the corner of the building across from the theatre showing the high water mark about 6 ft up the wall.

Orange was later to assume greater historical significance when the House of Orange was established there and William of Orange came to power.

To complete the tour of the other towns in the western Var, we would have to leave early and stay overnight. That way we could spend more time sightseeing. In spite of this we did manage one other major stop on our way back at St-Maximin-la-Ste-Baume. This is a very large basilica containing several important historical artifacts including the skull of Mary Magdalene, as well as an enormous organ with over 3000 pipes, considered one of the finest in France.

On our way back to St-Raphael, we finally found Géant and did some shopping. Leclerc is just as good and easier to get to. We returned to our apartment having a better idea of what was going to be possible.

You open the drapes in the morning and are met once again with dazzling sunlight. That was now 18 straight days of good weather. Even yesterday with a full scale mistral blowing, the sky was clear. We had better take advantage of it. The cashier at Géant last night said that a bad weather system was coming in this weekend and the forecasts were never wrong! Now that's another difference!

After yesterday's long drive we wanted to do something nearby, so we headed for St-Tropez, about 30 miles south. It was 10:40 when we left, and having learned the hard way that nothing is open between 12 noon and 2 p.m., we headed straight for the Musée d'Archéologie in St-Raphael which we had missed on our last visit.

It is a small but very professionally displayed museum with artifacts found around and in the sea. There are examples of primitive tools dating back 30,000 years or more. Immediately next to it is the church of St-Raphael dating to the 12th century. An archeological dig is under process which has so far unearthed earlier churches under it, one dating to the 4th century.

The attendant first directs you to the bell tower. She omits to tell you it's 10 stories high, so that when you do reach the top you are bushed. All in all the view is worth a visit.

It was now close to noon so we went back to the railway station to check out rates and schedules for Carcassonne. We determined (after failing to respond to our number for priority service) that it was going to cost over 1000F each for a return ticket. In addition, the best schedules leaving St-Raphael at 6:30 a.m. still took 6 hours to get there. It must be a milk run. It was clear that if we were going to Carcassonne, it was going to be by car, with a stopover on the way. Maybe Nîmes or Arles.

My stomach was growling so it was time to eat.

We found a very peaceful square in front of Église Notre Dame, which we had visited earlier and on which a very beautiful cenotaph had been erected. There were two stone benches, one of which was already occupied. We sat down on the other and began our picnic lunch.

Halfway through, an old white short haired retriever appeared with a bit of a limp, and a sad look in its eyes. Very politely, it sat down in front of us and began drooling.

Joyce tried to satisfy it with sesame bars. It got up with some difficulty which was when we realized it had a hip problem, sniffed out the sesame bars and decided that the rest of our lunch looked more interesting.

At this point we made an amazing discovery. Joyce was eating an orange and the dog began to drool profusely. She threw her a wedge and the dog gobbled it up. A second piece got the same treatment.

In due course a well dressed lady appeared and called to the dog, *"Nina, ne les déranges pas."*

I got up to talk with the woman. I had never seen a dog eat an orange before. *"Elle adore les oranges, et aussi les pommes, les noix, les fromages, mais pas les bananes. Elle a une problème avec une hanche, elle a treize ans."*

And with that, this amazing dog trotted off with the lady, probably for a bowl of fruit!

We were now smart enough to travel at noon when everything is closed, so we wouldn't spend our time killing time.

En route to St-Tropez we passed Ste-Maxime, a very nice resort area, then passed through Petit Grimaud, named after the Grimaldi family (Monaco). Its current claim to fame is that one entrepreneur thought it would be great if he constructed canals throughout so that it would look like Florida!

He didn't need to go that far. All he needed to do was put up a large shopping mall, place a walk in medical clinic on every corner and set up a few shops selling Disney souvenirs!

If Cannes was more refreshing than Nice, and St-Raphael was cleaner and more residential than Cannes, without the high rises, then St-Tropez had them all beaten. A beautiful harbour, quaint, tiny and clean streets in the old part of town and dozens of really interesting restaurants (upscale) and antique shops.

We saw a kiosque for the fondation Brigitte Bardot, but it was closed. We had hoped to see Brigitte herself, but she was probably out in the Gulf of St. Lawrence with the Newfoundland seal hunters.

Unfortunately, the Musée de l'Annonciade was closed on Tuesdays, even though our guidebook said otherwise. So we headed back to the Cap, stopping first at Leclerc for film and provisions. While there we found "tapenade", bought several jars and headed home.

Joyce was fading fast and planned to take it easy tomorrow. I casually suggested that I might like to try the golf course, "then book us both out at 1 p.m.," she responded. Obviously the competitive fire has not yet been quenched!

Well the fire may not have been quenched, but it is barely smouldering. Joyce stayed put in the apartment and did a large hand wash.

I decided to try the golf course. It is short but sporty. 7 par 3s and two par 4s. The view from many of the holes is quite spectacular. It costs 90F to play 18 *"trous"* and 60 F to rent *"batons"*.

On my first shot I blasted a slice right out of play and lost the ball. A few holes later I lost a second ball (I was given only 3 with the rental). By the time I had circled the area where we lived I was getting nervous, so I ran into the village sport shop and bought 3 used balls to keep me going. My game settled down and in the second nine I shot a 42.

When I completed 18 it was 1:15. The pro shop was locked. The pro was on the practice tee giving a lesson. He spotted me and ran up to the pro shop to take the rental clubs back, scolding me for not knowing that the pro shop is always closed between 12 and 2. (So what else is new?)

The only thing you can do between 12 and 2 is eat and buy gas. If you're going to have a heart attack you'd better plan it before or after because even the police close down for lunch.

I returned to the apartment and had lunch with Joyce. She had taken a walk among the village stores. She had gone into the sports shop to browse. There was a large sheep dog straddling the doorway with two Frenchmen. A German lady complained about the dog blocking the way. The Frenchmen said the dog had as much right to be there as she did. And so it goes.

After lunch we drove into town to Leclerc to pick up our film at about one-half the price Géant charged us. We received for the first time an index print of all the photos taken — the new Kodak avantix system. We are only beginning to see this at home.

On our way into St-Raphael we saw an attractive woman in her 40s hitchhiking, wearing high heels and a nicely tailored suit. They surely dress for all occasions.

The rain finally came — in spades! The cashier at Géant was right. The weatherman is never wrong.

When the cold and rain take over, the Mediterranean looks like any other body of water. Gone are aquamarine and cobalt blue, no longer highlighted by the sun.

We had to spend the day in nearby museums.

Draguignan looked interesting so we prepared, aiming to include Fayence and Bargemon as well.

All of the apartments have clay tile floors. In the unit over us there was a family with a small child. We drew that conclusion from the pitter patter of little bare feet on the floor running the length of the living room. It also sounded like the child had an educational hammer toy where wooden pegs are driven into a wooden frame. We also heard what sounded like a child's rocking chair but only at supper time.

The size of French families (at this family oriented resort at least) seems to be small — mostly single, occasionally two children. That doesn't prevent them from including the ever present dog.

The rain was fairly hard until about 9:20 a.m., then it let up a bit as we set out for Draguignan. The name comes from a legend according to which in the 5th century the local bishop, St. Hermentaire, slew a dragon. The statues commemorating this event suggest that it might have been a large alligator — but that would spoil the legend.

We arrived in Draguignan shortly after 11 a.m. A kind lady directed us to a public parking facility within two blocks of the two leading museums. The Musée Municipal is a small but excellent museum with many artifacts of a local prehistoric nature. It also houses a Renoir and a Rembrandt. There was no charge for admission and I would rate it superior to others where we have paid 20 or 30 francs.

By the time we had gone through it was close to noon. We crossed over to the Musée des Arts et Traditions de Moyenne Provence. It looked very interesting but once again we got skunked by the clock. It closed at 12 and requires an hour with a guide. There was still the *"Pierre de la Fée"*, a giant prehistoric dolmen — the only one in Provence.

We found it at the end of a very narrow lane just outside the city. I estimated the capping stone to be 14 ft by 9 ft and 2 ft thick. That would put it somewhere close to 9-10 tons. It stands on three upright stones about 7 ft off the ground. We took each other's picture under it. In the Musée Municipal there was a sizeable section devoted to it. It is some form of burial monument and important artifacts such as beads, semi-precious stones etc. were found under it.

The capping stone ranks up there with those we saw at Stonehenge. It was well worth the hunt.

We then set out for Fayence, a hillside town looking down on a fertile valley and a small airfield which is an important gliding centre. There is an excellent lookout which provides a view in 3 directions. We parked in a lot with immaculate washrooms on the crest of the hill. The only problem with the washrooms was that the lady logos are over the door where the pissoirs are and vice versa.

Right beside the municipal parking lot was a kindergarten for little children. They were just coming back to school about 1:30 p.m. On our walk to the lookout we went up a narrow curving lane which was undergoing improvements by the city.

I stopped to talk to a stone mason who was cutting and laying stone into flower gardens and stairs. I asked him if it was difficult to cut, he said no it was fairly soft. This is supported by what you see in the Roman ruins where many of the stones show a raked look from the cutting tools. I explained to him that I had an interest in stone walls having built one in Quechee, Vermont when we lived there, which required 120 tons of stone, most of it trucked in. So we were sort of kindred spirits.

We had many interesting experiences at our vacation home in the green mountains of Vermont. The first spring we had spent in Quechee, we had just settled down for the night and were appreciating the cool, clean mountain air with the bedroom windows wide open. A whippoorwill started cutting loose with his mating call. He probably could have been heard one half mile away, but just outside our window was enough to jolt Joyce out of bed. "David it's the police. Get up quick." I reassured her, and our lovesick bird must have found a girlfriend, because he never came back.

We became good friends with our immediate neighbours Zeb and Reedy Hastings from Springfield, Mass. And had many good times together. Early in the game we agreed to go downhill skiing with them. Joyce is a very good skier. We all started off together from the top of the hill and when we got to the bottom our friend complimented her on her graceful form on the hill. Then he turned to me and said, "And you Dave, you are obviously self taught."

In due course we became quite close and I was asked to give the toast to the groom's parents before the rehearsal dinner at their son's wedding. I said a lot of nice things, but I got the best reaction when I said "that it was customary to seek out a friend to say nice things about the family at such a dinner, but I was puzzled by why they had to go out of the country to find one." We remain good friends.

Just below the lookout at Fayence is the Église St-Jean Baptiste. We struck it lucky again. The organist was practising as Easter was approaching, so we sat down and listened to some very peaceful spiritual music for about fifteen minutes.

Right next to the church is the Bar des Compagnes which looked like it was doing a fair trade for that time of day. One of the highway cowboys that I had come to know in the past three weeks came roaring up, screeched to a halt and ambled out of his car, cigarette in hand , ready to add more fuel to what already looked like a full load.

We then went in search of the famous Saracen Gate and managed to walk through it before we noticed a sign pointing back to where we had just been!

Then, off we went to Bargemon. The road leading to it became quite mountainous and that butterfly feeling came back on a few hairpin turns. Bargemon was on the way back to Draguignan, but it was a bit of a disappointment. We had already seen most of what it had to offer, plus, nothing was open.

Finally at 3:15 a boulangerie opened and we bought bread, then took a look at Église St-Etienne and the Chapelle Notre-Dame-de-Montaigu. Both churches had brought sweet smelling cuttings of some fragrant local bush into the church, no doubt in preparation for Palm Sunday. It was difficult to see as only a few candles provided light.

The drive back to Fréjus was uneventful except that Joyce spotted a fabric store on the way in so we could expect to make a return trip!

By the time we got back to Cap Esterel the heavens had really opened up and it was raining hard. There was some uncertainty whether it would clear by noon tomorrow or later. There was a good mistral blowing while we were up in the hills.

The next morning it was still raining hard. The family upstairs had a problem about 2 a.m. which woke us up. So I was a bit slow to get started. Meanwhile Joyce was raring to go! So off we went in the rain to Aix-en-Provence. It was slow going even on the A-8. The sky had lightened up a bit as we arrived at Aix but we did continue to receive intermittent rain while there.

Shortly after 11 a.m. we found a parking spot in the Cours Sextius near the ruins of the Roman baths. There really wasn't much to see but we were also close to the estate Pavillon de Vendome considered to be one of the finest mansions in Aix. We were in the inner city so it was a short walk to the Cathédrale de St-Sauveur. The baptistry dates from the 5th century and contains 2nd century Corinthian columns.

The major work, a triptych of The Burning Bush (1476) by Nicholas Froment is hidden behind hinged doors on the wall near the baptistry and is only available for viewing Tuesdays between 3 and 4 p.m. We assume this is to preserve it. While we were in the church the main altar was screened from view by a light curtain. A rehearsal was taking place, presumably for a pageant with Easter fast approaching. It is a large impressive church containing many artifacts.

We continued our walk toward the Place de Ville, a very pretty square lined with upscale shops, boulangeries and small restaurants. We found a delightful eatery which seated about 12 which on arrival was filled with students.

Afterwards we walked down the cours Mirabeau which is lined with exclusive shops and restaurants. We were looking for a "toilette publique" and were not having much luck. By the time we got to Place de Gaulle it was becoming a bit urgent. We were told that there was one behind the post office which we couldn't find. We then went to the Gare Routière and finally found one behind it. It was 2F each, the attendant wanted to know if I was paying for both. There was one first class toilet which cost 10F. I'm not sure for what.

Restored to fighting trim we headed up to the Musée d'Histoire Naturelle. They have many interesting exhibits, but their dinosaurs are the junior variety compared to ours in Ottawa. The dinosaur eggs were of good quality and size.

It was now 3 p.m. and raining harder, so we returned to the car. Aix is an international university town. There are literally thousands of students. Those we saw in the restaurant we had lunch at were Italian. It is evident from the lifestyle the students lead, not only at Aix but also at Orange, that there must be considerable affluence in Europe. These kids were putting out the equivalent of 60F for restaurant lunches. They were also very well dressed.

On our way back to Cap Esterel we experienced a major downpour including hail, all the way to St-Raphael. There were five separate accidents on the A-8.

The lower streets of St-Raphael simply couldn't handle the volume of water and at one point we drove through flooding 12 - 15 inches deep for about 100 yards.

We got home safely, bought another baguette and settled down to relaxing with good Provençal wine. Always a nice way to end the day.

Reflecting on the day, Joyce was testing my French using colloquial terms. A pullover sweater which I would have thought was a *"chandail"* turns out to be *"un pull"*. You had better be careful how you pronounce it though, you might end up with a chicken!

After yesterday's wet ride we weren't up to any major excursions today. Besides Joyce was still preoccupied with the Provençal fabrics and wanted to get back to the outdoor market at Fréjus. There was at least one other interesting location nearby which we had not yet seen and that was Les Arcs, a few miles closer than Draguignan.

It began to clear. We made a quick stop at Fréjus where Joyce bought Provençal gifts and we then headed out to Les Arcs. On the way we passed a Roman amphitheatre which we had not seen in earlier visits to Fréjus. We made a mental note to take a few hours before we leave the south and really do Fréjus. It is known as a village Romaine.

Shortly thereafter we arrived at les Arcs. Sometimes you get an unexpected surprise. Such was the case at Les Arcs.

We parked in the square in front of the Mairie which proudly flew the flag of Provence above the "tricoleur". The French motto "liberté, egalité, fraternité" was prominently displayed on the face of this very attractive building. We had arrived moments before the infamous noon shutdown. Joyce spotted an artisanat shop called Lou Toupin. The door was not open but Lou was an enterprising lady — the first we had come across who came up behind us and asked if we wanted her to open up the store. We apologized. After all the entire nation seems to shut down for lunch. She was happy to do so and we entered on a guilt trip and ended up spending 140F.

She was a very sociable woman and in the course of the conversation we discovered that she had had a choir from Thetford Mines visit last year and had also met a couple from Ste-Anne-de-la-Pocatière, both lawyers who had bought property up in the old medieval village known as *"La Parage"*. We had just climbed up to the area and were absolutely taken with it. Every building is in excellent condition and each is privately owned. There are no commercial intrusions. There is an old church in La Parage which is no longer active. An elderly gentleman saw that we and another couple were trying to figure out how to get into the church — the Chapelle St-Pierre 16th century. He told us it was closed. He lived next door in a lovely stone home with a most unusual door. On it there were 12 carved panels, each depicting an activity common to the people for that particular month. March illustrated a man devouring a large meal so I guess we've become part of the family.

We were much taken with the homes in La Parage.

On the way back to the car in Place Charles de Gaulle we stopped and ate lunch in the square, having bought bread in the Boulangerie de la Tour just off the square. The place caught our attention because in the window were displayed marvellous loaves of decorated bread with artistic designs of the ingredients baked right into the surface. The young lady who served us was very pleasant and obviously proud of her husband's handiwork.

She gave us help in getting to *"La Chapelle Ste-Rosaline"*. This turned out to be something special. The chapel is dedicated to a young woman who by her deeds and a miraculous feeding of the poor became a saint. She was born in 1263 and much has been written about her. In 1968 Margaret Maight (la fondation Maight in St-Paul-de-Vence) was instrumental in restoring the chapel and in making it possible for Marc Chagall and Diago Giacometti to complete major works which are to be found in the chapel. The Chagall mosaic is enormous, probably 10 by 15 feet in size.

We had an animated conversation with an elderly man who volunteers a few times a week in the chapel. His son was an officer in the US navy and he himself had visited Niagara and the Thousand Islands.

On the way out we stopped at the Côtes de Provence principal outlet for its wines, located in Les Arcs. We bought 3 bottles reasonably priced at 28F, a Chausido Becasso 1997, a 1997 Nostre Souluou and a 1997 Domaine La Bouvière. We got into the Chausido and both of us liked it.

We got back to Cap Esterel about 4:30 p.m. and sympathized with the poor souls who were ready to check in but wouldn't be allowed to till 5 p.m. There seemed to be more kids coming in this second week, skateboards, roller blades, all equipped. The sky has cleared, the forecast was good and we were taking off for Arles and Nîmes at 7:30 Sunday morning.

Chez le marchand de fleurs

Chapter Four

Arles and Points West

It was clear, but a great mistral was blowing. We thought we had gotten off to an early start but found out that daylight saving began that morning so we had lost an hour. Traffic on the A-8 was light so we made good time arriving at Arles.

We used Frommer's guide and sought out Hotel Calendal, an absolutely charming small hotel reasonably priced at 380F and located 50 yards from the Roman arena! The garden which is off our door (nobody above us) is a walled area with garden swings and a huge chess game with pieces about 2 ft high. Joyce loved it instantly, so we booked it for two nights, and will use it as a jumping off point for Avignon and Les Baux.

We had parked the car in a public lot, but arranged to "*garer l'auto*" in a small garage belonging to the hotel which would handle four cars tops.

We ate lunch in the car, then accepted the challenge to try and get out of the old quarter. We succeeded by going downhill and eventually passed the fabulous Sunday flower market. Then on to the A-54 for Nîmes.

This is very flat land through which the Rhone flows before spilling into the Mediterranean about 40 miles south. On the highway there were markers reminding drivers of "*vents violents*" and every couple of kilometres there is a windsock to show just how hard the winds are. They weren't kidding! The mistral blowing that day had the windsocks absolutely horizontal! It is great agricultural country with thousands of acres devoted to roses and other delicate products.

Nîmes is larger than Arles and as you approach it high rises are evident. There is a vigorous industrial sector producing, among other things, blue denim used by the cowboys who ride the Camarque — a Texas-like parcel of land near the outlet of the Rhone.

It seems to be a very progressive city with many fashionable shops, particularly in the marble streets near the Maison Carrée considered to be the Roman world's best preserved temple.

We found a spot to park in a tiny street just off the Boulevard de la Libération and about 5 or 6 blocks from the Nîmes Roman arena. It is in excellent condition and is still used for bullfights, theatrical and musical events and in 3 days time it would be the home of the Davis Cup matches between France and Holland. The staff were preparing the red clay surface inside the arena as we toured it.

We climbed to the upper level and wandered through the arched supports for the upper tier. While there we met an American couple from Sacramento, California. They asked us if we would take their photos which we did, and they reciprocated.

They were also staying at Arles in the Calendal Hotel. They had travelled through France using the Frommer guide with excellent results. We agreed to meet for dinner.

We then set out for La Maison Carrée and got totally lost. It was because of this that we discovered the fashionable streets of Nîmes which led to it, and the major arts centre Le Carré d'Art. In the course of admiring the fashions Joyce stepped on the inevitable dog droppings and I was left with the much sought after task of cleaning her shoe. Yuk!

That was enough to call it a day. We tried our best to get out of Nîmes quickly and back to Arles, but no such luck. Out of the blue appeared signs for Ales, a town we had never heard of. Finally we circled around and eventually found a sign saying

Arles. Not so lucky, however, because every signpost had a blue A-54 sign for Arles as well as a green (local road) sign for Arles. Then the damned Ales signs began to reappear. We finally got out, fought the mistral on the way home, cleverly circled the arena and arrived at the front door of Le Calendal!

We had paid for indoor parking so in she went. Then into our delightful room and into the wine. We looked forward to seeing our new friends in the dining room.

The sequel to this part of the story is that while we were waiting to enter the dining room our friends from California arrived. Their car had been broken into in Nîmes and everything of value in it had been taken. Their suitcases, all the bags of gifts they had accumulated and all of the undeveloped film of all the places they had been. They were here with only their wallets and their documents. The Nîmes police told them there are 150 incidents of theft a day.

We did have dinner with them. But all we could do was console them and avoid falling into the same trap.

We ate breakfast in our room. The cold mistral was still blowing and I doubt if the temperature in Arles at 40 degrees F. was any warmer than back in Ottawa.

In any event we leaned into the wind and began a walking tour of the city. We passed the Théâtre Antique with a view to looking at it when the sun rose a bit higher. We continued down Rue de la Calade and came upon Place de la République which has a number of important buildings of interest including Église St-Trophime, a beautiful Romanesque church with several enormous tapestries. There were a number of niches, many of which contained tombs of martyrs and saints. Building started in the 11th century and continued through the 12th century when the splendid Romanesque portals were completed. For a church of its size it has surprisingly little seating room, possibly because of its enormous columns.

We arrived at the church early and a cleaning crew of 8 or 10 men and women, some volunteers, were working.

There is also an Egyptian obelisk in the centre of the Square. The Place de la Mairie is directly across from the church and has a fine clock tower.

We continued down to Boul. Georges Clemenceau and stopped at McDonald's for what I thought was going to be a coffee. Instead I got a demi-tasse sized serving of espresso with a miniature chocolate bar thrown in.

Then we walked to *"Place du Forum"* a square where Van Gogh often painted, especially *"le Café la Nuit"* in 1888, since restored to that era. We then worked our way up Rue de la Calade and I went into the Théatre Antique which is only 50 yards from our hotel and took photos. The arena is equally close on the other side of the hotel. It looks much like the one in Nîmes, also in excellent condition.

By this point we were ready to take on Avignon, so we had a quick lunch and headed out.

As you enter it, Avignon gives the impression of power. The old city is surrounded by walls nearly 3 miles in length. We parked about a quarter of a mile from the famous bridge and walked over to it; and then onto it where we took more photos.

The other major attraction near the Pont d'Avignon is the papal palace. It is enormous and at one time the centre of great religious and political power.

It has been stripped of most of its important furnishings but the designated rooms on the upper floor levels give an indication of how important it was.

We left the palace and walked into the commercial area looking for a place to cash travellers cheques. We hit upon Place l'Horloge by accident. That of course is the famous clock with two life-size Provençal characters.

By then we had done enough touring. We headed down toward the river via rue St-Étienne hoping to find the parking lot where we had left the car. A half hour later we found it, only it was in the next lot a quarter mile away!

On the way back to Arles we were determined to see les Baux de Provence so we detoured a few miles over and parked for 20F half way up the hill. This is another very touristy "village perché" from which you can see the Mediterranean 30 miles away. It is overrated. They clip you at each turn and everything is price inflated. Perhaps it has just become too touristy.

We left, and on our way back we picked up a baguette and a bottle of Domaine D'Adumar 1997 which turned out to be an excellent choice.

Getting into the old part of Arles we got hopelessly tangled in the confusion of narrow one way lanes, not to mention the impatient idiots who race down these narrow lanes. After about 4 tries we got to within 20 yards of our hotel, but we were faced with a dilemma — break the law and go 20 yards up a one way street, or begin circling again. We broke the law!

We had enjoyed last night's dinner at Le Calendal. After fighting the traffic all day, we elected again to have dinner at the hotel.

The charming young lady who had met us at the reception desk turned out to be the waitress, then the chef, then the dishwasher, at the same time answering the phone, taking reservations, keeping the cosy fire in the fireplace going, and looking after the front desk! Her name was Stephanie and she was a jewel.

There is a very personal touch at this hotel starting with Stephanie. The chambermaid was equally interesting. Probably in her late 40s she was a very handsome woman. At 8 a.m. this morning I was up and around before Joyce. There was a knock at the door and someone tried the handle. It was the chambermaid, almost as if she was giving us her wake up call!

When I checked in they did not ask for identification or for a credit card for security. They simply asked me to write my name on a piece of paper. No address or any of the other usual formalities.

Finally, we did the Luberon. We had been blessed with a marvellous day, 70 degrees F. and full sun. The mistral had blown itself out. It was quite a phenomenon.

Confident, having fought our way through the maze of narrow lanes last night, and expecting to be out in a flash, it only took 3 minutes to get hopelessly lost on our way out. Finally we found our bearings and began what was to be one of the loveliest days of the trip.

We headed northwest toward Cavaillon, first hitting St-Remy-de-Provence. Between St- Remy and Cavaillon we drove through mile after mile of secondary highway lined on both sides with plane trees which form a continuous shaded arch.

We arrived at Cavaillon about 11 a.m. and parked in La Place du Clos where we had a relaxing cup of coffee on the sidewalk of the forum café. It was there that we met a couple from Vancouver who also happen to be staying at Cap Esterel. They had stayed earlier at Menton near the Italian border (also Pierre et Vacances) and had made a one day trip into Italy by car. That was enough. Their friends were swarmed by gypsy girls and the fanny pack of the other woman was cut. They were robbed of about $500.

They were heading up to Gordes and we were aiming for Ménerbes. When we parted company we climbed halfway up the mountain which led to Chapelle St-Jacques and a great view of the Luberon. It was exhausting and we decided to quit halfway.

We returned to the square and took off for Ménerbes. This area is a major fruit growing centre and all of the pear trees were in full blossom.

Ménerbes is on the crest of a small rock hill not quite high enough to be considered a "village perché". It was, nonetheless, a lovely little village with wonderful views of the orchards below and Mont Ventoux in the distance, still snow capped. We walked up through the town, saw what we believe was the old Calvinist church, now inactive, and admired several private homes up top looking very luxurious.

We then continued our drive to Bonnieux, about 3-4 miles. We stopped to photograph a beautiful orchard and picked up Mont Ventoux in the distance from one angle, and Ménerbes from the other.

There is a museum of bread making in the town of Bonnieux but it was closed. We found a tiny art gallery, carrying lovely pastels of market scenes which we nearly bought.

From just about every angle Bonnieux offers superb outlooks. It was interesting to note two restoration projects underway where the contractors had set up high altitude jack cranes normally used in construction of multi-storey buildings. These had been placed in amazingly precarious positions on the side of the hill. I suppose they knew what they were doing.

When we left Bonnieux for Lourmarin we began a long downhill twisting drive through the Luberon Forest, breathing in the fabulous fresh air. There are many cedars and alpine pines contributing to this. When we finally reached the bottom, we came upon a clearing and the village of Lourmarin, where we saw the château owned at one time by the in-laws of Franz Liszt. It is a sizeable property and would be considered a château anywhere. When we walked up to the upper gate a set of not so friendly Alsatian teeth was waiting to greet us. Naturally, the château was closed on Tuesdays.

By this point we were "castled out" and glad that the road to Aix was just outside the grounds.

Happy at having seen all of these wonderful places, we thought how lucky we were. It was truly something to remember.

French picnic in the park

Chapter Five

Cap Esterel

March 31st was a bright sunny day, about 65 degrees F., but a slow day for us after our 3 day trip to the Arles, Avignon area. Joyce did a washing, but since a rocket scientist was needed to start the machine I was called in to launch the wash.

I also needed to make a long distance call to Nice to arrange for the return of the car on Saturday. I had some difficulty, so I walked up to the reception area, about 300 yards away, and wasted about 5 minutes before one of the clerks acknowledged me. I explained my problem. "It is very easy," she said. "Simply dial 0 then 4 and then the number."

So I walked 300 yards back to the apartment and tried again. A recorded voice said, "Call not authorized," so back I walked 300 yards and talked to another clerk who said, "Your apartment phone has not been *"branché"*. Give me your apartment key and I'll do it", which she did.

Back another 300 yards and presto! I completed the call. It has been our experience here that they take a lot for granted. Someone should have asked if we wanted the phone *"branchéd"*.

We were now in the last few days before peak season commences. I estimated that there were at least another 4-500 cars in the lot. With 1450 apartments, there was going to be *"beaucoup de monde"* here.

A rock group had set up near the pool and the kids had brought the blue cushions out from their room sofas and were sitting on them on the plaza where everyone including dogs walk with dirty or even wet feet. There were signs saying roller blades and skateboards "*interdit*" but there were plenty of them being used.

Later that afternoon we went to St-Raphael to pick up our photos. We also took a walk up to the top of the hill to see the view to the sea.

I showed Joyce the golf course and took photos as planned. There were quite a few in swimming and activity all over the tennis courts, the kid's basketball courts, and surprisingly, only a few golfers, especially considering the great day.

A group of artisanats had set up an outdoor market on the square. They were better than last week. We bought a couple of trinkets and then settled in for a quiet evening at home.

As I had made the appointment to return the car, we were now really winding down, with no more excursions planned. On Saturday we were to fly to Paris.

Just for fun I made a summary of the best and worst things about our month in Provence. Here it is.

NICE THINGS
French bread
"Villages Perchés"
Corniche d'Or
Lunches on park benches
Dogs that love oranges
Stephanie and Le Calendal
Fabulous produce
Les Arcs and
Chapelle Ste-Rosaline
Musée Maeght and Riopelle
Old St-Tropez
Picasso Museum — Antibes
Patriotism
Le Luberon

Conversations en français
The climate and weather
NOT SO NICE THINGS
French drivers
Incidents of theft
Tunnels at 120k
Dog droppings
Basement apartment at
Villa Francia
Gouging at Les Baux
Inability to sleep —
lumpy beds
Surliness of those in
hospitality trade

On balance I liked the place and would come back knowing the second time around what to avoid. I am jealous of all that France has to offer, the Alps, the South, the fabulous agricultural lands and their diversity. The cultural greatness. No wonder they are cocky. And no wonder so many others for thousands of years have tried to take it away from them. It is a land that has been truly blessed.

When we finished dinner I suggested that if tomorrow was a nice day we might consider playing golf. Immediately the competitive lights went on and she contemplated the situation for a moment; and then said, "Well I guess I'll have to practice on the balcony with a floor mop!" What can I say.

Throughout Provence in the mid to large towns it is common to see brightly decorated merry-go-rounds near or in the public parks. They are smaller in diameter than those usually seen in North America. However, many of them have two levels with staircases leading to the upper one. The amusing thing is the high percentage of adults riding on them acting in childish ways and having a great time.

April 1st was another great day so as agreed I made a starting time for golf at 12:20. Since the pro's shop was closed between 12 and 2 p.m., this meant getting there by 11:40 or so in order to rent clubs etc. I had been supplied 3 balls last time but this time no balls. I had to go all the way back to the sport shop in the "village" and buy 6 balls at 10F each.

When we got to the 1st tee there was a young Dane named Hendrick waiting to play with us. I had noticed him on the practice green because he hit every shot with his legs wide apart. So I wondered how his game was. Not quite as good as ours but he was a fine young gentleman who operated an Internet company in Copenhagen. He and his girlfriend were on a short holiday, 5 days at the Cap and then on to the Alps for some skiing. I hoped he kept his legs together.

He was only playing 9 holes because his girlfriend was suntanning.

After 9 holes I shot a 38 and Joyce had a 51.

We went straight to the 10th hole (which is the 1st all over again) and I hit off.

Out from behind the bushes which hide the ladies' tee, appeared an attractive blonde who asked me what our starting time was. She was alone. I invited her to play with us but she said she would prefer to go out alone, because it would go faster. We would bump into her later.

In the meantime from behind the rail fence appeared Bernhard and Monica a German couple who had been advised by "the club secretary" to join up with us.

We did, and this gave Joyce her golden opportunity to speak German. She counted to ten for them, rattled off her standard phrases such as "Wo haben sie deutsch gelernt, meine Eltern sprechen deutsch." and a few others. Monica smiled at everything we said, and understood nothing. Bernhard was more communicative. We got along swimmingly. In the final analysis it was a great day of golf.

Joyce hit her usual assortment of phenomenal shots and bloopers.

The walk back up to the village was a bit of an effort. We needed a few groceries, strawberries, yogurt and a large Coke for Joyce.

As we were walking down through the "village", the inner court of all the apartments, who should appear but the attractive blonde from the 10th tee.

Curious, I walked over to her and asked, "*Avez vous brisé le normal?*" Joyce thought I had asked her if she was having the usual amount of gas, and began to giggle.

The lady said no.

We climbed up to our apartment and got into the wine.

Golf itself is not unreasonably expensive but renting clubs and buying balls or tees certainly is. Used balls run 7F each. Tees are 1F each! You read it correctly.

With the high season beginning, every evening about 5 p.m. a rock concert starts up on the terrace near the pool, much to the delight of everyone under 13. The boom of the bass resonates across the valley — sort of a call to arms to every kid in the complex who felt the need to shake off the cobwebs. They squealed with delight.

This morning as I walked to the golf course there was a stretching class in progress on the same terrace, to music that was not quite so demanding. There was a wide assortment of humanity (mostly female) going through some of the wildest gyrations imaginable. Some looked ready for the Cirque du Soleil. I must be getting old.

After four weeks here I have found myself rolling my Rs when I speak French in a way that I would feel affected back home. When we were playing golf with Hendrick on the 7th tee he pointed out a shrub with tiny purple flowers called Lourmarin.

We had passed through a village and château two days ago at the eastern end of the Luberon called Lourmarin — so out it rolled! I was quite proud of myself. The shrub is a sort of a cross between lavender and juniper.

Joyce served up a very nourishing dinner of pistou with French bread, yogurt, bran cereal (petales) and Spanish strawberries.

We were working our way down our food inventory. The only thing we had to write off were some lemons and onions, both part of Joyce's Provençal recipes which she brought with her.

April 2nd was packing day. I had to throw my running shoes in the garbage to make room for her purchases.

Although it was another gorgeous day there would be no golf. Our bones said so.

It seems that the people above us found it necessary to rearrange the furniture every night. This went on for about an hour. Joyce got a broom out and swore if it went on past 10 p.m. she would start hammering the ceiling. I had visions of plaster coming down all over us, but fortunately it stopped about 9:45. It was then that I thought of the Desiderata, and remembered what peace there is in silence.

We bought the Herald Tribune, with horror stories from Kosovo all over it. There is a pretty good financial section so were able to track some of our Canadian stocks. Still nothing exciting.

The only good news was that the Ottawa Senators hockey team might win their division.

I had been curious walking by the boulangerie in the "village". All the baguettes are displayed standing on end. I asked the lady why. She said there were two reasons. It made for a more appealing display and there was less tendency for the crust to crush as it might if they were lying down.

Up by one of the sidewalk cafés I saw the huge Alsatian that Joyce had seen last week at cards. He wasn't playing cards this time, just sitting at the bar up on a chair like any other patron!

Off in the distance there is a twin rail line. Passenger rail is still a major and efficient mode of transportation in France. The TGV (train de grande vitesse) is expanding routes with space age looking bridge complexes crossing valleys. We saw a considerable amount of construction for the TGV west of Aix. Many tourists do not bother to rent a car choosing instead the fast and efficient train or bus transportation available.

Looking out at the Mediterranean Sea from our balcony and remembering the beauty of the various countries around it which we have visited, it is hard to believe that anyone would ever want to live anywhere else. Together we have seen France, Spain, Portugal, Morocco, Italy and Greece (also Britain). Joyce has also seen the former Yugoslavia, Turkey, Syria, Lebanon, Jordan and Israel (as well as many countries in the far east).

We still plan to get to Egypt and Israel, maybe this fall, if they would ever stop the violent incidents in that area. We did in fact have a trip scheduled in 1990 combining Greece and Egypt, but the Gulf war broke out and there was no way I was going to find myself 400 miles up the Nile with all that going on. However, friends who have toured Israel report that the degree of security evident is such that an incident is highly unlikely. So I'm hoping we can combine Israel and Egypt this fall.

We decided that we would get take-out food for supper so we checked out the restaurants open in the village plaza. A very interesting Provençal restaurant opens next week not far from our apartment. It looks like a full course meal might run 150F a head. The créperie is open. So is the pizza place which has interesting varieties at 40F. We'll probably go the pizza route.

While we were there we sat on a bench overlooking the pool and watched all the antics going on. Young musclemen showing off their acrobatic talents in the water. Girls in bikinis, some overflowing and some looking as though they were wearing a training bra. We watched for about an hour and then returned to our apartment.

We had been having some difficulty with the dishwasher. It didn't seem to open the detergent hatch and allow it to distribute "*la lessive*" during the washing cycle. On the third try we left the hatch open and also put one of the cookie sized detergent disks in the utensil tray. Third time lucky — they came clean. We'll do the rest by hand.

We were at the point where we had been away long enough (4 weeks) with another 10 days to go.

Joyce is already fantasizing about her own bed back home.

In another 2 or 3 weeks the forsythia in Ottawa would be blooming and if spring is as early this year as last , the golf course, which is right out our back door, would be open.

We have now lived in our home for 7 years and look forward to the return of the Canada geese which have nested there longer than we have in a pond 50 yards from our kitchen window.

Spring and summer in Ottawa are as lovely as anywhere in the world. The landscaping is now mature and we look forward each spring to the rebirth of all of the plantings which were under 3 feet of snow when we left.

So, as much as coming to the Côte d'Azur has given us a break from the cold and ice of an Ottawa winter, arriving home to the warmth and rain of mid April, and the unique smell of the sun once again reviving the earth will do the same for us.

At different times of the day here, the sun focused on different things within our view. For example about a half mile away there is a fairly good sized villa on the rise of the mountain near Dramont. I had been looking out there for two weeks and today was the first time I was conscious of the property. The sunlight had lit up a private tennis court and behind it up about 15 feet, an equally lovely private pool. The house was large but not a mansion. It must look out to sea with a view of Cap Esterel, the lighthouse and the red mountain behind.

From our vantage point there was a narrow rocky point which extended into the sea about 300 yards, creating a small harbour in front of us. In the morning the sun rose behind it. So it was difficult to see what was on our side of it. Yesterday, I noticed for the first time what appears to be a concrete docking facility for yachts.

This morning our electric power kicked out. I looked outside and it was only us. I walked up to reception. It was early and there was an employee eager to help. I said "O*n manque de la puissance.*" He looked at me quizzically and said "*La puissance?*" I said electricity. He said, "*Alors, depuis quand?*" "*Une demi-heure.*" I replied. To which he said "*Bon, on enverra un technicien.*"

By the time I walked back, the technician had arrived — by motorcycle. He checked out the breaker box and pushed the black button. The lights came on. I had tried the red button without success. He was thorough. He checked everything and was pleased to find that the bathroom fluorescent had an annoying hum. He offered to change it right away. We said wait till tomorrow when we check out. He was certainly Mr. Fixit. In his opinion the hum was an *"embêtement"*.

Joyce was constantly reminding me not to let the blankets we sleep under come into contact with my face — making sure that the sheets fold back to cover it. This afternoon I saw why. One of the residents was taking a patio chair out on the grass and had covered it with one of his bedding blankets, so that it was all over the grass.

The same grass that several dogs and the famous black cat had marked out as their territory! Better we don't know.

The path that runs down beside our unit is one that eager golfers from this section often use en route to the pro shop. We were able to see what kind of equipment they were playing with.

About 2:15 today a family group walked by. The father with a bag full of Big Berthas, the athletic wife sporting snazzy golf shoes and lady's Big Berthas, then a man with clubs I didn't recognize followed by a young teenager 13 or 14 weighing about 220 lbs with a flashy looking set of clubs and the only one of the four to sport a power caddy! About 5000F.

This made me think about the attractive blonde from yesterday. I hope she continued to *"brisé le normale"* for all our sakes.

Birds of all description were flitting excitedly around the trees near our balcony, common sparrows and what looked like purple martins busily doing their thing. In the countryside there was a very common bird seen in farmer's fields which is not known to me. It was about the size of a blackbird but had a brilliant white breast. We saw many of them throughout Provence.

We had a pizza for supper made with a very thin crust almost like a crêpe. It only took 5 minutes to prepare. It tasted all right but there wasn't much of it. We finished packing and were now ready to tackle the City of Light.

April 3rd. Happy birthday Vicky! We climbed out of bed at 6 a.m. as planned, finished off the food, cleaned up the place, and loaded the car. The extra charges were lighter than Villa Francia and the pretty young clerk who checked me out was actually interested in whether we had enjoyed our stay or not. I said, "very much." She wished me a safe trip and off we went.

This time we took the road we knew to the A-8 and arrived at the expressway in about the same time as the so-called short cut.

We felt more comfortable as this route was one we had travelled several times in the past two weeks as opposed to "the road less travelled" as Robert Frost might have put it.

We arrived at the Nice airport in good time. I dropped Joyce off at terminal 2 with all of our luggage but the *"chariot"* required a 10F coin. We had plenty of francs but none of them 10s, so Joyce took off in search of change while I had a conversation with a gendarme. As soon as she returned we picked up a *"chariot"* and she went inside to wait for me to return the car at terminal 1.

Peugeot had given me two cards to permit access to the parking lot and of course the one I had kept in my wallet expired on March 5th. I inserted the card and nothing happened. Cars began to line up behind me. The driver behind me supportively said, *"Appuyez sur le bouton."* Meanwhile the parking control centre across the street started barking instructions which I didn't understand. Finally everybody gave up and parking control issued me a new ticket by remote.

After placing the car carefully in a safe position, and with a sigh of relief, I headed for Peugeot. It was quite simple — I sold the car back to them. They were happy and I was happier. I then took the *"camionnette"* back to terminal 2 and found Joyce guarding our possessions. The anxious look on her face disappeared when I appeared and we wheeled our chariot to the cafeteria for café Americain and a chocolate brioche. We had two hours to wait before our flight to Paris.

One of the fun things about this part of the world is the amusing names they give to fast food outlets. One such stand that we passed many times entering St-Raphael was an ice cream stand called Lou Cigalou with a grasshopper as a logo. We always said we'd try it, but never did. Maybe next time.

Diana's Flame

Chapter Six

Paris

The flight from Nice to Paris was pleasant with several children on board, no doubt visiting relatives in Paris for *"Paques"*. We flew north, partly over the Alps. I cannot be sure but at one point I thought we could see the Matterhorn. If it wasn't, it was its twin brother.

On our arrival at Charles de Gaulle, we elected to take the Roissy CDG train to central Paris. We were able to stop at the Luxemburg Station, which unknown to us was only 3 blocks from the Hotel Trianon on Ave Vaugirard. We were actually looking for a taxi but began walking (under some difficulty considering the baggage) and stumbled onto the hotel.

It is a fairly old building, but has been upgraded and is considered a 3 star hotel. It is well located on the left bank of Ave Vaugirard near Boul. St-Michel.

We were only two blocks from the Panthéon. While I was writing this there was a large demonstration close by in favour of Kosovo with 3 busloads of police maintaining order. The red and black flags of Kosovo were very prominent.

We were of course right in the middle of the *"Quartier"* inhabited by students. The Sorbonne was only two blocks away.

We needed to get out and buy bottled water which we did, and then too tired to worry about it we found a McDonald's and pigged out on hamburgers and fries.

Sitting next to us was a couple from Texas who had been here for a week. Yesterday they had been in Lafayette Department Store where Monica Lewinsky was autographing her book. On Monday she was scheduled to do it again at Printemps Department Store.

Even though we were a bit weary, I did sense a surge of excitement when I saw the Panthéon and St-Etienne, and off in the opposite direction la Tour Eiffel. Things that I had read about for years but somehow never managed to come face to face with.

The Kosovo demonstration was peaking with orchestrated chants ringing out. There were only a few hundred of them but since they were only one hundred yards away it sounded like thousands. It was certainly becoming a dilemma for the western world.

Tomorrow would be Easter Sunday. We were only a 15 minute walk from Notre Dame Cathedral so we made plans to go to Easter high mass at 11:30. That promised to be something to look forward to.

We did not have a good first night. The room was small and near the elevator. Although we were able to open the French doors leading to a tiny balcony, we eventually had to close them and the room became hot.

What made matters worse was a commotion at 1 p.m. when a group of revellers came tumbling in after a night of carousing.

Joyce was determined that we weren't going to spend the next 8 nights there.

In the morning the buffet breakfast was quite generous and better than expected.

After breakfast Joyce put her case to the desk clerk who was sympathetic. She handed us the keys to room 802 and said, "take a look and let us know." Up the lift we went to the very top floor to an absolutely delightful garret away from everything with two dormer windows peeking out between a slanted roof ceiling. It was perfect.

We were able to look out over the rooftops straight ahead and see Montmartre. Looking to the left we had a wonderful view of the Eiffel Tower. And we couldn't hear a thing!

So there was peace in the valley once more. We moved in within an hour.

We then walked down Rue St-Michel to the river, and there was Notre Dame! One block to our right. I was surprised at how small the left branch of the Seine was, although the flow was swift.

We had arrived a half hour early for the 11:30 high mass presided over by the archbishop. There were already 8-900 people in line waiting to get in. The gendarmes were there in numbers wearing riot gear (except for face protection). It was an interesting commentary on human behaviour. Here was this large crowd of what we would have hoped were "*les fidèles*", most of whom were respectful of others in line. It was interesting to watch the games played by the few who thought they had a right to beat the system and jump the queue. Planting kisses on people they recognized in line, then snuggling closer in conversation until they thought that nobody noticed. Others simply barged in without blinking an eye, and nobody called them on it. Toward the end it became open season, as the last of the line (about 500) were allowed in the right hand door and everybody made a run for it.

The police did nothing. At that point we were about 30 people wide converging on a space wide enough for 3 or 4. Finally we got in. The mass was already in progress with dozens of television sets set up for those who did not have a direct view.

We were about three quarters up the right side toward the altar and could just see it live. We were packed elbow to elbow. A small child in front of us began to cry and was passed from mother to father in hopes of ending his frustrations. The music, singing, and readings were beautifully done as were the prayers and homily.

I wondered how on earth they would serve communion. There must have been 3-4000 people in the cathedral. Somehow they managed.

When the time came for the peace, Joyce leaned over and whispered, "I want you to shake hands with me for a long time. There are a lot of people coughing in here and I'm concerned about germs."

The peace came, she smiled and proceeded to shake hands with everyone in the church! Later outside she handed me an alcohol hand wipe and insisted that I wash my hands. Oh well.

From the outside the church looks smaller than I had expected, but once inside the extremely high ceiling adds to the immensity of it. It was a memorable experience.

Afterward we walked along the left bank of the river and bought some interesting souvenirs. Then we retraced our steps back up Boulevard St-Michel.

There are hundreds of restaurants in this area. We bought a Paris newspaper "*Le journal du dimanche*" and headed back to the hotel.

On the way we meandered a bit and came upon the Pantheon which was not only open, but free on Easter Sunday.

It is a tribute to all the great patriots recorded through French history. It is endowed with wonderful massive paintings depicting major events and the people involved.

There are enormous sculptures which the guard confirmed were cut from a single piece of stone. Totally beyond the imagination. Many great French patriots are buried there, including Voltaire, Hugo, Zola, Marie and Pierre Curée. Rousseau, Braille, Soufflot and others.

Directly across the Square is the faculty of law of the University of Paris where Joyce studied in 1959-60. We took a photo of it (with Joyce in front of course).

Just behind the Panthéon is the Église St-Etienne, which has to be one of the most beautiful churches I have ever been in. It is neither large nor ornate. It is constructed of elaborately carved stone — pillars, stairways and arches. The stained glass is superb. And yet it does not screech out at you as some overly ornate churches do.

We sat down and soaked in all its beauty for several minutes.

It would appear that Parisiens are a bit more concerned about dogs and excrement. There are by-laws directing dog owners to ensure that dogs do their business in the gutters and we saw several symbols of dogs doing just that, painted on the sidewalk. Progress.

We walked down Boul. St-Michel to a little restaurant on St-Severin that we had seen earlier in the day. They offered a 3 course meal of quite decent quality for 68F. On the walk back up to our hotel we decided to check out the exchange rates being paid. Two different wickets were charging about 15% more than we were able to get in the south. It was of course Easter Sunday in a tourist area. We declined.

In the Paris newspaper we bought earlier today there was a critique of the opéra Lucia de Lammermoor at the Opéra Bastille. There was a 3 p.m. matinée on Sunday the 11th. We thought about going.

Lying in bed I could not help but think of two incidents we had seen earlier while walking around near our hotel. The first occurred at a pedestrian crosswalk waiting for the green walking signal to show.

The light turned green and people began to cross. Just at that moment a thoughtless driver waiting to cross in the same direction suddenly accelerated and impatiently turned right and tore through the crosswalk 3 feet from the curb. Anyone who had chosen that moment to step off the curb wouldn't have had a chance. We were doubly careful from then on.

The second incident occurred near the Sorbonne. A group of 6 or 7 young boys were horsing around matching belligerent egos. A little guy about 8 years old (the same age as Philip my grandson) was taking on a bigger kid probably about ten. They were engaged in a violent contest using oriental kick boxing techniques with a bit of Kung Fu thrown in. They both knew something about it. The little guy was game and attempted a kick trip. The bigger boy retaliated and sent the young one flying to the sidewalk landing on his back. He was hurt. The others foolishly were egging him on — to get up and give more, but he couldn't, he was in too much pain.

The image of it bothered me during the night. The kid had gone down almost exactly in the way that had happened to Joyce in a skating accident 4 years earlier. She had fractured a vertebrae and for a while it looked as though she might never play golf or tennis again. By sheer determination and the skills of the Ottawa Rehabilitation Centre she did recover, and continues to love the sports to this day.

But that little guy had the same look on his face when he hit the ground. I hope his bones were young and soft enough to bounce back from it.

On Easter Monday we had another excellent breakfast and then set out about 9:45 toward the Musée d'Orsay. There was hardly a soul to be seen as we walked down boul. St-Germain until we passed Les Deux Maggots which was doing a brisk trade inside and out. When we turned toward the river it was obvious that the Musée d'Orsay was not open. But it would be on Tuesday.

We decided to head for Le Louvre and crossed the river on the Pont Royal which took us into Les Jardins des Tuileries at the west end of Le Louvre. In the distance we could see hundreds of people lined up on the Pont du Carrousel, leading to the museum.

When we got closer to the Arc de Triumphe within the square around which Le Louvre wraps itself, it was obvious that there were several thousand people in line. A carry over from the Easter holiday. A guard confirmed that it was unusually large and would lighten up in mid week. He recommended that we return at 9 a.m. Thursday when traffic would be lighter.

We did the lower area under the glass pyramid, then crossed over to a string of boutiques on Rue du Rivoli, where we found an exchange wicket giving 15% more than we had been offered the night before on boul. St-Michel. It pays to shop!

We continued up Rivoli looking for La Sainte Chapelle, missed it and ended up back in Notre Dame just as a mass ended. This afforded us a chance to look at what we had missed yesterday.

Eventually we did discover La Sainte Chapelle which is on the same property as the Paris Law Courts and the Conciergerie. It was very heavily guarded by armed policemen, and every visitor had to pass through an electronic security gate. We weren't completely sure why this was so.

In any event, after waiting in line for about a half hour during which we had an interesting conversation with a staff member from the US embassy in The Hague, we got in.

My personal opinion is that it was simply overwhelming, for my taste, overdone.

And yet it is considered one of the most beautiful Christian chapels in existence. This is largely due to the enormous and detailed stained glass windows which occupy about 80% of the exterior walls of the upper chapel, and which depict every book in the bible from creation to redemption.

On our way back to the hotel near Le Musée de Cluny we passed a large contingent of gendarmes — probably over 100 of them, waiting for something to develop. Perhaps another demonstration was expected. However, on our way to dinner we looked down St-Michel to see what if anything had in fact developed with the gendarmes. They were gone.

After dinner we walked down St-Michel to check out some of the stores — mainly a student's market. As we got near the Musée Cluny I commented to Joyce that it looked like a quiet night for the gendarmes. With that sirens wailed, and 4 busloads of them went flying by on St-Germain! Joyce thought they were probably going home for dinner.

After sundown, the major attractions in Paris are lit up. There was a marvelous view of La Tour Eiffel from our bedroom window, which I took a picture of.

We had four options in mind for Wednesday: Musée d'Orsay, Le Musée Picasso, buy opera tickets and reconfirm our Air France flight home.

Well 2 out of 4 ain't bad.

We walked to the Musée d'Orsay and got there about 10:15. There were already 3-400 in line, but it moved quickly and after about twenty minutes we were inside.

They have a great security system, with metal detectors and x-ray machines. Everything had to be passed through x-ray. Signs stating that no pack sacks or other large bags were permitted, and no flash cameras were allowed. They then proceeded to ignore it all. We saw several flash photos being taken and dozens of students with pack sacks on their backs. The guards did nothing.

The museum is housed in what was formerly the Gare d'Orsay train station. It is in itself a magnificent building and now a fabulous world class art museum. There are hundreds of priceless paintings, particularly impressionist, post impressionist and mid to late 19th century art.

I was not aware of the significance of it at the time, but when we were in Arles we stopped in "Place du Forum" and sat down on the yellow sidewalk chairs in front of "le Café la Nuit".

Vincent Van Gogh would certainly have been there many times in 1888 to paint this colourful building which he did from several different perspectives.

I remember the eye catching yellow of the café which still exists, and the many paintings of it I have seen in Paris and Amsterdam.

It struck me that he seemed obsessed with yellow. It stands out in the painting of his house as it does in "le Café la Nuit".

It provides a smashing background for the "Arlésienne" a swarthy woman in dark attire, a copy of which hung in the dining room of Hotel Calendal where we stayed.

I wondered to myself as we looked at his work, if this man, so obviously tormented, had finally found an escape from his depression in the brightness and optimism of yellow. His fascination with sunflowers, his home, his furniture and harvest landscape all emphasize this upliftng colour.

Perhaps in the last stages of his desperation it became his colour of hope. Not soon enough apparently. He died the following year of a self-inflicted gunshot wound.

We toured the museum for three hours and probably saw about one half of what was there. But did see most of the paintings we were interested in.

It is a fabulous collection and included all of the art formerly displayed in the Jeu de Pomme Museum. It would take several days to really do it properly. But it was very satisfying to have seen many works that are always included in art books covering the world's greatest art.

It is about a three mile walk from our hotel to "le Musée" via boul. St-Germain and back. So our feet were beginning to feel it. We stopped at rue St-Severin for lunch.

We also wanted to reconfirm our flight on the 12th. The map shows an Air France office one block from our hotel, on rue de Médici. We looked and looked and finally found what we thought was a travel agency. It turned out to be Air France; but there was absolutely nothing on the outside to suggest that it was. There were several people inside waiting for service. There was also a sign saying please take a ticket for service. But no ticket machine was operating, so we just muscled our way into line and it worked out. They do things very loosely.

Paris is a huge city. It is particularly active in the evening, when the entire population seems to come out of the woodwork and stroll down the streets or eat at restaurants. During the morning the city seems almost deserted except for those rushing to work.

While we were waiting in line at the Musée d'Orsay we chatted with a couple from New Jersey whose daughter is majoring in French at the Sorbonne. She is an intern at the Herald Tribune.

Later that day Joyce and I had walked down boul. St-Michel to a little restaurant we had eaten in the night before on rue St-Severin.

When we came out of the restaurant who should be sitting at a sidewalk café across the street but the couple from New Jersey! They waved and we had a brief chat with them. It is amazing that in a city this size, we bumped into them again a mile and a half from le musée.

When we bought the Sunday paper there was an ad in it promoting a unique little car called *"Le Smart"*. We have seen three of them on the street. It is a uniquely designed car with ample seating for two, about six inches more headroom than the Peugeot, a very wide wheelbase and an incredibly short length overall under 10 feet!

It is designed for city driving and costs 54000F. There was a reference to Mercedes Benz in the ad so possibly they were the manufacturers. It is probably the only car that would fit in our garage alongside our Camry. There happened to be one parked across the street from where we had dinner surrounded by an admiring crowd.

On our first visit to the restaurant everything was excellent. On the second, the fries were tired, probably warmed up, and they showed it.

So I told the waiter who was a very nice young fellow from Greece, named Yanis. He was very apologetic and gave us two cognacs on the house. I gave him an extra 10 F over and above the 15% gratuity already added. He gave us the name of another restaurant called Knossis just down the street specializing in Greek cuisine.

Once you get the sense of it, getting around Paris via the underground goes fairly smoothly. However if you aren't expecting it you can end up mixing metro trains with R.E.R. trains and that can throw you off.

This was the first day we had used the underground. If you look at a simplified map of the system, it looks like a plate of spaghetti. As a consequence in the first couple of hours we spent more time trying to analyze the route systems and connections than we did travelling.

One thing is certain, the system covers huge distances. As an example we boarded at Cluny en route to the Tour Eiffel, during which we passed Le Musée d'Orsay. It had to be over two miles, and we had walked it both ways yesterday! No wonder our feet were sore.

On the train to the Tour Eiffel we got talking with a Belgian gentleman and when we arrived he took our picture. This, only after we kept moving in front of la Tour to ensure that it was in the picture only to have him move aside to get it out of the picture. Finally his wife intervened — "they want la Tour in the background" — "Oh" he said when he finally "got" the picture.

We walked under and around the Tour but did not go up. The thing that impressed me was the unexpected enormity of its base. We wanted to go from there to the Arc de Triomphe but there was no simple route so we walked toward it over the Pont d'Alma. When we reached the right bank we came unexpectedly to the tunnel where Diana was killed. There is a bronze flame monument over the tunnel which was there before the accident, but it has now been transformed into a people's memorial to her, with numerous sympathetic messages written on it, and still, small bouquets around it.

We walked straight up Georges V a very ritzy and fashionable avenue which led almost directly to Ave des Champs-Elysées and the huge arc. In Paris everything seems to be done on a grand scale and this certainly applies to this magnificent avenue.

By this time we needed a chair and some nourishment so we stopped near the arc for a few minutes, then continued to the rond point where we took the metro to Gare de Lyon. We did this because the Picasso Museum was close and more particularly because a display room for "Le Smart" was across from the Gare. We had a discussion with a saleslady who told us about this amazing little car and also gave us a brochure and pricing. The car is only nine and a half feet long but the two passenger compartment is huge. It has a Mercedes engine and can be bought for export for about 50000F plus transport and import duties.

After viewing "Le Smart" we got back on the metro and headed with some difficulty for the Picasso Museum. It was overrated, and not as good as the one at Antibes.

We stopped at a tiny sidewalk café near La Bastille for a coffee and then made for the metro. As is the case at home the metro had a good selection of street musicians. There was a particularly good violinist at La Bastille and an excellent cellist at Gare de Lyon.

At certain points on the route the train rises above ground level. Near the Bastille there is a point at which riders can look out at one of the canals leading up from the river. It is very picturesque with many different types of barges and yachts moored there.

There is simply no end to the beautiful architecture one encounters when least expected. Little pockets of exquisitely designed buildings such as La Place des Vosges, which emerge from nowhere as you turn a corner.

We have been intrigued by the pace of activity in late afternoon and early evening, particularly in the area of Cluny/Sorbonne. There is an unrelenting stream of people in a hurry to go somewhere, many with baguette or panini sandwiches in hand, eating on the fly. There are people from many different parts of the world, Asians, Africans. And other countries not so easily recognizable.

Graffiti is everywhere. Where we took the metro to the Tour Eiffel a fairly decent looking young man was busy defacing the inside of the car with some political slogan.

It was now Thursday and our day to tackle the big one, Le Louvre. Its size is beyond comprehension. It has over 300,000 works of art of all kinds, many of which are not displayed.

However, with the help of Michelin and some very good direction signs in Le Louvre we saw a great deal, and many of the famous works including Mona Lisa, Winged Victory, Venus deMilo and hundreds of others.

The museum is helpful in identifying key works with a grey card alongside the work stating *"personal choice of the museum staff"*. We were then able to zero in on the key works quickly. That is not to say that the rest is to be ignored. On the contrary. There is just so much of such great quality that it is almost overwhelming.

Of the three principal sections we toured two of them, the Denon and the Sully. We did not enter the Richelieu. After three and a half hours we just had had enough and went to Le Louvre commercial level which fans out from the glass pyramid and had lunch.

By now we were feeling quite confident in the metro so we took off for Montmartre which required three connections. The Église Sacre Coeur is quite lovely, once you master the climb up. The view is also wonderful, but it is no longer a centre for artists. It is now strictly tourists.

We can see it in the distance from our hotel room window night or day.

I also wanted to see the famous Moulin Rouge which was about one half mile away, so we walked along past Place Pigalle seeing all kinds of characters on the way and took a great photo of it.

We got back on the metro at Place Blanche and worked our way back to our hotel with several transfers.

The underground network at Gare du Nord is enormous. In one case we had to walk about a half mile underground to connect with La Chapelle Station from Gare du Nord.

We were surprised to see several police and soldiers armed with semi-automatic rifles, obviously looking for someone in the metro stations. The other thing that bothered us is the extent to which graffiti is spoiling the beauty of so much of the city.

That night we had a wonderful Greek dinner at restaurant Knossos which was at 16 rue St-Severin, and was the place recommended to us by Yanis the young Greek waiter at Le Menhir, the French restaurant just up the street.

There were dozens of little restaurants in the area near St. Severin Church. Both of us had a brochette of the most sumptuous lamb chops we had ever eaten. I also had an outstanding Greek salad and we split a bottle of very good Cretan wine. Joyce and the waiter hit it off because he was a Turk, and she had been in Turkey in 1960 hitchhiking in the middle of the Turkish revolution. They exchanged stories and at the end, two snifters of excellent Metaxa cognac appeared on the house. Although we needed them like a hole in the head, we thoroughly enjoyed the restaurant. Dinner for two with wine and service 200F.

We were winding down a bit and feeling a bit mellow. I said to Joyce that if we could have the same room (802) at the Trianon I'd come back.

After dinner we walked along St-Severin to see how business was at Le Menhir, the restaurant we had dined at twice before.

Just next to it was another restaurant with tiny table level windows.

Sitting at a window table, in a chair just like any other customer was a white Sealyham terrier, with a cup full of ice cream in front of him. This was no ordinary dog. This dog had class. Tucked into its collar was a napkin and the dog was very politely enjoying the ice cream without spilling a drop. Across from the dog was a little old lady wearing a 1920s style felt hat, every now and then passing Fido a sugar cube which she consumed with dignity.

A crowd of amused spectators gathered outside to watch this performance, but the dog came from the right side of the tracks, ignored them, and continued to enjoy her dinner like a grande dame. *"Qu'arrivera-t-il ensuite!"*

There is no shortage of motorcycles in France. They first became evident to us in Cannes where they seem to defy all the laws of the road — including gravity. If city traffic is backed up they have a simple solution, just start another lane, preferably in the middle of the road where they can also borrow space from the oncoming lane. The day we drove from Cannes to Cap Esterel on La Corniche d'Or they passed us on sharp curves doing 120-140km with their bikes angled over 30 degrees. In Paris they have two specialties. In the first they simply move into the oncoming (and supposedly exclusive) bus lane and roar down the wrong way. You take your life in your hands even when the *"pietons"* signal is green.

The other stunt they pull is usually at 4 a.m. in the morning where they get to a corner, keep revving their engines and then break loose with a thundering roar.

Dogs! There are two distinct groups. The majority, probably 60-70%, are tiny long haired characters mostly Yorkies. The rest are huge usually Alsatians, the largest we've ever seen. You rarely see a mid-sized dog. They are a large and active part of the everyday life of the French people and very much included in everything they do.

A large group must have checked into our hotel yesterday. We were unable to get into the regular breakfast room and were fed instead in another quite nice dining room we didn't know existed.

We headed out to see Les Invalides, still an active military hospital, and of course the tomb of several important soldiers including Foch and Napoleon. It was a sunny warm day and several of the old vets were outside in wheelchairs, close to the tomb.

As is the case with most of the French national monuments, this too is on a grand scale. Les Invalides occupies a sizeable area, probably 50 acres, around which a fashionable residential district has sprung up. It is one of the few large areas where you see grass. It is located on the main line to Versailles. We had intended to do the Cluny Museum, but decided instead to continue out by train to Versailles, about 15 km from the centre of Paris.

We passed through a large commercial area with high rises, something you don't see downtown. Further out, once past Issy, you begin to see the equivalent of our suburbs, with attractive single family homes and well cared for gardens, especially along the tracks.

Eventually we arrived at the end of the line — Versailles.

Before walking over to the palace we stopped at a popular fast food chain called Classe Croute which operates much like McDonald's but serves much tastier and healthier food. We got into a conversation with a young businessman in his 30s who gave us an insight into many things we had been wondering about.

The armed police in the metro, for example, were there because of Algerian terrorist activity in Paris.

The municipality of Versailles had become very prosperous through a combination of tourism and the fact that a sizeable number of military officers had settled there. There is also a university.

The Versailles Palace and all of the surroundings are enormous and beautiful. The landscaping behind it is superb. In many ways the size of the palace reminds me of L'Escorial in Spain.

It is easy to understand the resentment among hungry peasants which resulted in the French Revolution, with the concentration of such opulent wealth in so few hands at the expense of the masses.

The walking areas around the palace are paved with cobblestones and are quite rough. Good walking shoes are a must. It is everything that it is reputed to be and more.

When we returned to the station there was a train ready to depart and somehow the trip back seemed faster than the way out.

We walked up boul. St-Michel, replenished our supply of bottled water and returned to the hotel.

We again went down to St-Severin for dinner. This time we chose to go where it appeared busy, at the Pregrille Restaurant. The meal was satisfactory but not as good as either of the two previous restaurants we had tried and cost about 20% more.

We ate inside but just outside, in the sidewalk section of the restaurant, there was a family of four, two adults and two kids about 10 or 12, the daughter being the younger. She was having a great feed of moules marinières and loving every minute of it. It was amusing to see.

When we got back to the hotel our ride to the airport was confirmed and we were handed an invoice for 170F of which a down payment of 40F was required. I paid the clerk in cash and asked him to receipt it. He was very indignant. A receipt is quite hard to come by in France. When I had checked out of the Villa Francia in Cannes I was handed an invoice for about 400F which I had paid, but it did not show a zero balance.

There must have been a sporting event of some kind going on involving some British team because we saw a lot of men in kilts, all having a great time.

Even though there were many things we had not yet seen I felt that we had seen as much as I needed to. We still wanted to see the Cluny Museum which was only about four blocks from us. If we were to duplicate previous visits it would be to the Musée d'Orsay which we both loved. Beyond that it was simply a case of winding down.

Joyce wanted to go to mass at St-Germain-des-Prés on Sunday. Very close to it is Les Deux Maggots, perhaps lunch.

We had been very lucky with the weather in Paris. Up to that point very little rain, but the forecast predicted 5 days of heavy rain. We were going home at the right time.

The situation in Kosovo was front page. Yeltzin was sounding belligerent. Germany was opening its doors to refugees. French public opinion favoured stronger intervention and some were even talking about a major war! God help us if that develops.

Very close to us was the Musée Cluny or Musée Nationale du Moyen Age. It was the former residence of Mary Tudor and was built over Roman baths. The collection is considered the finest in the world from the middle ages. There were fabulous tapestries including the famous unicorn tapestries in which each dealt with one of the human senses. They were as mysterious as they were beautiful. There were also numerous objets d'art from the middle ages, a superb collection of icons, and many beautifully detailed altar pieces. The museum is much larger than it appears from the outside and is the last of only two remaining examples of domestic medieval architecture in Paris.

Up to that point we hadn't ventured into any of the major stores in Paris. The nearest, Lafayette, was on boul. Raphael about a mile from our hotel. This is a prosperous residential and commercial area where the buildings are well maintained.

We did some comparative shopping and found Lafayette prices considerably higher than the equivalent design and quality at home. More than double.

We wanted to take a different route back so we left boul. Raphael and followed boul. Montparnasse for several blocks until boul. d'Observatoire where we entered Les Jardins de Marco Polo which led to Les Jardins de Luxembourg, where the palace, now the senate, is located. It was built for Marie de Médici in the 1600s.

While the gardens were open to the public, the senate was heavily guarded by armed police. The main entrance to the senate was on rue Vaugirard just two blocks from our hotel.

It seems that everywhere you walk in Paris you are surrounded by beauty. Not just the architecture, but statues, wide boulevards, and colourful restaurants and shops. Someone back home told me before we left that it was the most beautiful city in the world. I have seen a great deal to support that and very little to challenge it. One exception is dog droppings.

We returned for dinner to St-Severin at Knossos and had another excellent meal. We had a different waiter but the first one from the other night spotted us and greeted us like long lost friends. He was going to be working late that night. It was the Orthodox Easter and a huge party was coming in at midnight for a feast. It is a fun place with a personal touch and very good food.

We found out what all the big guys in kilts were doing in Paris. Scotland played France in English rugby and won! It wouldn't be quiet on the streets that night.

On Sunday morning we got up a little later, straightened out a few things in readiness for the final onslaught of packing and then went to Église St-Germain-des-Prés, one of the oldest churches in Paris, dating from the 6th century. It was nearly destroyed several times by the Normans. It was designed with outstanding acoustics and we were particularly fortunate to be there when a wonderful choir from west London was participating in the mass (in Latin) with several beautifully sung anthems. After the mass they sang additional works which were greatly appreciated by several people who remained to hear them.

Joyce and I had arrived there early and were sitting in the third row on the centre aisle. When the time came for the peace, the priest came down our side for only 3 rows and we both received the handshake of the peace of Christ. It was a warm and spiritual mass making us all feel a part of it, especially in contrast with the huge throng at Notre Dame which seemed totally impersonal.

After the mass we explored the areas surrounding the altar and came across a small sculpture which commemorated *"Nouvelle France"* and in particular the bishop of Laval and Montmorency.

Directly across the street from the church was Les Deux Maggots, the restaurant made famous by Sartre and the existentialists. We had decided earlier to blow the budget and have brunch there. Joyce had a Deux Maggots salad and tea, and I chose a ham omelette, coffee and a courvoisier. Cognac for breakfast? My mind was more on the cost than the quality. I made a Freudian slip and ordered *"une omelette jambon et un combien — er un cognac courvoisier!"* He probably had heard it before. It was a nice experience in a classy environment.

Later we had one final item on our checklist and that was for Joyce to see once again *"L'Institut de Droit Comparé"* which was on rue St-Guillaume. We found it and then proceeded to get lost again. We found ourselves on boul. Raphael and in the distance was Lafayette. We were headed in exactly the wrong direction.

In due course we made it back to the hotel and that brought our travels in France to an end.

We departed the following day full of good memories. We had seen a lot, had met some very fine people, and some not so fine, but that's life anywhere.

We saw great innovations still not commonplace in North America. Some of them should be.

We have never tasted bread to equal the French baguette. It must be possible to duplicate it and we wondered why no one had.

The quality of produce is vastly superior to home even when compared to Florida.

The quality fast food offered by chains such as "Classe Croûte" would seem a natural opportunity at home.

Design originality such as the amazing city use auto Le Smart which takes advantage of space utilization without sacrificing comfort and fuel economy. It is a brilliant concept with all kinds of possibilities for space related economies in urban areas.

In our wanderings around Paris we came across many interesting things including 2 or 3 different sales offices for Pierre et Vacances. In the window of one such office on boul. de Montparnasse there was an ad for one week at Cap Esterel in July for 7000F. We had just stayed 4 weeks including airfare for 5400F. I guess we did pretty well.

We continue to see hilarious scenes involving dogs in Paris. While eating at Les Deux Maggots a number of people arrived looking for a seat. One elderly and very well dressed lady had her tiny dog with her — sticking out of a purse.

About 200 yards up boul. St-Germain a young man had an enormous Chinese dog — the kind with the wrinkled face — with him. He was making money by allowing people to have their picture taken with him.

As in the south, people are usually dressed up. The other noticeable phenomenon is the way they dress up small children. Bright multi coloured outfits in striking designs which make them stand out.

The scarf is an essential accessory to every woman's wardrobe. All sizes, designs, colours, materials and prices. They can be bought on the street for 20 - 40F or you can pay 600 - 800F for something special. Shoes can be bought for 5000F a pair. The interesting fact was that fashion for the mass market was in our opinion extremely dull. Uninteresting colours, mostly shades of grey and beige. The high fashion outfits were clearly more colourful.

It is hard to walk more than a block without running into a Patisserie/Boulangerie. Some of the most sumptuous pastries can be bought fairly reasonably. In the Severin district there was a pastry shop specializing in middle eastern pastries which were fabulous at 6 - 8F each. They were catching the passing trade from people who had just eaten at nearby restaurants and cannot resist the temptation as they go by.

We also saw window displays of poultry with head and feet still on and what looked like bruises. They were absolutely revolting.

Food and eating is a way of life in France.

The restaurant/bar scene is often in clusters such as at St-Severin. Walking down the side street near St-Germain-des-Prés we discovered a whole new section of bars and restaurants probably a little more upscale than on St-Severin. One quite spiffy restaurant, Le Procop, had a plaque on its front wall claiming to be the oldest café in the world and laid claim to Napoleon, Voltaire and Franklin as its regular patrons.

In the same area we came across a group of street entertainers: three women — 2 singers and an accordionist. They were no spring chickens, but they sang in a robust semi-operatic voice and were a pleasure to listen to. You see other musicians playing violin, cello, saxophone, and some circus type acts such as jugglers — all working for tips in the street.

It adds immensely to the colourful flavour of Parisien side streets. And the people eat it up, milling around mainly in the evening, but also in early afternoons on weekends. It is the place to be.

All of this is multiplied if you happen to be in a metro station. The flow of humanity is staggering.

The tourists seem to be mostly German with Italian and English coming second. There are a fair number of Americans especially young students in large groups.

We saw one US school group at Montmartre wearing identical school shirts, huffing and puffing their way up the hill. (As did we!)

There were several classes of American students at Fondation Maeght in St-Paul-de-Vence.

In the Picasso Museum at Antibes there was an adult group tour from the Smithsonian Institute looking very prosperous and being guided through by a knowledgeable looking type.

Yesterday an elder hostel tour checked in at our hotel. They were off to see many of the places we saw including Le Musée Cluny which is nearby.

We had an hour and a half to wait for the transport to Charles de Gaulle airport. It rained earlier but the sun had come out so Joyce went for a brief walk through Le Jardin Luxembourg.

When she returned I did the same. While outside I noticed a team of erectors putting up a scaffold on the corner across the street next to the *"Place de la Sorbonne"* where the demonstration occurred.

Very few buildings in downtown Paris exceed 10 stories. Our hotel had eight and we were able to see easily over the rooftops in three directions.

There was an electronic sign on the corner of Vaugirard and boul St-Michel. It was about 8 feet square and the message kept changing much like a bulletin board. At first it was urging Parisiens who wished to help the Kosovo refugees to bring staple foods to city hall. Closer to my heart the sign then changed its message to a warning to dog owners. *"Si votre chien a des manières mauvaises vous risquez une amende de 3000F."* I sincerely hoped that they would enforce it.

Yesterday near St-Germain-des-Prés we saw more painted sidewalk dog logos indicating that dogs should do their business in the gutter.

Interestingly there is a system of gutter flushing which we saw frequently, where a flow of water comes out from under the curb and very effectively flushes the gutters downstream. Each sewer inlet is partly blocked by a burlap mat, allowing the flow to continue on past the sewer.

This has been a nice hotel to stay at (once we changed our room). The staff are helpful and courteous and the location is great. Two hundred yards to the Sorbonne, two blocks to Le Musée Cluny and Le Palais Luxembourg. A fifteen minute walk to Notre Dame and St-Germain-des-Prés and two metro stations on two different lines within two blocks.

The public spaces , lounges, bars, dining rooms are tastefully decorated.

The ride out to the airport was interesting. We had to make another pick up in the 2nd Arrondissement not far from the Boul. Marechal Foch — a very nice district. To get there we again crossed over the Pont d'Alma. There were more floral tributes to Diana since we were there a week ago.

The people we picked up were Australian and had been in Paris for eight days. A woman in her 40s and her daughter. They had been visiting a niece who was a dancer at the *"Lido"*.

The daughter was here applying for a similar job and got one at *"Le Moulin Rouge"*. Most of the dancers are Russian or Polish, one from New Zealand, and the rest French. Dancers in these establishments often end up nude, so when she got out we took a good look at her with her clothes on. Not bad!

At the airport there were hordes checking in and security as usual was very tight. A lady in line ahead of us had to open her hand baggage and voilà — a pretty good sized knife. They put it in a special security envelope and I assumed she'd get it back when we landed.

The cabin steward said it would be a full aircraft, although it didn't look that way in the waiting area.

Joyce commented that the south of France seemed a long time ago. We took bets on how much snow there would be at home.

The plane filled up. A woman and small baby took two seats behind the galley. Shortly after a lady arrived holding those seat numbers. A great discussion ensued but the lady holding the seat tickets became the lady holding the bag. No seat! Twenty minutes later she still had no seat. The plane was 1 hour late in departing (so what else is new). The cause, someone did not have the proper visa. Meanwhile we all just sat and waited.

So far 2 out of 4 Air France flights have been 1 hour or more late in taking off.

Finally we were airborne. I looked at my watch. We had been in the air 1 hour, 7 more to go.

Back in Paris it is 7 p.m. when the promenade begins for the evening. Joyce wonders how many dogs are being carried around in purses.

Dog in a basket

Coming Home

Chapter Seven

The Pond

Upon our arrival at our home in Ottawa, we were delighted to find that all of our perennials had wintered well and some were even beginning to push through with new growth in mid April. The ice that would remain for another week was still in the pond that lies just off our rear deck and continues for about 215 yards alongside the ninth fairway of the golf course. It then veers to the right at a 30 - 40 degree angle, forming the ninth green. Sitting on our upper deck we have a clear view of most of the ninth fairway and more interestingly the green itself, which presents an irresistible challenge to the parade of "jocks" who look at the shot from our end of the pond, flex their muscles and stand up to the ball brimming with confidence in their ability to hit a shot which must carry about 225 yards. They then proceed to hit the shot into the pond, and that is when we hear a selection of choice words not normally heard in places like churches.

We have learned by observation that there is no need to watch the ball, the player's body language tells us what kind of shot it was.

We had spotted a frogman in the pond two years ago and were told that something in the order of 5-6000 balls are taken out of it each year. Not being inclined to accept statistics of this type, we did our own calculation based on a minimum of one ball per foursome going into the lake and probably two during charity tournaments, and it's pretty easy to arrive at 5-6000 balls a season.

A neighbour of ours is a ball hawk. He is out on the course every morning at 5:30 a.m. I am also an early riser, and while I am having breakfast I see him returning most days with a plastic grocery bag which probably contains 15 or 20 balls. He pays for his golf with the proceeds.

The pond was here before the golf course although its shape was modified a bit when the course was constructed.

We take a great deal of pleasure from the wildlife which comes back to it every year, particularly the Canada geese, who breed here, some Mallard ducks who amuse us with their antics and a blue heron who fishes for carp.

The geese are fascinating to watch. They are completely disciplined and very protective of their young. We live on the opposite side of the pond from the ninth fairway and by early summer the geese must sense that they are safe on our side. About five houses down from us, a woman who loves nature, offers them bread crumbs quite regularly. As a result the parents will allow the goslings to come up on shore for treats.

When the babies are young, right through to August when they mature and can fly, they remain in formation at all times in the water and do what they are told when feeding on the golf course.

Geese seem to love bent grass, which is the most commonly used grass variety on premium golf courses. The problem develops because the geese have an apparently high volume digestive system and this disturbs the golf course owners and some members. It is ironic that while goose droppings can create a howl from the club owners and golfers, they are strangely silent on the subject of herbicides and insecticides, with all of the known serious health hazards these create.

Shortly after our return home in mid April the golf course, in its wisdom, ringed the pond with red and silver reflective tape about 18 inches off the ground which completely destroys the natural look of the pond and creates a major source of noise pollution in a strong wind. This was done in an effort to discourage the geese from breeding here and even more so from spending the summer here.

It has failed miserably. Last year it took the geese about two days to figure it out by simply walking under it. By putting it up a few weeks earlier they expected to solve the problem. They haven't.

It never was a problem for mature geese, they simply fly over it. It was really intended to thwart the goslings in the hope that they would starve or be killed by predators. Fortunately for the geese the humane laws disallow any act which would jeopardize the geese until they are able to fly and escape to safety.

As I write this, it is May 16th. Yesterday the first family appeared on the pond with seven goslings. Today a second family with 6 goslings showed up. They are a beautiful sight, and they have already figured out the deterrent. Our neighbours report each development to one another as these marvellous birds begin their life journey.

Now if we could only convince the golf course that the reflective tape is not only useless for its intended purpose, but a major irritation to those who have to look at it and listen to it.

Every year there are many fascinating and intriguing stories surrounding the experiences these birds go through. It will be interesting to follow their progress again this year.

While all of this has been going on, a dove has been constructing a nest in a blue spruce tree about 15 feet from our deck. Curiosity got the better of me yesterday, so I climbed up on a stepladder and lo and behold there was a pretty pink egg. It will be fun to follow this one.

Wild animals aren't the only attraction out back. There are also some house pets with a personality of their own. Three houses over to the left a miniature dachshund with a great pedigree and no brains resides. His name is Ludwig. He is a loveable little hound who thinks that it is his God given right to retrieve golf balls — especially those in play on the ninth fairway out behind us. He also imagines himself as the canine world's answer to Pele. He adores playing soccer with his owners' three year old, and can nudge that ball as deftly as many a world cup striker.

We also installed a 3 column bird feeder on the back edge of the property line. In cool weather it provides us with a lot of activity when purple finches, chickadees, wood sparrows and blue jays frequent it. In spring we greatly enjoy the gold finches and the occasional red pileated woodpecker.

Everything falls apart when the grackles arrive. They completely dominate the feeder and this year we gave up at the end of April and emptied it for the squirrels in the nearby woods. I suppose we really should confine our bird feeding time to the winter months anyway, in the interest of keeping the little guys actually hunting when their regular source of food becomes available in the spring.

As for us, the early spring enabled us to get out on the golf course to see if we could improve on last year. After five rounds Joyce decided she needed more lessons. I am stubborn but leaning in the same direction.

Both of us celebrate birthdays within two weeks of each other, Joyce first. This year we were in Montreal to visit my son and daughter and their families and we received the nicest gift of all — news that Sandy, my daughter-in-law, is expecting her third child. It will be a millennium baby expected between Christmas and New Year's. Her first two, Julie and Philip, are as excited as the rest of us. With little Sarah, my daughter Vicky's child making four, we have been truly blessed.

When my birthday came along two weeks later, Peter my son announced that as he had to be in Ottawa that day he would stay overnight with us and take us to dinner.

We had a great meal at Isaac's one of our favourite restaurants with wonderful Mediterranean food and a couple of bottles of wine.

The following week we both spent time at the dentist patching up the area where the daily diet of sesame bars in France had taken its toll. Next time we'll have to chew something softer.

Today I began a campaign to shed some excessive weight around my middle. I think I should lose 10-12 lbs which I have put on over the past three years. That should take eight or nine weeks. In addition to the health factor involved in carrying excess weight, there are economic considerations. I have four or five expensive suits which I can no longer get into.

Going on a diet is a bit like giving up smoking (which I did forty years ago). You have to psyche yourself up to the point where your will to achieve your objective totally dominates all other considerations. Once you take the first step, the second and third come easier. So we shall see in about eight weeks how I did.

I have known a number of people, especially in the business world, whose job required them to frequently be in 4 star restaurants. That can be a killer. You can only survive if you stick to omelettes or salads and club sodas.

A close associate of mine found it necessary to diet from time to time to offset the excess intake. We parked side by side in the Tilden garage on Stanley Street in Montreal. During one such period, I was picking up my car during lunch and lo and behold I spot this sad looking face sitting in his car eating a lunch of lettuce leaves and lemon juice from a plastic container. He looked absolutely miserable.

Another character I worked with was on just about every diet imaginable over a twenty year period from Metrical to Scarsdale to the steak diet and back again. He was a loud, outgoing guy, full of determination. At one point he went on a diet of Special K and bananas three times a day. He had been on it for a couple of weeks when we had to meet a third party whom we were considering for a job.

We met at an Italian restaurant on Dominion Square. I ordered lasagna, the man being interviewed ordered spaghetti, and my determined associate ordered Special K and bananas. The waitress fidgeted nervously and said she didn't think they had Special K. He asked her to check. When she returned with the bad news, he sent her back to see if they had bananas. She returned after a minute or two to confirm that they didn't. He squared his jaw and in a voice brimming with conviction, he said "Then I'll have an extra large pizza with double pepperoni." Oh, well.

———————————————

It is now early evening on the third week of May. The solitary goose has arrived once again as he has done for the past three years. He is without mate, presumably shot down somewhere while migrating. The social behaviour of the other geese somehow does not permit a ménage à trois, except under certain conditions. One of them is when the goslings are threatened by an osprey who normally hunts for fish in the pond. The osprey must have a taste for baby geese as well.

Two years ago, at the same time of year, the geese sighted the osprey circling above, 2 or 3 hundred feet in the air. Immediately the geese headed for the centre of the pond, placed the goslings between them and covered them with their wings. The lone goose also spotted the problem and he too raced to the water and added his own wings to the coverage. In due time the osprey took off and with a lot of gobbling and squawking, the all clear was sounded. The male parent who had welcomed the lone goose, now turned on him and chased him off of the pond.

Sometimes when the newborns have reached the point where they can be walked to another pond about three hundred yards away, the lone goose will land by the lake and stand for hours at a time on the fairway. Why? We have no idea. Perhaps waiting for the mate to return. Who knows. But this problem must work in reverse as well. One wonders why some widowed goose doesn't sneak up and tweak his behind. Maybe one will. In the meantime he is not allowed near the family until much later in the season when all of the geese will cluster together in the shade, presumably even him.

The goslings mature remarkably fast and within weeks exchange their beige baby fuzz for darker markings. Within eight to ten weeks they are almost adults. It is not until mid July that the first trial flights begin. At first it is only running with their wings flapping. This goes on for two or three weeks. Then they graduate to short attempts at flight, landing in the water. There is usually one straggler who has to be coaxed into trying it. Finally about the third or fourth week of July they are airborne! Even if it is only a matter of 40 or 50 feet. It must be as exhilarating for them as it is for us to watch them. Then in early August they take off and get into serious flight training for the big trip south ahead of them in November/December.

The degree to which they are under the control of the parents is something to see. Equally there is never a moment when one or the other senior geese is not on guard. In the summer of 98 a really interesting social phenomenon occurred. A third pair of geese arrived on the lake, and with them two small goslings. Normally third parties are shooed away but for some reason they were accepted. For two or three weeks they grazed together, swam together and mixed very compatibly. Then one day the two adults of the third group left, leaving the two goslings to be brought up by the original inhabitants. From that point on, where we used to see two adults and seven goslings, there were now nine goslings, and they all received the same protective treatment until they matured.

In contrast to the geese who will swim across the pond in a tight single file line with the parents at each end, the Mallard ducks are totally undisciplined.

Unlike the geese they do not remain on the pond all summer, and after two or three weeks, if we are lucky, we will see the mother leading a parade to a nearby stream. In this act they display discipline. However for the brief period they are on the pond it is utter chaos!

The mother attempts to lead the pack but some of the ducklings go off on a tangent exploring their own world. On one occasion last year the flotilla of geese was swimming neatly in a line straight down the pond. One of the ducklings was having a great time off on his own when he suddenly realized that he was about to be cut off from his family. Like a dart he tore across the water doing his own version of the road runner, and back to the safety of mother duck. It is interesting that while we see the male with his magnificent colouring for the first week or two he is seldom seen again. Just another deadbeat dad!

About the end of May a third family of geese arrived on the pond with five goslings. For the first day or two they went their own way, but gradually moved closer to the earlier arrivals, who by now were becoming quite brazen, lounging around on the grass near the ninth green, like polite spectators at the Masters. One of the earlier brood has disappeared, presumably hit by a golf ball or succumbed to a predator. That brings the original groups of babies down to 12.

While only a week or ten days older than the new arrivals, they have grown like wildfire and are considerably larger with darker colouring beginning to show.

The "bread lady" and her grandson were having a great time yesterday tossing crumbs to the birds who will now come right up on shore as long as momma is close by. They are a riot to watch, constantly scurrying from one place to another as the crumbs fall. Father goose will actually now take a piece of bread from the bread lady's hand, having developed a sense of trust.

As is the case throughout eastern Canada, water levels are extremely low and we are badly in need of rain. Some draught restrictions may have to be placed on ships in the St. Lawrence Seaway, about 70 miles from where we live, although the Ottawa River is not quite as bad as the St. Lawrence.

Our perennial garden is bursting forth, with every plant vying for space with its neighbour. This is the second year that we have enriched the soil with composted sheep manure and it certainly shows. If one is patient even plants which appear stubbornly slow will sooner or later surprise you. Three years ago we planted lily of the valley in a partly shaded area. This year for the first time it is flowering.

In about ten days we go to Toronto to try our luck at the two semi-annual art auctions which are held there. I am trying to collect small paintings by the Canadian "Group of Seven" who dominated the Canadian art scene during the twenties. It is expensive. However, several years ago I discovered that the Toronto auctions not only have the widest and best selection of Canadian art, they are in fact cheaper than buying locally. One local auction house in fact buys art at the Toronto auctions and then offers the works for sale in Ottawa at a substantial mark-up. So, if you're serious about buying art, Toronto is the place to do it.

About thirty years ago, while on vacation with my family, we came across a touring exhibition of the Group of Seven in Saint John, N.B., put together on the fiftieth anniversary of their first exhibition.

I was captured not only by the quality of their paintings but also by their story. In many ways it is similar to the experiences of many great artists whose work was rejected out of hand by the established "schools", but who persisted and eventually came to dominate.

Today, the major finished paintings done by them are worth hundreds of thousands of dollars and belong appropriately in museums where they may be seen and appreciated by all.

Years ago, when I was too young to consider buying art, a business associate from Ottawa and I were discussing the group. He expressed a preference for the small oil sketches that were done by them on site in Algonquin Park, Algoma, and eventually every corner of the country. That was because they truly reflected the artist's impression at that specific time and place, without later modifications to "improve" on it.

Even today it is still possible to buy very good oil sketches at auction for less than $10,000. For some this may seem like an outrageous amount. Ironically they wouldn't think twice about laying out thirty or forty thousand for a fancy car which would be a bucket of bolts in ten years!

And so, about every three years I take a run at it. I do not do so as an investment, although it seems to be more profitable than papering the walls with Canada savings bonds. I do it because I have great admiration for the skill of its creator. I do it because it is important Canadiana which I am proud to own.

That, plus the element of discovery, is what brings me to Toronto auctions.

Early on we travelled to Toronto by car on highway 401, the main throughway in southeastern Ontario. We found that travelling highway 7 was not only just as fast but far more scenic, with much less traffic to contend with.

Now we can get back to improving our golf game. Joyce, having taken one lesson of a set of four has already greatly improved, so I too have bitten the bullet and will begin with the same instructor this week. We shall see.

It will be a busy summer. We will go to the Maine coast in early July to visit our friends David and Kathy at Biddeford Pool. En route stop off at West Brome, Quebec, to visit with our friend Thérèse. Then on the way back see our old friend Mika at Rawdon, Quebec.

Then in October we go to Quebec City for Joyce's Aunt Christine's 90th birthday, which may allow us to tag on one or two other destinations in the east as well.

Today is the 29th of May. The very intrusive red and silver reflective tape is either down or removed. Once again it has been a dismal failure. The geese have quickly figured it out. So nature continues to triumph. The newborns are adding weight at a phenomenal rate and the training lessons are becoming more and more obvious.

Watching the three families yesterday, there was a disciplined parade taking place with each brood following a parent, seemingly farther and farther from the security of the pond. When they had reached a point about 100 yards from the water, the leaders turned around, nodded a command and the little ones began racing back to the security of the pond.

This year's crop of new families seems increasingly more sure of themselves than was the case last year. Now they will simply continue lounging beside the pond, on the edge of the fairway and stay right where they are even when a foursome of golfers comes across and gets within ten yards of them. The one thing that gets them back in the water in a hurry is an approaching golf cart. They've probably heard about those wild Ontario drivers!

So, whatever other tricks the golf club has up its sleeve, the geese are winning the battle for control up to this point.

More training sessions continued in early June for the geese, which are growing at an astonishing rate. The flock had been walked on the ninth fairway back to the tee and the security of the second pond which guards the 8th green. There is a creek which connects the two ponds which is heavily wooded. I had stepped out onto our upper deck to soak in the fresh air when out from behind the woods emerged this parade led by an adult at double time with all the young goslings in a row behind it. The remaining adults took up a rear guard position with one of them, body low to the ground and neck stretched out, harassing the goslings from the rear in an obvious attempt to push them along. They were almost at a run as they finished the last 150 yards to our end of the pond and safety. Every day this exercise seems to be extended further as this strengthening program gathers momentum.

Chapter Eight

The Art Auctions

It is amazing what things can be done to a photograph of a painting by those skilled in colour separation. A painting which is in fact drab or which requires special lighting to bring out its brighter colours can be made to look entirely different in the catalogue illustration.

And so what one anticipates from studying a catalogue can sometimes prove to be a disappointment in the flesh.

Nevertheless there is an air of excitement attached to attending an auction preview. Viewers stroll up and down the displays trying to look coolly disinterested, while each in his or her own way is slyly calculating how much lower than the estimate they might be lucky enough to successfully bid when the hammer drops.

Dealers and others in the trade stand around in groups of two or three, exchanging tidbits. "This is the third time around for this painting," one will drily comment. Another will brag about the fabulous buy he made recently. It is easy to recognize many of the dealers if you occasionally drop into galleries. Sometimes the auction is simply used by those in the art business to test the market value for a particular artist.

Everyone connected with the business loves to see records set for a given artist and if it happens, it becomes the subject of animated conversation.

But when you do get into competitive bidding for an item you have decided you want, if you really like what you're bidding on, you'd better be prepared to back that up when your competitor beats your so called predetermined top price. If you end up losing out on a painting that you dearly love, by $500 or $1,000, you'll hate yourself for a long time afterwards.

Sometimes it is easier to remain calmly detached if you place an absentee bid. The danger of course is that, if what you are after turns out to be hotly contested , you will be left at the gate.

Last year I did precisely that. The estimate for a very small Casson painting was $1,000 - $1,500. I thought I would be clever and place an absentee bid of $2,200. It went for $3250!

So, we've now ruled out the one painting I was interested in, a small J.E.H. MacDonald. Tomorrow we will get a chance to see the other possibility, also a MacDonald.

The hotel we are staying at is not far from the first auction so we were able to walk to it. We picked the hotel from the CAA listings which gave it 2 stars and red lettering for good value. It is "The Executive" on King St. West. It is excellent value at $95.00 a night for two, including parking and coffee and donuts in the morning.

About 50 yards up King Street is a small, clean restaurant called Oscar's Bistro. Joyce and I had one of the best restaurant meals we've ever had. Everything was fresh, temptingly prepared with exactly the right spices and herbs and served by a helpful, personable lady. We would go back.

The down side of what was otherwise a good day was that I had parked our car on a busy street in a metered space. Neither of us had noticed signs under the meter and down the street stating that parking was authorized only until 3 p.m. I had bought plenty of time with one hour showing after my loonie dropped and decided about 15 minutes early to go back and feed the meter. To my horror, a police officer was finishing writing up a $40.00 parking ticket while his buddy was attaching my car to a tow truck to be taken away — God knows where. Five more minutes and it would have been gone! Oh well.

Toronto continues to astound us with evidence of new growth popping up again. The confidence is back. There was a time when a genuine rivalry for national leadership existed between Montreal and Toronto but that is long since gone. Political uncertainty has taken its toll in Montreal. Every year more and more of those who are not *"pure laine"* simply pull up stakes and leave. So Toronto is by far and away Canada's leading metropolis.

It is also a very clean city. By comparison with Paris, it is spotless. Although, one must admit, still a long way from the cultural excellence of Paris, something that has taken hundreds of years to develop. Nonetheless we can be proud of Toronto. It's getting there fast.

Wednesday morning we drove downtown to the TD Centre, Ernst and Young Tower, where the second auction preview was taking place in the Design Exchange.

Now, entering the underground parking area of the TD Centre is an experience in itself. Most of the spaces are *"strictly reserved"*. You begin to feel as though you are driving around aimlessly when an attendant appears out of the blue. He permits you to occupy a space which remains unoccupied, but you must leave your keys with him. With seemingly no alternative, we agree, and head for the Design Exchange. We are immediately taken with a sense that we are somehow in a rich man's private club. The preponderance of very expensive luxury cars is almost overwhelming. People look at us in our humble V6 LE Camry as though we have crashed the party. As we pass the car grooming area a flashy blonde in a halter and very short shorts pulls up in the longest lowest slung sports car I've ever seen and trots on ahead of us. A sympathetic young businessman notices the catalogue under my arm and offers directions. I comment that the management consulting business must be very profitable. He smiles.

The preview is nicely displayed. Two very large security guards discreetly look everybody over as they enter. It is early, about 9:45 a.m., and we are relieved that not too many viewers have arrived. We will be able to get a good look at those paintings we are interested in. There are little niches with about a dozen paintings in each, quite well lit with flood lights. We eventually get to the other MacDonald I had been interested in. It is very nice but again not quite as nice as I had expected.

Nearby, there is a Varley landscape, group period, which I like, even though it tends to be a bit dark. We hold it under direct flood light. Several areas of the painting then show very interesting colour. One of the staff points out that the varnish may be working against it, noting that even varnish has a limited lifespan. Joyce still doesn't find it bright enough.

We divert our attention to the Jackson. Kluane Lake, Alaska Highway 1943. A very fine painting — strange that it wasn't pictured in the catalogue — it is nicer than some that were.

Joyce falls in love with a couple of works by other artists that we haven't even considered. That is the danger. It takes discipline to stick to your objective. We mull it over and conclude that we'll wait until the fall to see what comes up then. We leave.

On the way up the Don Valley Parkway, I suggested to Joyce that "Tilley Endurables", the renowned marketer of travel clothing, is close by and we might find it useful to check out, especially since Egypt is now firm for November. I didn't have to persuade her, any opportunity to shop gets top priority. The designs and quality of the outfits are first rate, original in concept and beautifully implemented. We spend about an hour there as Joyce sizes up a very smart ensemble of separates. Eventually, this decision is deferred and we aim for the 401 east and home.

The volume of tractor\trailer traffic is extremely heavy until we get east of Oshawa. About 150 kilometres out, Joyce asks how much mileage we could cut off our usual planned day trip to Watertown, NY, if we just turned south at the Thousand Islands bridge on the way home. About 100 kilometres is my estimate. "Then why don't we just take a run down today and save that extra mileage?" I agree.

We arrive at the Salmon Run Mall about 3:30 p.m.; one of our favourite day shopping excursions. When we get there we find that the depressed value of the Canadian dollar has taken its toll on Canadian trade at the mall. Two of the larger anchor stores have pulled up stakes. The other majors, Sears and Penneys, are still going strong.

Both of us make good buys on sharply reduced items that are standard clothing with us. In my case a 60% reduction on brand name casual shirts. So even at 1.50 to the US dollar you can still do well if you hit it on the right day.

Watertown was one of the communities severely damaged during the great ice storm of January 98. We have been watching mother nature do her slow but deliberate repair job, shooting new growth out of many of the trees that were damaged. There remain however, isolated areas 2 or 300 yards across where the ice damage was so extreme that it will take years to recover — if at all.

Tomorrow we both have golf lessons in the morning. We shall see what progress we have made.

Our teaching pro Don uses a driving range located just east of Manotick which is on the Rideau River, about 20 miles south of Ottawa. He is an excellent teacher with a very upbeat approach and a way of explaining the effect of muscle position on a golf shot.

For the first time I am conscious and confident of making a wrist cock, a key part of the swing.

Since it is about a twenty mile drive from home, we schedule our lessons back to back. Today Joyce goes first, but I think that she'd prefer it if I did. After logging over 1000 kms in the past two days we are both a bit stiff. Don says he'll be gentle with us!

Manotick is a beautiful residential community which has mushroomed enormously over the past thirty years. Both sides of the Rideau are lined with homes which vary in size depending on when they were built. The older homes are generally smaller, while the attraction of the beauty of the area has resulted in a sizeable influx of wealth; and as a result, some very large homes being built in recent years.

The charm of the community is enhanced by Long Island which causes the river to fork into two streams for about two miles. Some of the choicest properties are on the island, which is accessible from either shore by two bridges.

Manotick was a fairly early settlement, benefitting from the fact that the Rideau canal system passes through it. There is, as a consequence, a strong interest in boating. There are several quite good golf courses nearby which is another appeal.

There is an historic grist mill on the river which is now a museum. It is the Long Island Mill which began operation in 1860 and became the commercial centre around which Manotick developed. Originally a grist mill it later added a woollens mill. Today it is an historic site lovingly restored and cared for in a beautiful pastoral setting.

Manotick was also the home of one of Canada's foremost painters for a number of years in later life — A.Y. Jackson one of the original members of the group of seven.

As is the case throughout North America, golf is undergoing an explosive period of growth. I had played on and off since my early forties but only really got into it when we moved to Kanata six years ago. It was at that time that we both started taking it seriously, and for six years enjoyed being members at Kanata Lakes Golf Club, a 2 iron from our back door. However the acquisition of the club by a Toronto corporation resulted in a sharp increase in the annual cost and simply put it out of reach for many a pleasure golfer, as opposed to someone who is in a position to write the whole thing off as a business expense.

Fortunately there are outstanding alternatives nearby, so we will continue to pursue this wonderful game at a much more reasonable and realistic cost than before.

As I write this I am sitting in the car waiting for my turn with the pro. In the distance (about 100 yards away) I can hear Don hooting and hollering as Joyce gets it right. She deserves to. She is certainly working hard on it and with a little more consistency she'll be shooting in the 90s this summer.

Although she tends to sell herself short, she is a natural athlete, with a strong flexible body, capable of hitting a golf ball as far as some men. Once I saw her drive a ball 240 yards! On another occasion, using a 7 iron from the first tee at Hidden Lakes, near Smyrna Beach, Florida she belted one out about 160 yards. Several men, mostly duffers, were waiting to tee off behind us. I overheard one guy say, "Holy —— did you see that? I'm glad I'm not playing with her."

She expects to hit every shot perfectly — and we know that's not going to happen. She writes pages and pages of notes which Don is trying to get her to tear up. He calls it paralysis by analysis.

She probably has the right genes for an athlete. Her father was an outstanding athlete.

Her body language and facial expression will tell the tale when she comes off the range in a few minutes. She is smiling. It has been a good day.

When my turn came I regret to say "There was no joy in Mudville." Although I was making excellent contact with my irons, I got hung up on a slight tendency to pull to the left. The required corrections to my swing, although subtle, left me hopelessly confused, and although my teacher felt I had made progress, I did not feel that I had. It wasn't his fault, I was tired from the two previous days and was fighting the adjustments. However I'm not that far off the mark that the gains made a week ago were lost. They weren't, and with practice my iron game should begin to show results.

We had decided to proceed with our long sought trip to Israel and Egypt. So I dropped in to CAA travel, looking for someone knowledgeable and experienced in that part of the world. Up pops Ruth Shulman. What a going concern. In a matter of 2 or 3 days she had the whole package put together including our preferred airline — something the tour company had initially refused to do. She has a list of great restaurants in Israel visited first hand by her which we are looking forward to checking out. She can talk first hand about hotels in other European cities, which is an enormous advantage. So on Monday we will sign on and begin the preparation for these very exciting destinations in the fall.

We are getting mixed reactions to our travel plans to the Middle East. Most people tell us it will be the trip of a lifetime, filled with sights of unparalleled beauty and historical significance.

Others tell us we are crazy and won't come back alive. There have been frightening examples in the past of violence. But those who have made the trip report that security is now so extensive that an incident would have to be a quirk of fate.

We are determined to go. This is the third time we have planned a trip to this destination. The first cancelled out because of the Gulf war, the second by the massacre in Luxor. Sooner or later the time will be right.

———————

In mid June mother duck finally emerged from the creek which is well sheltered by bushes and mature trees — a great place to lay eggs. We spotted her scampering across the 100 yard stretch of golf course toward the pond with 5 tiny ducklings close behind.

They all moved quickly into the security of the pond, then once in the water the ducklings pulled their usual stunt and began swimming around independently. Mother must have quacked some command from about twenty feet out because the stragglers suddenly shot out from shore, literally sprinting across the water to her, from which point the family resumed formation and swam out to the centre. Still no sign of deadbeat dad.

Yesterday the blue heron also showed up, gliding lazily over the pond, checking out the supply of carp which seem to be larger and more numerous than previous years.

So the natural cycle is complete. All summer residents are in their rightful place, and we can look forward to a continuation of the usual shenanigans.

In spite of the explosive development of housing and commercial support systems, deer are still being seen in the early evenings on the golf course. We have the regular collection of squirrels, chipmunks and racoons as well as muskrats. We haven't seen a fox for over two years and the porcupine which frequented the 10th fairway (about a quarter of a mile away) is long since gone. We still see the big turtle who lives in the pond from time to time but less frequently. Civilization is gradually taking its toll.

But these are the survivors. They aren't going to give up without a fight. So far they have succeeded in the face of a determined effort by the golf course to get rid of them, the destruction of nearby forested areas which provided them with refuge, and all of the contaminants that development brings. Weed killer, exhaust and other destructive effluents which come with heavy industrial equipment and two car families. So far nature has held on, but one cannot help but wonder for how long.

Sitting on the upper deck with Win and Barb Cotnam, our neighbours, in their rear garden which also overlooks the pond, and is in fact, closer to it than our home, we were treated to another example of young geese in training. They had once again spent the day at the smaller pond in front of the eighth hole of the golf course. About 6:30 this beautifully disciplined parade emerged from behind the trees which line the creek along the ninth fairway which links the two ponds.

In a line as straight as an arrow, the young geese were being made to sprint toward the home pond. Every one was in sync. It was as though they were being taught to run, first from danger, and probably more important for the long term, as a prelude to conditioning for the flight trials which are now only 4 - 5 weeks away. Once again they do exactly as they are told, receiving their commands through a soft high pitched verbal signal given them by the adults.

There are now very few stragglers, and any that slow down get the head down, stretched neck body language from dad which signals attack.

All of the baby fuzz is now gone, and with the colour changes to their down and plumage they look like junior versions of the mature geese. The count is now down to 14, so somewhere along the way we have lost 3, from a total of 17 goslings when they first appeared on the pond.

Our neighbour Win has just retired after a long career in the high tech industry.

During a conversation with some friends we got on the subject of old age and senility and when a court of law finds reason to judge someone to be suffering from dementia. Joyce recounted a law case where the will of an elderly man was challenged, based on whether he was of sound mind when he wrote it since he always wore galoshes when visiting the bathroom.

There are those who might argue that this was a perfectly reasonable thing to do, for someone whose age was advanced and whose aim had lost its accuracy, and that in itself might suggest careful planning and complete competence.

Chapter Nine

Weir

Today we are setting out to visit two of our old friends from Montreal, Denis and Lynn Courte. After a few years in Toronto, they have settled down in Weir, Quebec, a small town in the Laurentians about two and a half hours from Ottawa or Montreal. Weir is also Denis' birthplace.

It has probably been 15 or 20 years since we have been "up North", since most of the intervening years were spent going in the opposite direction, to our vacation home in Quechee, Vermont.

We have never been to Weir, although it is not that far from Morin Heights, where as a teenager, I raced downhill on the Kicking Horse Trail — aptly named for an extended run over moguls which can not be avoided.

It is also fairly close to St-Sauveur, where I had my first beer among other things.

Farther North is St-Jovite and Mont Tremblant, always the biggest ski hill in the Laurentians, which has undergone massive development in the past 10 years. We shall see them all!

On our way up from Ottawa through Montebello we were surprised at the flatness of the land near Notre-Dame-de-la-Paix — which is famous for potatoes — particularly since this is the beginning of the Laurentian Shield.

En route we noticed police on the highway and in due course saw two separate autos pulled over for speeding. Initially we thought their revenues were behind budget, but later we heard on the radio that with *"La Fête Nationale"* approaching, they are clamping down on speeders in an effort to reduce traffic accidents.

We continued on to Weir which is a small settlement on Round Lake, originally established by farmers and woodsmen and later by a lumber mill. Round Lake was a marshalling point for logs which were consumed by the J.W. Duncan Lumber Co.

Long after lumbering ceased, perfectly preserved deadheads were being pulled from the lake until most of them were removed some twenty years ago. 18" hemlock, long since gone from the region, was common.

The Courte's cottage was acquired in 1968. However the family dates back into the first half of the twentieth century and was typical of that era. Denis is one of eight children. There were 6 boys in the family. The old Courte family home had an enormous bedroom for the boys which contained four double beds. Even so, there was still enough room left to permit the boys to play ball hockey in the remaining space. Denis recalls his mother pleading with them to put away their hockey sticks and get to bed.

Victor Courte, Denis' father, operated a garage for many years in Weir. In 1934 he modified a motorcycle, by attaching a ski in place of the front wheel, thus patenting an early version of the snowmobile. In the early 1940s he purchased one of the earliest Bombardier snowmobiles with an enclosed passenger compartment, permitting him to operate it as a snow taxi. In those days the roads were not ploughed, they were rolled. Later, Victor Courte was recognized by Bombardier as one of the pioneers in the use of snowmobiles. He also used it to deliver mail, which he picked up at St-Jovite, and brought back to Weir for distribution. He operated a successful restaurant into the seventies.

In the early half of the century, the Round Lake Inn was a popular vacation spot with a strict dinner dress code. This was also extended to the tennis courts and Lynn can recall her mother describing ladies in knee length tennis dresses, always in pure white of course! The era ended in 1963 when fire destroyed the Inn. It was never rebuilt.

Round Lake drains into Bevin Lake and eventually spills into the Rouge River. The Rouge itself passes by the Harrington Nature Centre (where Joyce and I spent many arduous hours learning French), and eventually becomes a tributary of the Ottawa River emerging at Calumet.

From Weir, the nearest settlement of any size is Arundel, which is situated along the north side of the Rouge — so named because of the red sand along its banks.

Arundel is home to a mature, sporty, golf course founded originally over 60 years ago by Doug Cooke as a nine hole course, and later expanded to 18 holes when Dickie Moore and Stu Forbell became partners. It is a very pretty course which looks out over the Rouge to Huberdeau on the opposite bank, but its beauty is a bit misleading. We didn't exactly bring it to its knees.

Always hospitable, Denis and Lynn served up a delicious dinner. We had a great evening reminiscing about the many good times we have had together, ending in utter nonsense when I suggested that we play a game in which we pretend we are part of a symphony orchestra while a CD is playing the real thing. Denis handled the woodwinds, Joyce the percussion and brass, and Lynn the strings, all the time acting it out as though they were really playing and producing the sounds for their instruments. They got better as we got deeper into the wine. It was hilarious.

The neighbours must have thought we had gone completely mad. Probably thought it was some form of therapy.

The following morning I awoke early as usual, and watched all of the natural activity going on outside. We were lucky.

Another glorious day was ahead. The sun had not as yet appeared, but the sky was absolutely clear of clouds. It is fascinating to watch the morning mist rising off the lake. The sound of crows cawing in the distance, and all the rest of God's little creatures signalling the beginning of the day, long before our watches allow it.

There isn't much of real wild life visible, although we know it's not far away. Last night at dusk, a pair of loons were ambling along the water about two hundred yards offshore. Ten years ago Denis spotted a small bear just in front of the cottage, but that was a very rare sighting.

Although there are outboard runabouts on the lake, so far we have been spared the roar of high speed power boats, although I suppose they are out there. The lake itself is not that big, probably three quarters of a mile across and about one and a half miles long, so that tends to discourage the mega boats.

There is a hummingbird feeder hanging just outside the kitchen window which has been well visited and needs refilling. Lynn says the hummingbirds will attack predator birds such as hawks. I suppose their versatility in being able to dart quickly or hover gives them a competitive advantage over the more cumbersome hawks, which makes up for their size.

This place is full of memories and Denis' large family is evident everywhere. A local resident, Bevin Jones, edited a history of Weir published in 1988. The Courte family appears prominently many times throughout the book.

It is now 6:30 a.m. The sun has risen to the point where its rays are able to reach over the hills behind us and highlight the cottages across the water. Vapour plays games at this hour. The mist which drifted upwards a half hour ago is now collecting about 100 feet up and has enshrouded the northwestern side of the lake in fog. It is now moving eastward and very shortly I will be unable to see the water at all. That will be short-lived. Once the sun gets high enough it will burn off quickly. But for the moment, we get a sense of isolation, as though we were the only ones here, which of course is not the case.

In only a matter of fifteen minutes the opposite shore is visible again, almost as though nature is changing the set in a theatrical production. Time for the next act. Time to get moving. Unfortunately most of the actors brought in for the occasion are still in bed. Probably exhausted from too much wine and last night's hard work performing in the local symphony orchestra!

Joyce and I live in different time zones. I am up at dawn and she reads late at night, often past midnight.

Just offshore a duck and her babies have silently swum past the dock. They are quite tiny. Probably a week or two younger than the brood back at our home pond. We are now a little farther north, not far from wilderness, so their chances of survival are much better.

Across the lake there is what looks like a water spout moving silently down the lake towards the sun. It can't be, of course, or we would surely hear it. It is only about 100 feet high and ten feet wide and moving quite quickly. Strange.

There is always something special about the relationship between old friends. Perhaps it is because we have been through many of life's experiences and the veils are off. We know enough about each other that we can afford to be open. Each in our own way has gone through our share of difficult times to really appreciate those occasions when we can share the happy, lighter moments, which seem much sweeter for the contrast.

When my son Peter was married, we met many new friends on his wife's (Sandy) side of the family. I had to propose a toast on the occasion of the rehearsal party. I think it's original, it just came to me at the time:

Some of us are old friends. Most of us
are new friends. May we all become old friends.

Mont Tremblant

We had been led to expect a tremendous change from when we last saw this facility and we were not disappointed.. The developers expect to put over $500 million into the conversion over a five year period and are well on their way. Canadian Pacific's Chateau Mont Tremblant is consistent with the high quality in spectacular settings that are synonymous with this chain. Marriot Residence Inn is there. Literally hundreds of first class condominiums are already in place, supported by an excellent selection of shops and restaurants. Two championship golf courses which look absolutely spectacular are now operational, Le Géant and Le Diable. The latter will host the skins game in a week's time. The lift capacity for skiers has been substantially increased. All of this first class in every respect. It will surely become the world class resort that the mountain deserves.

During her years at university Joyce worked every summer as a waitress at the C.P. Banff Springs Hotel. It was a wonderful experience in a breathtaking environment.

On days off, rock climbing was a popular form of recreation, scrambling up the mountains often a couple of thousand feet.

And so, when back at McGill, someone mentioned that a handful of students were heading to the Laurentians north of Montreal for a day of mountain climbing, Joyce jumped right in. After all with all this experience in the Rockies , the Laurentians would be a breeze.

Serious mountain climbers usually carry their own equipment; pitons, hammer, rope etc, in small packsacks which Joyce noted, thinking to herself that everybody must have brought their lunch in those packsacks and she hadn't.

When they arrived at the hill, not far from a well known Laurentian hotel famous for its food, she looked up at a small mountain with a sheer vertical rock face of about 100 feet. She was looking at the day's challenge.

When the experienced climbers opened up their packsacks out came the tools of climbing and not lunches. Joyce was petrified. As the novice she was positioned in the middle of the team and the climb began, pulling and clawing up every foot of the way.

About two thirds of the way up she began to have second thoughts and told the leader she didn't think she could go any further.

"Look down" he replied. "It would be far more difficult to pick our way down." So filled with trepidation she dug in, and with experienced guidance made it up the last part of the way to the summit.

Most people with no climbing experience would have stood at the bottom, looked up and said "no way". Joyce simply thought if they can do it I can do it. But she promised herself that the next time she'd bring a lunch!

Everywhere in the surrounding communities there is evidence of the economic impact that Tremblant has had on the economy. The town of Mont Tremblant, the properties which border the huge and beautiful lake nearby, and even over at St-Jovite, the largest town in the area, everything is on the upswing.

We had lunch at *"Le Brunch"* a sidewalk café in St-Jovite, one of several excellent eateries in town.

Across from Le Brunch is Antiques Coq Rouge, which although pricey, has a very good assortment of Canadiana pine furniture and artifacts which are rare. As a plus, they do not appear to have compromised with reproductions.

There has been a good attempt at preserving the nostalgic symbol of a key part of St-Jovite's past — the railroad. Restaurant Antipasto moved the former CP rail station and converted it on Rue Ouimet where it seems to be doing a roaring trade.

Metro Richer managed to fit in to the image of the town with a cleverly designed supermarket which almost looks like a boutique. The town looks like it is doing well.

We then set out on the eastern side of the Rouge River, past the extensive Buddhist temple set among beautiful surroundings, and continued down about 10 kilometres to the Harrington Nature Centre now operated by Bowaters. It was encouraging to see the tree nursery, started by CIP in the forties under Vernon Johnson's tenure, continuing its program of reforestation under Bowaters.

Then, back to Weir where we passed Teleglobe Canada's earth station Weir, with its massive satellite dishes, the largest of which is 90 feet in diameter.

Denis seems to know most of the population and as we passed, we received a friendly wave from many of the residents on the way by.

It is Wednesday 5:30 a.m. Once again I am the only one up. All of the rest are still getting their Zs. It is cooler this morning, so much so that I had to shut the window in the bedroom to stay warm. That is the nature of the climate in the Laurentians — almost 90 degrees F. during the day and probably below 50 degrees at 5 a.m. It reminds me of scout camp in the early 40s at Tamaracouta, near Morin Heights, not far from here. We slept in tents. It was the chill of morning rather than the sunshine which got you moving.

That was an experience. Rain or shine, every scout had to take a skinny dip swim at 7 a.m before breakfast. Then breakfast at a long table which could handle 30 - 40 kids.

The toilets were something else. Usually a 2 hole privy which had extended handles on the end so that when one site was filled to capacity, the privy could be moved a few feet away to another position over a new pit.

If for any reason you were given demerit points, one of the favourite tasks you were assigned, was to dig a new pit, using the fresh earth to fill in and cover the old one. Not exactly an exercise to improve your appetite!

As I write this I am again at the kitchen table overlooking the lake. Nothing spectacular happening this morning. A large blue heron loping down the lake in search of breakfast. Four mature ducks feeding directly in front of the cottage among some reeds. The mist still doing its act.

There is a racoon which showed up again last evening at "crépuscule". He climbs a huge oak which stands at the water's edge to the right. I think Lynn is spooked by him but other than getting into garbage they seem harmless. There is a chipmunk squeaking down below. Unlike destructive squirrels, chipmunks can be fun. In Vermont we even had one who would respond to his name — Leonard. We always kept a supply of peanuts for him. Joyce would get out on the deck, call him by name in a high pitched voice and then from 50 - 75 yards away we would hear the rustle and crashing of twigs and leaves coming closer and sure enough it would be Leonard. He would wait eagerly on the ground below the deck for his treats and eventually became at ease enough to take the nuts directly from our hand.

Finally the rest of the team surfaces. Lynn proposes a boat ride around the lake, through the outlet creek and into Bevin Lake, slightly larger than Round Lake. After a hearty breakfast we are ready. The boat is a four seater runabout equipped with a 55 HP outboard. Big enough for the kids to water ski but not overwhelmingly powerful considering the size of the lake. Denis knows who owns every cottage. Again we exchange waves on the way by.

The creek which makes its way through a wetland for about half of a mile is spectacularly beautiful. All of the marsh is thick with lush tall Indian head. The passage itself is bordered for hundreds of yards with white and yellow water lilies on both sides. The water, though somewhat shallow in the channel at 3 - 4 feet, is clear as a bell. We see sunfish everywhere and pike 20 - 30 inches long swimming alongside our boat. Dry land is 50 - 75 yards away from the channel on either side. Denis tells us that this is a favourite spot for the blue heron.

We break free of the creek channel and out into Bevin Lake. There seem to be fewer cottages along its shore. The terrain on the west side is more rugged with cliffs rising 30 - 40 feet up from the water. I make a mental note that there are some choice cottage locations on the west side. There are also 2 or 3 clean sandy beaches tucked against the rock ledge.

The east side is more pastoral and is for the most part being farmed. At the far end is a larger, more open creek which is the outlet which drains into the Rouge River.

In another corner of the lake is a third creek which one could use to access Macdonald Lake, but only by canoe.

The whole mix stirs the imagination as to what kind of magical summer days could be spent canoeing through the 3 lake chain. It is a nice way to end our stay with the Courtes. They have invited us back in the fall, when we will test our golfing skills at Mont Tremblant's "Le Géant".

Chapter Ten

The Pond

In late June a crowd was gathering on Campeau Ave., about 300 yards directly behind our house and over fairways 9 and 1 of the golf course. Elephants were walking along Campeau on their way back to the Corel Centre where Ringling Bros/Barnum & Bailey are presenting a circus, here in Kanata, to children of all ages! Elephants!

These along with the other circus animals were being walked through the town, in part for exercise, and also to promote the circus. Joyce could see them going by from our kitchen door, each elephant hanging on to the tail of the one in front with its own trunk.

The construction of a modern 18,500 seat arena has resulted in Ottawa now being "on the tour" for many shows which heretofore have bypassed the city.

Earlier this summer the super dogs came to town. They are clever, marvellously conditioned animals who love to compete, and display this eagerness the minute they arrive on the arena surface.

The trainers are required to put their dogs through several very difficult manoeuvres and the fastest, error free dog wins. It is a wonderful show for dog lovers and particularly for children who love dogs.

During the show a mother and two young boys about 8 or 10 years of age sat beside us. They really got into it. The finale is designed to maximize audience involvement. It is a relay race.

The race courses are set up, one on each side of the arena. The dogs are divided into two teams one per side. The children are asked to cheer for the team on their side and the MC does a masterful job of getting the kids involved. The contest is two out of three.

Our side won the first race but it was close. Then the second race was taken by the other side by a healthy margin. When we got to the run off, the excitement level of the two kids beside us had reached fever pitch. The race began. There are about 10 dogs of various breeds on each team. Our side got ahead at first and then the other side overtook them. With about three dogs to go, the kids were frantic. They jumped up excitedly yelling "Come on! Come on!", and our last dog just beat out the other side by a nose. It was more fun watching the kids than the dogs. After the show the audience was allowed down on the floor to pet the dogs. They absolutely loved it.

The main purpose of the arena is for NHL hockey. After 3 or 4 years of being in the league cellar, our Senators became contenders in 1997 & 98. This brought with it outrageous salary demands from some key players.

The promotion of professional sports in an indoor arena has become the noisiest experience imaginable. During commercials, the sound level is cranked up almost beyond endurance.

It isn't cheap to take a family of four to an NHL game. Even seats three quarters of the way up in the stands are 35 -40 dollars each. Add to that popcorn, french fries and soft drinks at 3 - 4 dollars a pop and you have a $200 night on your hands. The volume of fries consumed is such that cooking oil is delivered in a jumbo fuel tank truck, much like gasoline.

Frankly, I don't know how a young family can handle it.

Other major draws which usually sell out, are rock concerts and super stars like Celine Dion. In the past year we also had the Billy Graham crusade here which packed the arena for several successful nights.

The success of the building has resulted in a huge increase in vehicular traffic when events are held. It is becoming evident that with this and the explosive growth of industry and population in the west end, additional traffic lanes will have to be added to highway 417 to accommodate the volume.

A day or two after our return from Weir, we could see a huge plume of smoke rising in the distance to the southwest as we drove west along highway 417. You cannot help but wonder. It is obviously a fire and something very big is going up in flames.

It has been tinder dry in Ottawa this spring. The garden is parched, even after only three days away. I had better get some water on it. Outside on the back deck we and everyone else are being showered with white fly ash, almost like an early snowfall.

It is coming from a massive forest fire near Almonte about twenty miles away. It has consumed over 150 hectares and is out of control. Every available fire fighter in the district has been called out — even our own force is there. It is described on the radio as the worst in memory in that area which is relatively civilized. Major forest fires normally occur in the northern unpopulated forest regions. By morning it was still burning but being brought under control.

Joyce once had an experience with a fire when she was a young struggling lawyer trying to make ends meet.

Her first new car was a Valiant which was treated with loving care and guarded with her life.

In her single days she lived in a very nice apartment on Olivier Ave. in Westmount, just west of Green. The car was carefully parked every night in the building garage away from thieves and vandals.

One evening the fire alarm went off in the building. The fire was in a dumpster stored in the garage. Someone must have forgotten to squinch their cigarette properly. Several reels of fire fighters charged in to do battle.

When she realized that the fire threatened the car, Joyce tore down to the garage and drove it out of the building to the safety of the Canada Post parking lot on the corner of Olivier and Ste-Catherine. Then, like Mr. Bean, she stood on the street with a smug look on her face waiting for the fire fighters to do their job.

They did it all right. Moments later the smouldering dumpster was pulled out of the garage, towed to the street and then parked — still smouldering — right beside her car in the postal parking lot! Just one of life's little ironies.

On June 25th, Vicky, Frank and Sarah came to visit for the long weekend. Sarah was fascinated by the geese. After a Bar B Q we sat on the upper deck. We are very close to a full moon. Probably tomorrow. A fat groundhog was scampering around out by the creek. Tomorrow we will all go to the lawn supper at St. John's Anglican Church.

The St. John's Church lawn supper has been held almost without interruption for over 75 years. The church itself was constructed in 1839 probably by stone masons brought over during construction of the Rideau Canal. It has thrived and survived through many different phases of demographic change. Originally strictly rural, then strongly affected by the early urban development of Kanata when Beaverbrook was created in the

1960s, it is now a mixture of both urban and rural parishioners and is quite healthy.

Along with Frank, Vicky, Sarah and Joyce and I, Joyce's sister Lois and her husband Gary all went to the supper. Sarah was a big hit.

The lawn supper takes a lot of organization and hard work. They usually feed over 400 people. If the weather is good (which it was) tables are set up on the rectory lawn under the shade of the old sugar maples planted years ago. The rector, David Clunie, who is a talented cellist, joins with others in the parish, or others who are friends, in a recital played inside the church during dinner. It is very pleasant for young and old.

The mayor and some councillors were there. In an election year you can be sure that the incumbent members of parliament or the provincial legislature will be there along with competing candidates. There is always a strong rural representation at these events, where the church remains a centre of both spiritual as well as social contact. Those who work the land have a greater understanding of the meaning of dependence on God and nature.

The Anglican parish of March consists of three small churches, St. John's (my home church) in Kanata North, St. Paul's in Dunrobin and St. Mary's on the sixth line road west of Pinhey's Point, the original settlement in this area. The three churches are served by rector Rev. David Clunie, who resides besides St. John's, and an assistant minister. Between them they manage, with the assistance of lay readers, to look after all three churches. This requires them to move quickly from one to the other which can be a bit of an adventure in mid winter.

The very first time I ever entered St. John's was on Christmas Eve eight years ago. I immediately sensed that this would become my home church. It is a warm and friendly place which derives its beauty from its simplicity.

It will seat a maximum of 110 people. There is a provision for a choir of nine persons. Somehow the organist and choir director can make this tiny group sound like the Red Army Chorus!

There is an old cemetary on the property shaded by mature maples. Several pioneers are buried within it, some whose lives began in the 1700s.

The church itself sits on a small rise of land with a lovely view of the Gatineau Hills across the Ottawa River. There is ample space for outdoor activities, such as scouting, on the fifteen acres of mixed pasture and forest with the added benefits provided by Shirley's Brook which crosses the pasture land behind the church.

It is a very special place.

Originally all three churches were rural. St. John's has now become increasingly urban as a result of the explosive growth Kanata has experienced in recent years, related to the hugely successful high tech industries which have been established here.

The parishioners at St. John's tend to be less demonstrative in their demeanor than the other two; as is typical of city folk. St. Mary's and St. Paul's are still primarily rural, although some very sophisticated families, attracted by the beauty of the countryside, reside there as well.

One senses the interdependence of the population in the two rural churches to a greater extent than in St. John's. Even so St. John's tries to continue the traditional values of its rural history with events such as the lawn supper, which has wide appeal.

You see a difference between the churches during "the peace". St. John's parishioners share in the joy of wishing each other peace but usually confine it to those in surrounding pews. By contrast, when "the peace" is offered at St. Mary's, everyone gets out of his or her pew and extends it freely to the entire congregation. It is obviously an important and joy filled moment for everyone.

While St. John's main social fundraiser for outreach is its lawn supper, St. Mary's holds an annual raspberry social. The berries are grown and supplied by two of the family parishioners. The shortcake is baked by other members and enthusiastically served by them loaded with berries and whipped cream.

This year there was some concern with the hot dry weather in June that the crop might be adversely affected. However the recent rains have helped, although it has been necessary to advance the date of the social by a week or two.

The church itself is set on the edge of a heavily wooded area, and is the second St. Mary's church, constructed in 1902. It replaced the earlier St. Mary's church built in 1827 at Pinhey's Point, which was left in ruins after a wall collapsed.

St. Paul's church is located in Dunrobin. It is a smaller church than its two sister churches and is basically rural. A significant amount of new housing has appeared in Dunrobin in recent years and hopefully in time will strengthen St. Paul's which celebrated its centennial 2 years ago.

Joyce was reminding me that it was time that we had Father David Clunie of St. John's and his wife for dinner. It was probably overdue.

David is a very sociable individual who enjoys getting out with members of his parish. He likes golf but doesn't play enough to score well.

About three years ago when we were members of the Kanata Lakes Golf Club I invited him for a round of golf. Kanata Lakes is a championship course with undulating greens, plenty of deep sand traps and two lakes to contend with.

He greatly enjoyed it even though he was a bit out of practice.

The following Sunday, as he sometimes does, he reported to the congregation on his social activities, mentioning that he and I had played golf together on one of the nicest courses he had ever played, but that it certainly ranked up there as the closest he had ever come to a walk through the valley of death in his entire life!

The congregation loved it.

There are many fascinating people to be encountered in the course of a year at St. John's.

One such person is a retired priest who occasionally substitutes for our regular clergy. He is a very experienced minister who virtually knows the service by heart. Although he might be considered a bit eccentric, he is very professional and delivers with enthusiasm.

When it is time for a hymn, he belts it out as though he was Ezio Pinza on the stage of New York's Majestic Theatre. He does not drive. So he is always accompanied by an assistant who has a supply of orange popsicles at the ready, which he polishes off upon arrival before getting started.

He owns a miniature schnauzer which goes everywhere he goes.

Once, when the service began and he walked up to the altar as we sang the opening hymn, his tiny dog was right with him.

The dog is usually very well behaved and respectful of the surroundings, however even he can be "human". On this occasion, it was the week after Thanksgiving for which the church had been decorated with all the offerings of the harvest, sheaves of corn, pumpkins, squash and other vegetables such as beets. When the cleaning staff had removed the Thanksgiving offerings, they had missed a small beetroot which looked amazingly like a mouse.

When the dog spotted it we were in the middle of prayers of the people. The dog began to growl and then pounced on the beet and shook it. The good reverend ignored it all and continued as though it was an everyday occurrence. He was a very likeable and interesting man who had been many places and did things his own way.

At the end of the service he shook hands with everyone and then he, the dog and his driver took off down Sandhill Road for points unknown. The beet went into the garbage.

Many of the Brits who emigrate to North America are Anglicans. They bring with them a strange assortment of colloquial expressions. Someone who is attired in their Easter finery might be referred to as "all dressed up like a tailor's dummy". If the attire happens to miss the mark it might become "all done up like a dog's dinner".

I was in a conversation with one of our British parishioners who like many others in Kanata works in the high tech industry. We were talking about an interesting high tech I.P.O. which was covered in the weekend's financial papers. I pointed out that there were several important industrialists who were associated with this offering and that it might be worth investing in. He nodded and said "always bet the jockey not the horse!"

I have never been a truly long ball hitter in golf. That is not to say that I have not hit some pretty good shots when I least expected it. Typically I am 200 - 210 yards off the tee. But on a few rare occasions I have belted out 250 -260 yards.

When I try to analyse what I did differently, at least up to this point I draw a blank. Obviously my timing and coordination on those really big shots must have been close to perfect — within my own limitations.

And yet I stand in awe of those who can regularly and seemingly effortlessly hit a golf ball consistently 275 yards. Size has little to do with it. There are some outstanding long ball hitters who are probably 5' 8" or less such as Woosnam and Player. They have simply learned how to hit a ball properly.

When I was a teenager, about 14 years of age, I was fascinated with the concept of kicking a football. I watched and marvelled at the ability of senior high school or college players to punt or place kick 50 sometimes 60 yards.

I bought myself a football with my allowance and began trying different techniques starting with place kicking. I reasoned that if I trotted up to the ball with my upper body weight forward and brought it back to upright at the time of impact with my foot I ought to be able to generate more leg speed.

It worked! Suddenly at age 14 I was consistently able to place kick 45 - 50 yards — even 55 yards on occasion.

Punting was a different matter. If I kicked 30 - 35 yards I was lucky, but I kept at it. I used to go down to the baseball diamond at Macdonald Park with another kid and for hour after hour we would kick punts back and forth.

Then one day it happened. I noticed by slowing down the process I was able to punt high spiralling kicks about 50 yards, particularly if I contacted the ball with the arch of my foot. I was even more consistent if I tried it with my right shoe off.

By trial and error and the development of "memory" in the muscles of my legs and torso I had taught myself to kick. My high school coach noticed it and I became the team place kicker.

But no matter how much analysis, or time with golf pros I spend, my plateau remains consistently at 200 - 210 yards.

Golf of course is very much a mental game. Although I have won team events on a number of occasions, I have only once won an individual championship. That was the "C" championship at Kanata Golf Club in 1997.

It was a 3 day 54 hole event. After the first 2 rounds I had a comfortable 7 stroke lead over the rest of the field.

I was paired with a younger and frankly better player than I was. He began on a hot streak and my game decided to go south for the winter. When we stood on the 10th tee we were all even.

I looked to the sky and asked the good Lord to show me the way. Immediately my game improved and ironically my opponent's began to deteriorate.

I hit shots that I didn't even know I was capable of. 100 yard wedge shots to 4 feet of the pin, 50 foot putts over weird undulations, and when we at last dropped the final putts on the 18th hole I had regained my lead and won.

What had happened? There is no explanation for it other than the spiritual connection. I played far over my head on the final 9 holes. Some of the shots I could not duplicate again if I hit them 100 times.

It is 6:15 a.m. The geese have assumed their usual place in the 9th fairway. A duck is sitting on the aerator on the pond, which in deference to those who live next to it, is shut off on weekends and at night. She would get a rude awakening if she chose to sit there at 7 a.m. on a weekday. That is when the timer kicks in and she would learn the true meaning of white water rafting.

A newly discovered duckling family of 11 is clambering around the water's edge near the fairway. The mother carefully leads her brood up the bank, looks in all directions and then signals the ducklings to come up. With much stealth she moves out on the fairway, ducklings close behind her. It looks like she may be going to try for a run to the creek with all of the duck victuals that it contains.

Slowly they start across. She stops, takes another careful look around, then starts again. About twenty yards out she stops again — then suddenly turns around and chases her little ones into the safety of the pond. A moment later the giant blue heron appears, gliding on its enormous wings to the pond. A trip it makes most mornings. He is not really interested in the ducklings. It is the carp in the pond he is after. He takes up a position on the shore, watches and waits. He usually gets one.

In the meantime, Paul the ball hawk comes out to make his usual rounds, ball retriever in hand.

One of the golf course maintenance men goes by in a golf cart, then quickly reverses and takes a run at the geese in an effort to get them off of the fairway and into the water. When he leaves they climb back out and resume their position. Yesterday we spotted then all lounging around the ninth green, waiting for the next foursome to arrive. They'll sit there while the golfers putt out. By now they can probably recognize the better players!

It continues to be extremely hot and dry. The Colorado spruce's leader is wilting a bit, so I'll have to soak it again. The sky is clear, and the forest fire which raged for two days near Almonte is now out.

The deadbeat male duck just made a hasty fly past over the pond, quacked at mother duck and the kids and probably yelled out something like — have fun, see ya later!

Chapter Eleven

Sarah

Sarah is now 27 months old. Typical of little children her age, she is bursting with energy and doing very well with the English language. She is now quite capable of carrying on a conversation and she has a mind of her own. She is used to other children as she spends several hours a day with a sitter who also has a young child of the same age, while Vicky recovers from several operations.

She is very gregarious. Our neighbours, Win and Barb Cotnam, also became grandparents to Cameron, born one month after Sarah, although Cameron is slightly taller.

We were curious to see how these two would get along so I walked Sarah over to the Cotnams where Barb and Cameron were sitting on the rear deck. I introduced them. Sarah moved right in and sat down close beside Cameron. He immediately burst into tears!

The following evening when we came back from the church supper Barb was walking Cameron out to see the geese. I brought Sarah and several slices of white bread which the geese love and we all took turns feeding them. The children loved it.

When we were done, we turned away from the water and the two kids started running around like puppies. Sarah then walked to our deck and Cameron followed. Next thing we know Sarah is giving him a big hug and a kiss. From then on the two of them got along swimmingly.

When my granddaughter Sarah was born to Vicky I wrote a poem dedicated to her. It was a very high risk pregnancy and we really didn't know how it would turn out, for Vicky or the baby. We were truly blessed on that occasion and I was moved to write the following poem especially for Sarah.

> They've called you Sarah
> Your tiny hands and lovely face remind me
> Of thoughts I had I'd rather leave behind me
> Against the odds you made it here to show me
> What faith can do, when you are old enough to know me
> They've called you Sarah.
>
> They've called you Sarah
> So as it was in olden days we waited
> You brought us joy we'd not anticipated
> Your tiny presence gives a special meaning
> To all the hopes in life that we've been dreaming
> They've called you Sarah.
>
> So tiny Sarah
> Be blessed in life with love and peace around you
> May harmony and happiness surround you
> May angels guard your sleep at night and keep you
> And every morning sunshine rise to greet you
> You're special, Sarah.

Chapter Twelve

My Parents

I grew up as an only child. My parents were very caring, loved me as a child and were proud of me when I became a man.

My father Ray was born in Australia where he grew up, was educated at Sydney Technical School and joined Cable and Wireless Ltd. In the early 20s he was transferred to Canada and posted to Halifax where he met my mother. I once asked him shortly before he died, how he met her. As was commonly the case, bachelors lived in boarding houses. He was sitting on the front porch on Robie St. one evening with some fellow boarders when my mother, Dorothy, walked by. She of course was a lovely young woman at the time. He asked her who she was and was immediately smitten.

They courted for about two years and then married. In due course my mother gave birth to a son Jackie, who from the old photographs must have been a beautiful child. Shortly thereafter my father was transferred to Suva, Fiji. They had a very good life in that primitive part of the world. I remember them recalling invitations to Government House on several occasions. Life was pretty good.

Then disaster struck. At age four, Jackie contracted diptheria. There were no antibiotics and immunization for this terrible disease was not yet available. It was a horror story which was to impact on them for the rest of their lives.

Jackie was under the care of a physician but was being treated at home. When the disease reached crisis stage the physician came to their home. It was going to be necessary to perform an emergency tracheotomy and my father was called upon to assist. There was no anesthesia. It was a terrifying last ditch attempt to save the child's life. The sight and the horrifying sounds as his throat was slit open must have affected my father for the rest of his life. Jackie died in surgery in his own little bed. It was more than my father could take. He staggered out into the garden and vomited.

I do not know who took it harder, my father or my mother. They never spoke about it. The following year they returned to Halifax where I was born.Years later, when I was about nine years of age, we went to a movie in Verdun, Que., the town closest to Montreal which permitted children under sixteen years of age. The story was remarkably close to their own experience and my mother wept openly as we watched it. I was too young to understand why. Afterward she had to go to the ladies room to compose herself. It was then that my father partially explained why.

I was never told the whole story until after my mother had died, and shortly before my father's death, which was only three months later. They had lived for one another and once she was gone he had lost the will to live. I believe that he knew his own time was coming. We sat up late one night and spoke of many things never before discussed. It was then that he told me the whole horrible story.

Both my father and mother were people of principle. As I grew older I found myself constantly asking how they would have done it. I began to act as they might have acted and I hope that their principles have rubbed off on me.

In a sun baked Anglican cemetery in far off Suva, Fiji, Jackie is buried in a tiny grave with a white marble headstone. John Walter Garred, aged four.

I would like to have known him.

Chapter Thirteen

West Brome/Knowlton

The area of the Quebec Eastern Townships with which I am most familiar is Knowlton/Brome Lake where for many years my family weekended on Fisher's Point on the lake. I have many happy memories of sun filled days spent with my children who adored those things that a cottage on a Canadian lake can offer.

I kept a "Bluejay" sailboat (which I built myself) at the lake. Brome Lake is marvellous for sailing. There is almost always a stiff breeze and the lake is large enough to permit long reaches in most directions.

I had also been a member of the Knowlton Golf Club which is renowned as a very sporty course with rarely a flat lie to shoot from.

September is the time for small town fairs in the townships east of Montreal. Early in our courtship I had decided that it was time for Joyce and I to go on an old fashioned picnic.

I was having a few drinks with a couple of business associates in Toronto, one, a kind of rough and tumble Englishman, and the other, a Torontonian with a considerable artistic talent. The pastel portraits of my children were done by him.

We were discussing the proposed picnic. I mentioned that there was this lady who was becoming more important in my life and that I wanted the picnic to be something special. "You need to wear a tweed jacket with leather patches on the elbows", suggested the Canadian. The Brit came up with a menu of cucumber sandwiches.

It was a beautiful late September day. The goldenrod on the hill was about 4 feet high, and we had climbed to a height of land on which there was a television relay transmission tower. To the west there was a fabulous view of Brome Lake, which looked more like a duck pond from that height.

I spread out the blanket, turned on the portable radio to soft music, poured a couple of glasses of chilled white wine, and was about to tell her how wonderful she was, when three young children about 7 or 8 years old poked their heads through the goldenrod, pointed their pistols at us, and yelled — "bang bang bang bang"!

We became quite philosophical after that.

The cucumber sandwiches were great, but I never did get leather patches put on my tweed jacket!

_____

When planning a trip to Biddeford, Maine offered us an opportunity to stop off at West Brome and visit Thérèse Bernard, a close friend of Joyce's, we jumped at the chance.

An outstanding skier and horsewoman, Thérèse purchased a tiny heritage house on the Yamaska River in 1986 and settled down in this community. What she has done with it is nothing short of amazing.

She has a soft spot for animals and in particular stray cats. She has four of them. Oscar, a ginger coloured short hair, was the first. He arrived two years ago, lost and hungry by the edge of the river. She took him in and advertised throughout the neighbourhood without success. They became buddies. Some two years later a neighbour recognized Oscar, but seeing how well he and Thérèse got along, let it be.

A friend then made a presentation of another male, fluffy ginger variety. This took a bit of adjusting, but in due course the two agreed to a Mexican standoff. Two stray grey kittens have since been added.

Lady friends arrived to visit while we were there, Nicole, who had met Joyce before, accompanied by Alexandra, a young woman from Toronto who was spending time in Quebec in a total immersion program in French. Most of the afternoon was therefore spent in French in deference to Alexandra. I'm not sure that the others were grateful to us, but by God they encouraged us to learn it so they will just have to accept the consequences!

Nicole and Alexandra wanted to see a bit of Knowlton so we drove over to the Mill Pond Mall which was not there in my days. When they took off for Montreal, the three of us took a tour of old Knowlton which hasn't really changed a lot — except for a spiffing up of the commercial district.

We continued around the lake along the east side where the important estates and the golf club are located. Joyce had the bright idea to check out my old haunt on Fisher's Point, which is now jammed with cottages. Lo and behold my ex and her husband were entertaining. We were greeted with open arms. They were delighted to show us the changes made under the new regime. They were substantial improvements, which added to the use of the cottage (which I designed). I had not been there in 23 years and was curious to see how the landscaping changes which Peter (my son) and I had made during the summer of discontent had held up.

We had also added immeasurably to the property.

We toured the additions made to the second floor and the biggest surprise I had was to see the excellent oil paintings done by my mother hanging proudly. She was very good, and should have pursued oil painting commercially.

———————————

When my first marriage broke up, I needed legal advice. There was this cute lawyer working for our company whom I barely knew. As a typical male chauvinist pig, I had generally consulted one of the other male lawyers on staff when I had to.

Nevertheless friends suggested that I talk to Joyce. She was well liked and known to be a good person to talk to when one had a problem, particularly of a personal nature. She gave me the names of two or three excellent lawyers and guided me with sound advice, as I was going through this difficult period.

During the first 3 or 4 months (which happened to be in summer) I was facing a sizeable financial hit, and so my weekends were spent lying in the sun in my back yard. By the end of July, I had developed such a deep tan that I must have looked like Aristotle Onassis.

With the help of a *"dutch uncle"* whom I had known for years and done business with, I devised a totally reasonable plan to refinance using my home as collateral which was entirely doable and far more economical than surrendering a 6.25 % mortgage and taking on a much larger one at 11.5 %.

I approached the bank where I had done business for over 20 years. I had an excellent credit record and a history of early payment of any loans I had taken out. I put my proposal to the pompous lending officer for review.

A few days later I dropped in to the bank to be informed that although my proposal made reasonable economic sense, it was rejected. The grounds — lifestyle! It was then that I learned that banks are only as good as the people representing them. This clown had looked at me with my Onassis tan, going through a divorce, put the two together and concluded that I was a swinger and therefore a poor credit risk. The exact opposite was true.

Shortly thereafter I changed banks. I had to take the more expensive route but within three years had retired all debts and went forward from there.

Several months later, in the fall, I thought that I had better show my appreciation to Joyce for her considerable help in getting my legal life in order. We had dinner one Friday night in Le St-Amable, a great restaurant in old Montreal, and step by step she became the centre of my new life.

In the spring the divorce proceedings were being heard, in the middle of a raging blizzard on St. Patrick's Day. Always the protective one, she supplied me with a book to read, while waiting for the hearing, and taped inside the cover was a tranquillizer! I didn't need the tranquillizer and the clerk of the court wouldn't allow me to read in court.

In July we were married and began a lifetime adventure filled with love and laughter. We set out for Nantucket Island for our honeymoon at a quaint historic inn known as The Woodbox. It had great food and we have many happy memories of it.

Now it takes a bit of time to get used to a new wife (or husband) when you have just been divorced from the old one. It so happened that my ex had also remarried within a week or two of our wedding.

Joyce had gone downstairs at the inn and was waiting outside for me. We were going bicycling across the island to Siasconset. When I came down the stairs, the inn keeper said "Hello and by the way your wife is outside." I said with alarm, "Good God, don't tell me she's here too!" Anyway we got that straightened out and as we were cycling across the island I got a flat tire. It was a rented bike and like AAA they service it on the spot. Joyce spotted a police car about a quarter mile back and pedalled over for help. Still not quite into this Mr. and Mrs. thing she said to the understanding officer, "The man I'm with has a flat tire. Could you call the bicycle shop." Oh, well, we eventually got used to it.

───────────────

We thanked our Knowlton hosts for the cake and apéritifs and tour and left for dinner at Sutton — probably the best ski area in the townships, and the place where Joyce had first met Thérèse years ago on the mountain top. Thérèse had offered Joyce to share their wine. That was the beginning of a long fun filled friendship valued by both of them.

It had been too long between visits, nearly eight years, although they corresponded regularly, so our visit was all that more enjoyable. Thérèse continues to be active and may well have the opportunity to visit Ottawa to complete a project she is working on.

We look forward to sharing our home and wine cellar with her.

On Wednesday morning we all rose before 6 a.m. and left at 6:45. Thérèse to a business rendez-vous in Montreal, and ourselves on the next leg of our trip to Biddeford Pool. We didn't see a soul until we hit the US border. We arrived at Freeport, Me., about 3:30 p.m.

There are dozens of retail outlets at Freeport including the granddaddy of them all, L.L. Bean. Not too many red hot deals left though, even in the factory outlet. We had a light dinner at the Jameson Tavern on US #1 which is historically significant as the place where the state of Maine was born when the forefathers broke away from Massachusetts in 1820. Tomorrow morning we'll take a quick look at Portland en route to Kathy and David's at Biddeford Pool.

Bagel

Thou shalt not covet

Chapter Fourteen

Biddeford Pool

We had been told that Joseph's and Carla's on Fore St. in Portland were the best sources of fashion so we headed there first. Joseph's covers both the female and male requirements, good, but pricey. Even on sale I couldn't find anything priced low enough to make me spring for it. Joyce showed interest in an outfit in deep navy blue, surprisingly, since she resists anything resembling black.

The real fun was when we hit the Maine Mall in south Portland, especially at Filene's basement. We made several fabulous buys. It was a great shopping mall with every opportunity for real deals.

Joyce's friendship with Kathy dates back to school days. Both Kathy and her husband David are intellectuals, Kathy a university professor who specialized in women's literature at Concordia, and David who became a journalist, and later a producer at the CBC.

They are generous fun loving people, open and easy to mix with. Their daughter Juliet is following in mother's footsteps in the same field, and Chippy, their son, is pursuing a career in the theatre.

The problem is they have a beagle dog. His name is Bagel.

He is without question the ugliest, most disagreeable, most oversized cur that God ever created. I am convinced that the man who wrote the song about "bad, bad Leroy Brown — meaner than a junkyard dog" had him in mind when he wrote it.

If there is food on top of a table he will steal it. If you stand anywhere near him he will jump all over you with his grimy paws leaving their imprint.

Now, I like dogs. But this one was clearly at the end of the line when the good Lord was handing out personalities. So that is what is ahead of us for the next four days.

David was rocking back and forth on the upper deck of the cottage when we arrived. As we pulled into the driveway he stood up to greet us. Bagel also stood up with his paws on the railing. I suppose he thought his dinner had just arrived. Chippy was there to help unload the car. David said they thought we would be there early in the morning. We explained about Freeport and then got into the wine.

The cottage keeps getting better. David and Chippy have continued to improve it in the off season. It is now worth quite a bit even though it's unfinished. The house across the street, which is on the beach, has just sold for over $500,000 US.

It was fun to relax over a glass of wine with David. Kathy and I always spend the first hour jousting back and forth about the power of men vs women. She is an avid feminist.

She is also a marvellous cook, and we enjoyed a great dinner of baked haddock with fries and a lot of Chablis to wash it down. It was a fun evening as always.

Tomorrow David and I play golf at 9:30 at Gorham. Bagel was generally well behaved. He only jumped up on the dinner table twice.

As usual I'm the first one up. Bagel is in the other cabin with Chippy, so I'm safe for the moment. Then one by one they surface, Kathy then David. We wonder who is leading the British Open so I place an armchair in front of the TV and wait. Without cable no news from the outside world. Lots of weather reports and predicted high and low tides along with winds but only news of local interest.

In the meantime Bagel has decided that I look like fair game for a tug of war with a knotted rope shaped like a bone. I try to ignore him but he's not buying it. All 37 lbs of him. He becomes increasingly insistent, pushing the rope bone at me trying to engage me in this game. Kathy finds it amusing. I don't. Bagel takes a lunge at my knees with the rope in his mouth. Then in disgust he barks and growls at me. Kathy then comes out to see what's going on and has to lead him away.

Shortly thereafter, she placed a child security gate on the stairs leading up to where Joyce is still sleeping. Bagel simply leaps around it and heads up. We have visions of him climbing onto her bed and scaring the daylights out of Joyce. Kathy runs up and drags him down the stairs.

In the dining room all the chairs are tilted forward into the table to prevent him from getting up on it. Right at the moment someone has forgotten and left one chair upright. Bagel has seized the moment and is currently sprawled all over the dining room table asleep. He is totally unmanageable, but they haven't the heart to do anything about it.

After David and I came back from golf I went for a dip in the sea. It was an invigorating 66 degrees. It felt warmer than what I remember of Florida. The tide is up and so the pool behind us, which is about a mile in diameter, is filled. This has an amazing effect on the atmosphere and cools the cottage down quickly even with the temperature in town in the 90s.

David and Kathy were very clever at the time of the purchase to have bought five feet of direct access to the ocean from their neighbours across the street on the beach side. This not only adds to their enjoyment of the property and the beach unrestricted, but adds substantially to the value of it.

Joyce and Kathy have gone off to play tennis at the club. David is asleep. We were supposed to play doubles with them but after 18 holes of golf we just weren't into it.

David is quite a philosopher. He generally reasons very logically. Last night we got into a discussion about how candidates for the PhD program at Oxford can corner the adjudicators by developing expertise in rare fields that few if any can challenge. For example becoming an expert in the use of the Bantu language at Khartoum. Who is going to challenge them?

It reminded me of a story told to me by a personal friend who had worked for the US parent company of the one I worked for in Canada. At the time he was a forestry engineer in the woodlands division of the Southern Kraft business.

As was the case with all operations within the company, they were required to submit their capital budget each year which was presented to a head office review committee consisting of senior financial and engineering officers of the company, all flown in for the occasion in the luxurious corporate jet.

Harvesting pulpwood has changed immensely since the times when a man with an axe or men with a two handled saw cut down and trimmed full grown trees.

Today it is done with largely automated mobile harvesting machines capable of cutting, stripping, and placing logs of a predetermined length on a carrier for transport to the mill. Some of these high priced head office executives sat silently in their shirts with buttoned down collars, as each of the major items were submitted and approved (usually involving millions of dollars). Finally, the last item on the budget called for a station wagon V8 capable of performing on logging roads. The head office committee sprang to life. Why do you need a V8, why not a more economical V6? It was the only item they had the slightest understanding of, and after approving millions of dollars for equipment they knew nothing about, they weren't going to pass on something they knew something about without a fight. The budget stood up as presented but the committee had had its say. One wonders how they would have handled a major capacity expansion proposal involving hundreds of millions of dollars.

It is Saturday morning 6:00 a.m. We continue to have wonderful weather, clear skies, warm, and a constant 10 - 15 knot breeze from the southwest.

We always associate the fresh moist smell of the sea with a holiday at the ocean. Wild roses seem to grow so easily in this environment and their fragrance is another scent we associate with the sea. Closer to the commercial areas the smell of deep frying, whether potatoes, or seafood, is another way to identify with the sea.

Even though it has been dry, the marsh grass dances luxuriously in the breeze. Deep green gorse-like bushes grow vigorously in nearby clusters. David tells me that is usually an indication that a septic system leech field is buried underneath.

I'm not sure how I feel about keen joggers or cyclists tearing around at this hour of the day. They are forcing themselves to get their rate up. A bit like going to a physical training centre and working out. Good for you, but not much fun. I think I'd rather get my cardiovascular rate up with tennis which is more enjoyable.

From time to time a lone car passes. Normally you wouldn't be conscious of them. But by virtue of the fact that the only other sounds are the birds, the low hum of the breeze and the never ending motion of the breakers, the sound of auto tires becomes magnified by comparison.

I have always admired the way that Americans fly the flag in the rural areas of smaller towns. Less so in the cities. I guess like many other differences, city folk take a lot more for granted. The flag becomes more of a symbol of the struggle to survive to country folk.

I thought I could hear a wind chime nearby, but it's the flag rope tapping on a nearby metal flagstaff when the breeze hits it.

The tide is now about halfway out, so the tidal pool is nearly empty, sailboats lying on a slant, supported by their keels.

Across the pool I hear hammering. It is now 7 a.m., the legal time for construction work to begin the day.

There isn't a dress code in place, everyone does their own thing, but shorts are generally the order of the day. It seems that the fatter the legs, the shorter the shorts. Sandals have become a part of the current fashion statement. Most people now have them. The Velcro closures spiked up an interest in them. They are practical as well. Cooler, they allow your feet to breathe and dry out.

There is a fund raiser antique show on today at the University of New England, not far from here. We'll probably go and see it, even though what passes for an antique today is a far cry from my idea of one.

Years ago I used to collect pine furniture, mostly in Quebec, where even as late as the 60s you could still find outstanding examples of early pine furniture for a few hundred dollars. The same articles today, restored, would be worth thousands.

I used to love to tackle the restoration of huge armoires, vaisseliers and other large pieces. I would spend hours in my garage, painstakingly removing layer upon layer of old paint. It was some time before I discovered that you need only three things in addition to paint stripper. An egg spatula with rounded corners, which eliminated the risk of scratching the surface if you slipped, fine steel wool to rub off the dissolved paint without spoiling the patina, and a teaspoon, the shape of which would allow you to curve into the various mouldings without damaging them. A few feet of fine jute twine is useful for cleaning out turnings.

Sometimes if I had a business or other problem to resolve I would go to work for hours restoring an antique. While doing so my subconscious would take over the problem, and many times a solution would come to me while doing it.

The old New England adage about busy hands keeping a sane and happy mind. (Or something to that effect). Joyce had a nun teacher who always said that an idle mind is the devil's workshop. I suppose it is.

Most of the Quebec pine furniture that we own was bought in the late 60s in the eastern townships or around Quebec City.

During this same period I was often asked why I was interested in this "junk", as I wandered through old barns or ramshackle sheds stacked to the rafters with old armoires, tables and chairs. Trying to recognize rare and basically sound articles under layers of blistered and scratched paint became a game.

More often than not there would be absolutely nothing with the potential to justify the hours of laborious restoration it required. Only once in a dozen outings would I discover something of interest.

But on those rare occasions when I did make a discovery I usually pounced on it.

If you knew what you were looking for and were able to examine the underside unpainted areas to determine what woods and what joining techniques had been employed, it was possible to acquire something of considerable value for very little money and a lot of hard work restoring it. It also took you to some wonderful small towns off the beaten track which you might otherwise never have known about.

Thus, over a period of about ten years, I found dozens of great pieces of Canadiana which had defiantly survived neglect, abuse and even vandalism. What had permitted them to survive was the masterful craftsmanship, mortice and tenon joinery utilizing pegs instead of nails and the fabulous quality of wide width native woods taken from enormous trees which were common at that time.

There was one dealer in particular, who was trading in Mont St-Hilaire in the Richelieu Valley, with whom I did a lot of business. He had an interesting background. He got into the antique business shortly after his grandfather's estate had been sold off before they realized how valuable the house furnishings were. He vowed to make it back. He operated what was at the time a small road stand on a family apple orchard. They also sold other produce. The quality was good, the prices were fair and he prospered and grew. There was a good volume of passing trade, many of whom were interested in Quebec antiques. He had a network of pickers who kept him supplied. He never got greedy. When other dealers were asking $3 -500 for an armoire his price was $125 -200. He had, over a period of 5 - 7 years, many rare pieces. On one occasion he had just found a rare diamond point armoire and I happened to be the first to see it late one Friday evening. He was asking $550 for it. I missed a golden opportunity to buy it simply because I didn't have that much loose cash at the time. Today it would command $20 - 25,000. I will regret it to my dying day.

I did manage to be there at the right time when a pair of Louis XV armoire doors showed up in the rough which I bought for $350. At the Toronto auctions this year the estimate on a pair of comparable doors was $8 - 10,000. Not a bad return for junk!

When the Quebec government began issuing licenses for cider production he was one of the first to get one. He never looked back. Although he had not done well academically he had a gifted business touch, and grew a small apple stand into a highly successful business.

There will probably be nothing at the local antique show to equal what I used to find at St-Hilaire. Nevertheless I'll probably go and check it out.

A jogger is just passing in front of the house with a golden retriever on a leash. The jogger is struggling with a pained expression on his face. The retriever patiently trotting beside him looks like he'd just as soon get this over with, and get on to some real exercise.

We were going to watch the British Open on TV, however John Kennedy Jr. is reported missing in his private aircraft en route to Martha's Vineyard. That family is jinxed.

I had to go into Biddeford to buy some necessities so on my way I stopped in at the M.A.D.A. Antique Show at New England College. It was really quite good, and contained several things I might have considered. Prices are well up from the last serious look I took at a show. They are probably inflated over normal in any event to cover the cost of exhibiting.

Sophie, Chippy's girl friend, has arrived. She is very pretty and David tells me she is a kind and considerate person. Joyce and I took a drive over to Kennebunkport and past the Bush Estate, still swarming with curious tourists, taking photos, checking it out with binoculars. What a way to live. A celebrity becomes public property. They'd probably like to be able to go out to a restaurant occasionally and not be recognized. Keating's antiques and auctioneers were preparing for a 3 p.m. auction. It was hot as blazes. It was at Keating's in 1978 where I bought a serpentine front butler's chest which is now used by me as a combination chest of drawers and desk. It is Delaware Valley circa 1790.

Joyce and I also drove to the point where the inlet to the pool is located. We had lunch in the rear garden behind Goldwaithe's Store. It has a lovely view of the gut and in the distance about 7 or 8 miles away you can see Old Orchard Beach, a favourite haunt of Quebecers. Several people were learning how to kayak in front of the point. Some learning faster than others.

Joyce, God bless her, has a mind as quick as a whip, but sometimes even she gets things backwards. We have visited our friends at Biddeford Pool, Maine a number of times. When their son, Chippy, was a young boy, he took Scampy the family pooch for a run on the beach and Joyce went along for the exercise. About an hour later Joyce came back to the beach house and Kathy asked her how it went. "Fine," Joyce replied, "except that Chippy peed on every single towel on the beach."

David barbequed a marvellous boneless lamb along with zucchini. It was a great combination. We had some inexpensive Almaden Burgundy which was surprisingly good.

Bagel continues to try to charm me. But I'm not buying it. When he leaps onto my lap Kathy approves. I don't. Finally Bagel goes to the small cabin with Chippy where he will spend the night out of harm's way. He has to be watched constantly. He has a voracious appetite. Anything from roast lamb to old facial tissue.

Tomorrow we leave for the north. It has been fun and we will see them again.

Chapter Fifteen

Mika

After a quick check at the standings in the British Open we took off down I -95 to Kittery. A quick look at the outlets, then onward to Concord, then to Burlington. We called Mika from Burlington to confirm that we would be there a day early, which presented no problem.

Then on over Morse's Line into Canada. We set our bearings for Boucherville, immediately across the river from Montreal's east end connecting with highway 40 which runs up the north shore of the St. Lawrence.

I had travelled the route hundreds of times when I was marketing manager of the paper products division of a large paper company. It was the centre of heavy industry in Montreal, oil refineries, chemical processing, cement kilns and foundries. The air quality leaves something to be desired. It is also the final destination for most of Montreal's sewage. So we will have traded the scenic beauty of the mountains for something less spectacular.

Once off the island the pastoral qualities resume. Some of the earliest settlements in North America were established along these shores as evidenced by the number of early French Canadian stone homes which remain as testimonials to the courage and determination of the pioneers who battled punishing odds and survived.

Heading north from the river inland, the countryside is mainly rich farmland for about 30 miles, yielding gradually to rolling forested hills, once the source of valuable timber, then pulpwood and later giving in to the ever increasing incursions of recreational vacation properties. We are not quite far enough in to find the important mountains and lakes for which the Laurentian region is famous. Nevertheless the air is clean and there are enough small rivers to support the tiny settlements which are found there.

Near Joliet, tobacco is an important crop while deposits of limestone beneath the soil support the cement and lime industries. Politically it is usually conservative.

There are also many dairy farms to be found along this route predominantly populated by Holsteins.

We are not really superstitious in our house, we just appear that way.

Driving through the countryside, if Joyce sees a herd of cows lying down, she will open the window and yell out, "Get up you fools, you'll make it rain."

Rain also comes into play if you happen to put your underwear on inside out with the label showing. Once, I met a good business associate for lunch, and had a lump on my forehead. "What happened to you?" he asked. I explained that that morning while getting dressed I had broken the house rules and was putting my jockey shorts on inside out — label showing. She grabbed them yelling, "You'll make it rain!", and sent me flying across the bedroom and I hit my head on the dresser. Such are the perils.

Joyce's friendship with Mika dates back to the late 60s when Joyce met her in Montreal at the Mount Royal Tennis Club. She is a very good tennis player. Her family emigrated to Canada after World War II from Poland. They had been a very prosperous family in Krakow and the old family (Zamoyski) mansion still stands there, having been taken over by the post war communist government. It is now a museum.

It is interesting to listen to her story, and that of others we have met through her, of the life they left behind. Many of their relatives spent time in concentration camps. One cousin we met who lived in the US, on the Maine coast, still has fragments of her husband's prison uniform with which she had covered her diary.

When Joyce and I were married Mika and her husband Raymond were very kind and generous to us. I had just lost both my parents within three months of each other. Raymond had rented a lovely beach house on Drake Island near Wells Beach for many years. We were their guests there on two or three occasions. Drake Island is relatively unpopulated by comparison with other beach communities in Maine.

It has a small but lovely clean beach. The cottage was right on the beach, divided into two self sufficient units. It had a large patio overlooking the ocean surrounded by wild roses. I can still recall their fragrance.

Mika owned a wonderful springer spaniel named Ponjy. I used to take him for early morning walks on the beach. He looked absolutely regal, head up, back straight, trotting along on the sand. On days when Mika and Raymond had to go in to town on business, I looked forward to minding him. Occasionally I'd throw a raw egg in with his dinner. He loved it. He was a real dog.

Nearby at Kennebunkport there was a Franciscan monastery and church where mass was said in Lithuanian. Joyce and I went there with Mika. We both still recall with amusement the sight of the Franciscan fathers in their long brown habits. But these were modern guys. Instead of brown sandals, they sported jazzy looking running shoes.

We have many warm memories of the time spent on Drake Island.

Later, Mika and Raymond lived in downtown Montreal at Chelsea Place, an exclusive cluster of enormous town homes just up from Sherbrooke St. They loved to entertain and did so beautifully.

Raymond was a successful entrepreneur eloquent in French, English and Spanish. Trading on an international basis, he travelled extensively, and he died in the US, while on a business trip.

Mika chose to move to a family cottage in Rawdon, Quebec, in the early 90s to rethink her life. In due course she developed a relationship with her friend, André, who spoke very little English. In time, Mika's French improved immensely!

We had not seen her in 5 years. She looked wonderful, and has settled happily into her new lifestyle. She has an uncanny ability to create a marvellous meal from simple ingredients, which she again did on this occasion. Ponjy has gone to dog heaven, but Mika's great love of dogs is now reflected in another Springer Spaniel named Notnot.

Mika's gifted artistic touch has enabled her to convert what was a very simple cottage in the woods, into a cozy home in a lovely setting.

We spent over 5 hours with her reminiscing about old friends and good times. She brought us up to date on the status of her 3 children now reaching their 30s.

When we reached home, Joyce expressed her thanks for being in her own bed that night, and quickly settled in to all those mysterious things that wives always do when they get home from a trip.

Chapter Sixteen

The Pond

This morning's paper, The Ottawa Citizen, contained a front page story reviewing an article written by Stephen Budiansky in the Atlantic Monthly about animal behaviour. In it he says people are being duped. Dogs are con artists who pick our pockets clean and leave us smiling about it. He says if dogs were people, we would be calling a lawyer or police to deal with them.

Pretty soon there will be nothing left to believe in. For now, I'll continue to believe that most dogs are man's best friend.

This summer seems to be flying past us. Maybe it is in part due to the activities we have been involved with. In ten days it will be August and then in 3 months we will be off to Egypt and Israel!

During our absence we must have lost another goose. They were feeding this evening directly behind our house. The count is now 18. Even in the space of one week their markings are more pronounced and they have almost reached full growth in size.

My neighbour, Win, tells us that the older group attained flight this past week. So we should see the whole group airborne in the next week. A very exciting time!

While we were talking, a flurry of activity started up out in front of us on the 9th fairway. The head goose took up a position about 15 - 20 yards away from the flock and began to honk out commands. The entire flock stood up and turned facing the pond and away from him. It went on for about 3 or 4 minutes.

Then the other mature geese began honking. Then suddenly it happened. The entire flock began running full speed toward the pond and for the group who were among the first born, it was lift off! The second born group of about 5 young stopped, and in fascination, watched while their young cousins flew about 50 yards and landed safely in the pond. They then began to move swiftly along the water's edge like a platoon of soldiers, still staring at the new aviators, as if they were thinking — how did they do that?

It is wonderful to watch.

On the property next to Win, a groundhog with a fine brown furry coat, is out feeding in the backyard. He seems to like some leafy looking weeds growing on the edge of a flower bed. He is quite brazen. He can't be more than 35 - 40 feet away from us, and must surely hear us talking, but that doesn't deter him. Win is concerned that we will wake up some morning and find half a dozen baby groundhogs out there feeding with him.

We exchange opinions on our respective gardens, which this year seem to have behaved differently. We both have Asiatic lilies, among other things, which have attracted tiny red beetles. We are becoming increasingly concerned about using pesticides, with everything being written about their link to cancer. We may just have to dig them out and plant some perennial more resistant to insects.

This morning another branch of the goose family showed up on the 9th fairway. I counted a total of 61 geese including the permanent residents. These are geese who have been raised on another pond and have now learned to fly. They are all accepted in the territory, although every now and then we see the males pretending to be aggressive, running around with heads down, necks stretched out, but never following through, which they would do if they were serious.

From now on as each brood masters flight we will see more and more geese on the fairway, and then for several days even the residents will take off on exchange visits to other breeding ponds.

In the fall during late November there will be as many as 300 all over the fairway or in the pond. That is when the owners of the golf course pull their hair out in total frustration. All the reflective tape they can buy is not going to deter the birds.

One of the golf pros has come along in a cart and begun to harass the geese to get them off the fairway. Back and forth he drives right at them until most of them are in the pond. But not the solitary goose. He stays about 40 - 50 yards away from the flock and they still won't admit him. Suddenly the head goose takes a run at him flying at top speed. He doesn't catch him but there he is again, all by himself. At one point he came into the pond swimming towards us. I looked at him through the binoculars and he is a pretty good looking guy. Maybe that's the problem! Maybe that's where the term jailbird originated!

Two years ago I was playing down the ninth fairway when one of our foursome hit a bad shot which struck a goose. For several minutes he lay there and then with great effort pulled himself into the water. Later we were to see him limping along behind the flock. But he did learn to fly and we spotted him last year. He made it again!

It is always an event when Peter and Sandy arrive from Montreal with our grandchildren Julie (8) and Philip (7). As they become a bit older we don't quite have to batten down the hatches as we did 3 or 4 years ago. However age and growth have not in any way slowed them down. Bursting with energy and enthusiasm they are ready to take on the world, preferably at double speed.

What do you do to amuse 7 and 8 year olds? Suggest a museum and you draw a dull response. When you ask them what they would like to do, the first response is always to swim at the wave pool or go to the big water slides at Mont Cascades. That is where we are today.

It is a hot sunny day, and we arrived shortly before noon. It is bedlam. There are probably 2 or 3 thousand parents and kids already here. There are tables set up at various points on the grass and if you are lucky enough to find one, there are awning covered patios under which more picnic tables are set. Most of them already have occupants. Peter says it's open season and you just have to barge in and share a table.

There is every conceivable size, shape and colour of humanity here. Some fabulous figures and some less than fabulous. Most people have brought picnic coolers which are inspected on the way in to be sure they aren't bringing in glass bottles, since most are in bare feet.

The owners have pulled out all the stops in creative imagination here. The main slides are quite straightforward with 4 tracks with humps on the way down to give your stomach butterflies as you rise and fall. There is a black tunnel through which you can slide on huge tire shaped rubber rafts which spin as you descend.

Fountains galore, and a fairly large wading pool with kids bouncing up and down in it. In the lower corner mushroom shaped waterfalls which the kids get under and get rained on.

And everyone squeals and yells as the kids excitedly urge one another on.

There is an arcade, if you need other forms of amusement, as well as a snack bar selling all kinds of junk food. Peter went to change into his bathing suit and came back with a face full of ice cream.

The turbo twister looks a bit steeper. Everyone lies on their back with arms folded behind their head and shoots down the slide feet first. It all looks like great fun.

On the ride up here (about 30 miles) along the Gatineau River the kids were all jazzed up and acting like 7 or 8 year olds. Interestingly they quieted down very quickly when Peter put the radio on and we all listened to a peppy piano concerto being played. Something to remember!

Meanwhile Joyce and Sandy were back at the house and will probably end up shopping.

At the water slide nobody owns or reserves a table. As is the custom at ski hills space is shared. There was a family at the end of a table with a few things on it. So we sat down at the opposite end. We had just started lunch when her cousins and aunts and uncles and brothers arrived with a load of coolers stuffed with food. "You're sitting at our table." one of them said. Peter had a brief dialogue with them about sharing and then we decided to move to one in the open sun which was vacant. That is where I wrote this.

The picnic hampers were getting opened and all of the ethnic cooking smells were floating through the air. Peter and the kids had gone back into the pools, and the sound system continued to play picnic music — whatever that is.

For the past week there have been as many as 70 geese on the pond. They appear to be part of the extended family of the permanent residents. They have been having a great time alternating between the pond and the 9th fairway, even extending their munching as far as the 1st fairway, about 150 yards away.

The golf club was becoming desperate. The staff worker who has been harassing them all week with a golf cart (with limited success) showed up with a very large black and white border collie which he let loose on them and which forced them into the water.

The geese moved to our side of the pond, feeding down near the trees to the right of the 9th hole. The worker and the dog were hiding behind the huge rock which separates the 9th fairway from the 1st tee.

Slowly, sneakily, the golf cart and canine marshall came around. Suddenly the whole flock headed for the water, the dog in pursuit. A lot of squawking and honking. The dog understood his job. He swam out into the middle of the flock which dispersed, then back to dry land he went — to lots of praise from the worker.

After waiting patiently for about half an hour the geese then began to climb back up onto the 9th fairway. About one third of the flock were up and feeding. The dog and worker were nowhere to be seen — yet. Eventually all of the geese were back in their usual position on the fairway. Other golf carts went by and the geese ignored them.

The dog and worker once again showed up. It was a waiting game. The golf cart parked about 50 yards away, dog at the ready. There was a foursome coming down the ninth. Was he waiting till they passed? He had moved into position. He let the dog loose! Most of the geese hit the water immediately. A few didn't bother, then they too jumped in. The dog followed but only part way. The golfers praised the dog who responded with his tail. If he succeeds he will become a folk hero in the clubhouse. No doubt his picture would be hung beside the trophies. It was a female. It had squatted near the sand trap. It was getting a lot of attention and enjoying it. Curious golfers pet the dog as they pass. The geese were back up near the green. The dog and cart moved closer. Back into the water for the geese.

She didn't look like a vicious dog. There was too much tail wagging with strangers for that. Hopefully this game would go on without incident.

It was interesting to observe the interaction between the geese and domestic animals. A year ago a large marmalade cat decided to take them on. The cat of course wouldn't venture into the water. It simply sat down at the water's edge and stared at them. The geese in turn lined up like a classroom of children and stared back at the cat. If the cat ever did get to a full confrontation with a fully grown goose it would be in for a surprise. There's a bit more to it than a sparrow!

Never underestimate the intelligence of the geese. The flock had now split into two groups, one at either end of the pond. (No doubt after a strategy meeting). The dog couldn't be at two places at once. That way when one group was being chased, the other group could jump ashore and begin eating, and vice versa.

For the better part of the afternoon there was no longer any sign of the dog. All of the geese resumed their normal feeding pattern on the 9th fairway.

As of mid August all of the geese are now flying and are visiting other ponds in the area.

The largest of the Kanata Lakes is about a mile away. It is known as the Beaver Pond and is about 350-400 yards in length. A wonderful wet land continues at its source for another half mile and is home to a great variety of birds and other waterfowl.

The city recognized this part of the community some years ago and has preserved a large tract of it in a natural state with an extensive network of walking trails through a mature stand of beautiful trees known as the Trillium Forest. In spring, the forest floor is a mass of brilliant white flowers as far as the eye can see. The trillium, of course, being the official flower of Ontario.

In a walk through this area this week I passed by another flock of geese, perhaps 30 -35 in number. There are also no golf carts to threaten them, so that I passed within 10 yards of them without causing them concern.

Peter, my son, and I played Eagle Creek Golf Course, about 10 miles from here last week. It has considerably more water than Kanata, which originates in Constance Lake and ends up on the Ottawa River. It too has its resident flock of geese in a much more natural setting, unspoiled by development.

Yesterday Joyce and I played Loch March Golf Club, closer to us by about 5 miles and also blessed with a sizeable amount of water. There too, there are resident geese. On the 14th hole I hit an errant shot from the tee which settled on a sandy strip of beach where about a dozen geese were sunning themselves. When I approached my ball I began talking to the geese in order to avoid a sudden surprise. I walked right by them within about 10 feet. They recognized me as a golfer and literally ignored me. Other than gingerly stepping around droppings I had no problem hitting my ball. So I guess it is possible for us to coexist!

Chapter Seventeen

Algonquin Park

We had always been curious to see what is so special about Algonquin Park, a huge provincial park located south east of North Bay, and about 125 miles west of Ottawa. Although it is only a two and a half hour drive from Kanata, we had never been there.

Algonquin was made famous in the early part of this century through the spectacular paintings of it done by the Group of Seven, and by Tom Thomson. Anyone who has visited the National Gallery of Canada, the Art Gallery of Ontario, or the McMichael collection at Kleinberg, where their major works are displayed, is immediately taken with the raw beauty of the Canadian wilderness depicted in them.

And so, we decided to take a run at it. Barb and Win, our neighbours, have had a family cottage for years at Round Lake, just outside of the park on the east. When they learned that we were heading there, Barb told us of a very nice lodge located not far from the park's east gate, called Spectacle Lake Lodge. We were booked to spend Thursday there. God willing!

In the morning newspaper, there was an article covering a major traffic accident involving a tractor-trailer on the bridge over Smoke Creek near Tea Lake Dam (painted many times by Thomson). The vehicle caught fire and so did the bridge, effectively closing route 60 in both directions. The highway department have said it would take several days to restore circulation, and all through traffic was being diverted around the south end of the park.

We were assured that we could still access the park via the east gate as far west as Canoe Lake (where Thomson died). The resident wolves would get a brief respite from the intrusions of visiting tourists, at least for a few days.

The east gate is accessed via highway 60 which runs through Barry's Bay and Renfrew.

There is an excellent golf course in Renfrew which is considered to be one of the prettiest in the region. We had intended to play it on Friday on our way back from Algonquin. However, Joyce, who is never one to do anything in half measures, injured her knee on Wednesday probably in a tennis round robin we played in at the West Ottawa Tennis Club. The swelling was such that we had to cancel our golf plans and spend 3 hours Wednesday night at the Ottawa Civic Hospital emergency room, ruling out problems such as another clot that might prevent us from going into Algonquin. We managed to do so.

We set out at 8 a.m. Thursday morning en route through Renfrew and Barry's Bay. We arrived at Spectacle Lake Lodge about 10:30 a.m. in full sunshine. It is a well run, reasonably priced resort on the edge of the lake. The owner, Maurice Mahusier is an affable individual who sets the tone for his guests. The lodge itself is host to about a dozen wedding and other receptions annually. The food is good and the service friendly.

After checking in we headed off into Algonquin which was our raison d'être for this trip. Although we were not aware of it ahead of time, August is the month when the park staff organize "wolf howls" which are always on a Thursday night. We had lucked out! Since 1963 when they began, there had only been a total of 82 "howls" or an average of 2 to 3 a year. When we purchased our park entry permit, there was a notice advising all that there was to be a "howl" that night, with the public invited to attend an information session at the open air theatre at 8:30 p.m., followed by the "howl."

Joyce had heard Michael Runtz speak to the CFUW in Kanata two years ago and had been fascinated by it. We weren't going to miss this opportunity!

We continued on to the west on route 60 which accesses most of the park with gravel roads which lead to the more important sites, stopping first at the outdoor theatre to see what we were up against. Then on to the Two Rivers Store for a quick lunch. We also stopped at Killarney Lodge to do some window shopping. It is beautifully situated on an exclusive point on the Lake of Two Rivers.

En route we came upon a large number of cars stopped at the side of the road, with people milling around excitedly. We stopped as well, and lo and behold, about 50 yards from the road, in a lily pond, was a very large and totally unconcerned cow moose having lunch. I took its picture while we watched it for a few minutes, and we then pressed onward, to the Algonquin Art Gallery which is a small but well organized facility with three exhibition rooms and an art shop located next to the admission area.

The first two rooms are hung with wildlife paintings and sculptures done mostly by Canadian artists. It is possible to purchase the works which are of excellent quality.

The third exhibition room was given over this summer to a "wilderness reunion" of Tom Thomson and the Group of Seven, curated by Brian Meehan, director of the London Regional Art and Historical Museums, London, Ontario.

There were several fine examples of works by the Group, including at least one which was a featured work by Lismer in the National Gallery of Canada's "Art for a Nation" exhibition, 1995. The Group of Seven artists represented in this show originally painted together in Algonquin in 1914.

It was a fine exhibition in very pleasant surroundings.

We continued on to the Portage Store and Canoe Centre on Canoe Lake (where Thomson's Memorial is located). We were taken with the enthusiasm and capability of all of the staff at the facility. While waiting our turn to ask a question, we watched while a young father and his son obtained permits to venture out. They don't miss much. Itinery and destinations are recorded, colour of tent, colour of canoe, car licence, people in party. Each group is given a numbered trash bag. They are reminded that no cans or bottles are permitted.

We had now worked our way west as far as we were permitted on route 60. A road barrier was still in place reminding everyone that the bridge over Smoke Lake Creek was still out, because of the accident and fire.

We headed back to the lodge.

When we sat down for dinner about 5:30 p.m. the lodge keeper came out on the patio and began opening all the sun umbrellas. It was curious. He explained that if he closed them bats would work their way up inside them for the night and the tables would be covered by morning with their droppings.

It was interesting to watch the other guests and families using the various canoes, pedaloos, and kayaks available. One very athletic man whom we estimated to be in his late 50s/early 60s, began a vigorous solo swim across the lake to the island about a half mile away. Before we had finished dinner he appeared in the water heading back, still swimming vigorously. We thought when he arrived that was it. Such was not the case. He climbed into a kayak and paddled enthusiastically back and forth, for another 10 -15 minutes. Next, he jumped into a canoe and took off for a further 15 minute paddle. When we headed back to our cabin, he was showing off a huge motorcycle with more chrome on it than a public washroom.

This pattern of vigour seemed to be present all over the park, where we observed water sports or launching sites, for those heading out into the wilderness to camp.

The people who are attracted to Algonquin are not the Las Vegas crowd. All of them from 6 year olds up are bright eyed healthy people filled with enthusiasm for what they are doing. This continued to be evident as we took our seat in the outdoor theatre, for the information session on the "howl". Wonderful young families from hundreds of miles away, some even from Europe and Japan. They all had one thing in common. Vigour, enthusiasm and respect for those around them.

We got to the theatre an hour early. It was already half full. By 8:30 p.m. the crowd was overflowing into the forest. The leader told us this was only the second "howl" this year. They estimated over 2400 people in attendance. That meant over 700 cars in the convoy which was to come.

Michael Runtz gave an excellent presentation with his immense knowledge of wolves, with an appropriate dash of humour. We listened to Michael and an aide offer their versions of the wolf howl, followed by a recording of an earlier howl which had been successful, with the remarkable sound of the wolves' reply.

With military precision, 700 carloads then took off for a "howl" destination some 12 miles to the east, down the Coon Lake campground road. Finally, we had cars bumper to bumper with engines off and lights out on both sides of the gravel road, for a distance of about a mile in each direction.

All 2400 enthusiasts stood silently in the dark beside their cars waiting for the "howl" to begin. They were amazingly well behaved. I stared at the cloudless sky trying to get my bearings — usually via the Big Dipper. But it must have been partially obscured by the trees beside us. We were almost directly under Cassiopeia about 20 degrees to our right. I can thank my boy scout days for recognizing it.

Even though the moon was only about one third full there was enough light to clearly make out the details of our car, and the others near us. It was eerie.

Joyce was very excited, anticipating a marvellous new experience. We waited silently and then it came.

Our howlers were about a quarter of a mile south of us, so we heard the call clearly. No response. The second howler joined in. Still no response.

There was, as agreed beforehand, a 10 minute pause during which complete silence was maintained. Howlers began anew. No response. Way off in the distance both Joyce and I heard a very faint sound of what we thought was a howl, but nothing like the tape.

The howlers gave it one final try, without response. Slowly, reluctantly, the auto lights and engines came on. It was over, and it was unsuccessful.

In spite of attentive tracking for two days by the park staff who had confirmed the presence of wolves in the immediate area earlier that day, we had not been able to raise them.

The success ratio to that point had been 84 per cent from a total of 82 "howls" over a 35 year period. It is difficult to explain the lack of response, but this had been the largest group by far ever assembled for a "howl".

My suspicion is that 700 carloads or 2400 people is simply too much. Too much engine noise, exhaust, too much scent of humans. No self respecting animal is likely to hang around in the middle of that.

Nevertheless, it had been a remarkable experience of human behaviour with a common objective, of observing the talents and knowledge of the howlers and the organizational skills of the park staff.

Given another opportunity, I would leap at it.

Moving 700 cars out of a secondary gravel road late at night in an orderly efficient manner can be a formidable challenge. And yet we were out of there and heading east on highway 60 in a matter of 10 minutes. Joyce dearly wanted to hear the wolves, I suspect we'll try it again next year.

A small consolation prize was given to us on our way home, when I spotted something ahead on the highway. It turned out to be a handsome red fox snooping around where he shouldn't have been.

It was midnight when we rolled into bed. Some lodge guests and their children, two cabins over from us, were gathered around a campfire beside the lake.

It is remarkable that as we stood on that gravel road for nearly an hour, there wasn't an insect to be seen, heard, or even felt. The sky and stars always seem immense when you look at them away from the city.

The following morning at breakfast, I asked Joyce what she thought was notable about our experience. "I think the fresh clean look of all those wonderful young people doing something I would have loved to have done at their age," she mused, "the pristine beauty of the place, water you can see through at 10 feet." "The energy."

I thought to myself that in Kanata where we live, development goes on without any regard for animal habitat. Every tree is razed, every rock outcropping is blasted flat in the name of efficiency. You are then left with a look that is anything but natural. They might just as well pave it all over. Over the past few weeks a wooded area of over 80 acres has been flattened. Two years ago I bumped into a deer in that same location while walking home from tennis. That is now long gone.

So, we are indeed fortunate that our forefathers saw the need and potential, in preserving this oasis called Algonquin, even as we surround ourselves deeper and deeper with asphalt and industrial grime. There is still one place left to get away from it and back to the way it was.

On the drive back to Kanata we stopped at Wilno, an early Polish settlement near Barry's Bay, to see Round Lake, some 12 miles away from the Wilno lookout. It is a lovely view. Which will soon be obscured by trees planted across the road.

We drove around the north side of Round Lake and into Pembroke, where I had been a delegate to the Anglican Synod held there 3 years ago. The downtown area of Pembroke is cleverly covering unsightly old blank walls with historic murals. The town of Deland in Florida has done the same thing, using them as a fundraising medium by selling the space for the faces of the people shown, to residents who would like their own faces painted in. Some very worthwhile community causes have been financed this way.

We also toured the Pembroke Historical Museum which has an excellent display of mid 19th century artifacts particularly those related to logging.

At Cobden we stopped to look at the Oaks of Cobden Golf Course and close to home, near Arnprior, the Mountain Creek Golf Course, which looked especially interesting. We will probably try it out.

Chapter Eighteen

Mountain Creek Golf Club

Joyce has been seriously trying to play golf for 5 years. During the time we were members of the Kanata Golf Club, she tried her utmost to master the game, but in spite of lessons and hours on the practice tee, she was never quite able to develop the consistency in her swing to score well, even though she was one of the longer hitters among the ladies in the club.

On lady's day, she was usually put with other women of the same playing level, which in itself is very discouraging. Anyone who has ever played any sport competitively knows that the opportunity to play with someone whose skill levels are greater than your own, invariably results in your own game rising a notch or two. But, golf etiquette being what it is, that rarely happened.

During this period she worked very hard to improve her game, but after the ladies round on Wednesdays, she would go to the computer to enter her score, and it invariably told her that her ranking was 57th out of 60.

There were very few women who could drive a ball farther. Last year after a Friday night nine and dine when she had hit the longest drive of about 210 yards, the only comment made to her was by another lady, who simply said, "I thought I had hit the longest drive." (Earlier this summer she belted one out about 240 yards!)

And so in the fall of 98 she was in the middle of her lessons with Don at Manotick. Week after week. The poor man must have been driven insane. One week she'd hit them out of sight, the next week she couldn't hit them at all.

There have been many occasions when her problem was obvious to me, but I knew better than to comment.

Finally, today, we played Mountain Creek Golf Course, on the White Lake road near Arnprior. It is a user friendly course, in the middle of farm country, about 7 years old and in very good condition. The greens are excellent, but sloped so that putting can be tricky. The fairways are mature and in great condition. It is reasonably forgiving except for about half of the holes where it is tight and an errant shot will jump out and bite you.

Joyce had a very solid front nine coming in with a 46. I was keeping score, and was getting inwardly excited. Was this finally going to be the day that she breaks 100? We started out on the back 9 and she shot bogey for the 10th through 13th. Well on target to break 100. On the 14th a 90 yard par 3 on which a farm fence runs tight along the right side of the fairway, I said to her, look at all the open space to the left of the green. Play left of the pin.

She lined up her shot, and I could immediately see from her set up that the ball was going to go right and over the fence, which it did. I was pulling so hard for her to make it, that I began to get uptight. The second try (her 3rd shot) followed the first over the fence. My heart was sinking. Finally the third try (her 5th shot) made it to the right hand side of the green from which she got down in 2 for a 7.

Any more like this and her round would be blown.

When we arrived at the 15th tee, there were two young boys about 9 or 10 years old who asked if they could join us. We said yes.

When Joyce teed up, I was more assertive with the instructions and the kids looked at me quizzically. I was literally coaxing her down shot by shot. One of the kids turned to her and asked, "Why does he take it so seriously. It's only a game." She took a six on that hole and I was getting completely up tight, watching it slip away.

She parred the next hole (par 3) and on the 17th hit a weak but straight drive up the middle. She was still over 200 yards from the green and chose to experiment with a long wood, which she did not hit properly. A third shot was flubbed. Finally she was beside the green in 4 and I had visions of her blowing the whole day.

Instead she chips in from about 25 yards for a bogey!

At last we are on the 18th. There are three different ponds to contend with. I offer advice to her on playing target golf. She places her drive perfectly but it settles on an area of hardpan. She is debating whether to play her 7 wood or an iron, at which point the 10 year old steps in to offer advice. "You have a better chance of good contact with an iron," he says. So she plays it and weaves her way over the right side pond and bogeys the 18th. She has shot a 92! She has never broken 100 in her life and she has shot a 92!

I think of all the hours of practice. Of the humiliation that goes with being on the lower end of the scale on ladies day. Of the glaring marshals, who follow every move of a duffer, trying to whip them along so the 4 hour round can be realized.

I thought of the yards of notes she has taken and the tossing and turning in bed fretting over missed golf shots. But now, she has done it. If she gains confidence from this she will bring her handicap down markedly. It would be interesting to see whom they would match her up with on ladies day, once this happens.

On the drive home she kept looking at the scorecard with inner satisfaction. It is a wonderful milestone to pass.

When we got home I broke out a bottle of good French Chablis that Peter had given me on my birthday. We took it over to Win and Barb's to share our celebration. One bottle quickly turned to two, and Win began waxing philosophical about his youth in Pembroke in the 1950s.

His father had been a prominent physician and surgeon in Pembroke, doctor to the Pembroke Lumber Kings who contested the Allan Cup, president of the golf club, and later coroner for the province of Ontario.

His parents entertained often, and because of their association with hockey, Win got to meet and get autographs from the greats of that era, Irvin, Richard, Belliveau, Howe and many others.

Win told us stories about town characters of that time. One enormous man named Simon, with a grade three education, was useful in locking up folks for misdemeanours. One night a very cantankerous woman who had had a bit too much to drink had to be locked up.

In the morning, Simon was responsible for feeding the prisoners. He passed by the cells asking whether they would like Corn Flakes or Rice Krispies. The lady replied, "Neither but I would like some Kotex." Simon came away muttering, he'd never heard of a cereal called Kotex.

Another gentleman, named Eddie, ran an appliance shop. He also had a franchise for testing applicants for drivers' licences. It became a local joke when it was evident that all pretty women were automatically flunked. This was so Eddie could get to know them better.

Oh, the pleasures of living in a small town.

Chapter Nineteen

The Rideau Canal and Waterway

One of these days we are going to charter a boat and do the Rideau Canal from Ottawa to Kingston. Since my navigational skills are limited to outboards, that is a while away. In the meantime we'll have to settle for short excursions to the towns along it where locks are located.

One such town is Merrickville, approximately 40 miles south of Ottawa by the canal and 25 miles directly inland by overland routes from Brockville. A former boss of mine, John Kroes, built a lovely retirement home not far from Merrickville, at Burritts Rapids. The stretch of shoreline between these two towns contains a number of outstanding stone masonry heritage homes, constructed between 1800 -1840.

Merrickville itself was considered of such strategic importance that a military blockhouse was erected near the locks. It is now a museum. The town has become trendy, with several good inns and B & Bs, Sam Jake's Tavern being noteworthy. The surrounding farm country was settled in the early 1800s and there are many historically significant homes and mills still remaining. The countryside is pastoral, so we decided to bring a picnic and take in an antique show at the community centre while we were there.

Heading down the east side of the Rideau from Kemptville, we thought it might be nice to drop in on John Kroes at his retreat on the Rideau. On our way, we spotted a sign directing us to the Burritts Rapids locks, so we took a short detour to check the locks out.

What a pleasant surprise. The grounds surrounding the locks on both sides and including the river bank were beautifully landscaped and set up with picnic tables in several wonderful locations overlooking the locks and also the river. What more could we ask for?

We chose a table close to the mooring wharf of the river. Several runabouts tied up while we were there. We spoke to one family asking whether an 18 foot runabout got bounced around entering the locks. The father laughed and replied that he did not know. That was why they had stopped to watch the locking process. A few minutes later we both got our chance to find out, as a similar boat came in to enter the lock.

The whole process takes under 10 minutes. The lockmaster and two assistants manually operate the valves which allow water to escape from the bottom before the gates are opened. The inner masonry walls of the lock have vertical drop cables every 6 feet or so which enables the boat crews to loop their lines around , to maintain position as the water rises or falls.

The total lift at Burritts Rapids is about 10 feet. And within 10 or 12 minutes the boat was up and away. I was curious to see what level of competence was required to handle a small boat in this situation. It does not appear to be an overwhelming challenge. Perhaps at a later date we will try it, maybe even on a rented pontoon houseboat.

The Kroes' property is only a few miles farther upstream. They have owned it since 1973. It was originally 12 acres on the river, but they have since sold off about half of it. The red pines which he planted as seedlings are now about 30 feet high, and make a nice privacy screen from the road and the neighbours.

Since retirement, John has kept busy working with stained glass and other creatively designed articles in woodwork, which he has sold quite successfully.

We reminisced about old times and the people we had worked with for many years, and passed a very pleasant hour together, before moving on to Merrickville.

What was billed as a major antique show, proved to be a little more than a glorified flea market. In contrast with the show I had seen a month earlier at Biddeford, Maine, which was excellent, and had genuine Americana in it, this one was a bust.

We didn't spend much time at the show, and instead toured around Merrickville among the lovely old stone masonry buildings and trendy shops that have sprung up since I was last there. The town has grown immensely in the past 5 - 10 years. Not surprising in light of the beauty of its location on the canal system.

On our way home we stopped off at Manotick to visit our friends from Montreal, Paul and Joan Coté, and share with them the good news about Joyce's golf game. We will play with them at the Carleton Yacht and Golf Club in two weeks time. Both of them are excellent tennis players. Paul is also very good at golf and Joan made a hole in one last year at Carleton. But, she is a perfectionist, and is struggling with her game at the moment.

On our way to Toronto earlier on we stopped at a coffee shop just east of Peterborough. It was extremely busy and we ended up sharing a table with another couple. Originally from Ottawa, they had retired in Rideau Ferry, a small community along the Rideau canal system, about 8 miles from Perth.

Although we had been in Perth a number of times, and through Smith Falls as well, we had never seen Rideau Ferry or for that matter any part of the lower Rideau lake.

So off we went, by the Carleton Place turn off from highway 7 down route 15 to Smith Falls. We continued down until Lombardy, where we turned west toward Rideau Ferry. Other than the bridge and a few service facilities there is nothing of significance clearly visible from the highway.

Certainly the shores are heavily built up with cottages and boating services. There is also a large houseboat facility about a mile east of Perth.

Once again though, what caught our eye were the beautiful stone masonry homes along the Perth road. En route to Perth we passed the Beveridge Locks Road, so out of curiosity we turned into it. We had discovered the entry point of the Tay Canal which leads from Lower Rideau Lake to Perth.

The historical display at Beveridge Locks described how after several attempts over nine years, the Tay Canal was finally completed. Unfortunately it never realized its potential as a commercial venture, but continues to have recreational importance.

Although it had only been three days since our trip to Toronto, there had clearly been a deterioration in the quality of the foliage, perhaps caused by a frost we experienced two nights ago. We certainly had timed our earlier trip to advantage.

We came away with renewed determination to travel the Rideau system in earnest. There seems to be no end to the number, size and variety of lakes to be explored.

The following week we set out with our neighbours Win and Barb to play golf at the Blue Heron Golf Club near Lanark. It is a short, sporty nine hole golf club which is fun to play. Probably more challenging than it would first appear.

After golf, we took the road over to Balderson and stopped at the Balderson Cheese Factory Store. In 1893 Balderson became famous for producing an 11 ton cheddar cheese which required a reinforced steel casing around it in order to allow it to set firmly in the desired shape. It was then shipped to and exhibited at the Chicago world's fair, which put Balderson on the map. When the fair was over it was taken to Britain where it went on tour. It must surely have been ripe at that point!

The Balderson Cheese Store continues to draw tourists and regular customers, as a result of excellent marketing of cheese and other local products, such as maple syrup and sugar, and specialty jams and jellies, as well as gifts. It also serves utterly delicious ice cream in many fabulous flavours which are produced on location. Naturally, we tested them out!

We then drove over to Perth which was one of the earliest settlements in eastern Ontario. It was originally a military encampment because of its strategic location between Kingston and Ottawa. It had direct access to the Rideau Canal, via the Tay Canal, an extension of the Rideau.

The downtown area of Perth is blessed with dozens of historic stone masonry homes and buildings, erected in the early 1800s. They are in excellent condition, and the town has made the most of it.

We had lunch at Peter's Cafe. We then walked about in Cameron Park through which the Tay River flows. The huge maples took a real beating during the ice storm of January '98, but they are sprouting new life, and within 4 or 5 years will probably look normal.

How lucky we are to have the legacy left to all of us by the stone masons who remained in Upper Canada after the Rideau Canal was completed.

Win expressed interest in renting a boat with us and cruising the canal system next year. He is an experienced yachtsman as well as a licenced aircraft pilot. Having already done the Trent Severn System he would make an excellent ship's captain, and we would be a willing crew!

Chapter 20

The Pond

About 10 days ago, our resident family of geese took off as they do, to explore other waterways and stubble fields. They are probably out on the Ottawa River which is cleaner and colder at this time of year than the pond on the golf course. Prior to their departure the maintenance crews had stepped up their aggressive tactics with golf carts, so who knows, perhaps the geese have simply taken a holiday.

One thing is for sure, they will be back in a few weeks with reinforcements, usually a couple of hundred of them. Then the last 150 yards of the 9th hole will be covered with geese and all that goes with them!

One also wonders if the water quality of the pond had deteriorated. The aerator which operates most days automatically, has been out of order for about 3 or 4 weeks. The heat hasn't let up during that period, so the water quality had to have worsened.

The aerator was back on two days ago, so we'll see what impact it has on the pond.

Win has been concerned about the woodchuck who seems to have set up house under his neighbour's ground floor deck. More so, since he has spotted baby woodchucks scampering around recently.

Very soon the squirrels will begin stripping the acorns from the huge oak 4 lots over. It is fascinating to watch. They get up on the outer limbs and bite off the ends of the branches, felling them to the lawn below which becomes strewn with acorns. Then they begin the endless treks from the oak, back past our house, and into their nests in the woods along the 9th. They will make dozens of trips back and forth until the harvest is in. So much so, that a tiny path will be worn across our lawn as they scamper from the safety under Win's deck, to ours.

On the ride back yesterday from Mountain Creek we saw that the birds have begun to congregate on the telephone wires along the Arnprior Road, in preparation for their fall migration, which for some varieties is only a few weeks away.

The dry weather must be tough on the robins. I gave the back lawn a good 3 hour soaking the other night, and there were several robins taking advantage of the watering, as they hunted for earthworms.

Branta Canadensis

What is it about you that makes them hate you?
You do not threaten us. Nor are you destructive.
Is it the sound of exuberance that you make in flight
Or the disciplined behaviour of your family?
Surely they cannot object to the caring way you raise your young.
Or the graceful form you show us, flying high.
You who astound us by your military precision.
You who amaze us by your family leadership skills.
Until that day arrives when all of you have learned it all.
And off you go, like a flight of Concordes,
To unknown places near and far.
And even when you feed in fields of stubble,
It is not the farmer's crop you steal or threaten,
But that which lies forgotten.
So how can anyone possibly hate you?
They accuse you of being unclean.
You who constantly bathe your feathers and preen and groom.
And still they hate you.
Are they the same ones who pollute with smoke
Or condone the use of deadly pesticides?
Or have we as a society become so delicate
As to be offended by what creatures of the wild leave behind?
Do we prefer the filthy trade off spewed over our highways?
Do we really believe that we are in a position to judge you,
Even as our refuse dumps become mountains,
And potential sources of disease and infestation?
No, we still do not leave the land better than we found it.
We should be grateful to share our turf with you.
You who were here before us.
Grateful for the uplifting sound you make in Spring,
Which tells us once again that the cycle of life
Is renewed once more as sure as God intended.
I for one am your friend.

Chapter Twenty-one

Carp

We live within one mile of pure rural countryside. The advantage of this is, that in season, strawberries etc. can be picked, within a 5 minute drive, fresh from the fields. Cycling enthusiasts can find miles of rural roads to travel along without the roar of heavy trucks bearing down on them or belching black soot from their diesel engines as they pass.

Typical of rural communities in this area is the Village of Carp, about ten miles from us. Carp sits on a ridge overlooking the mighty Carp River, which must be all of 15 feet wide as it passes by.

The river, which is of little significance other than to farmers of livestock, gained notoriety about five years ago, when the new hockey arena in Kanata, the home of the Senators, was on the drawing board. Many rural residents who opposed displacing a cornfield with an 18,500 seat stadium, tried every means possible to defeat the proposal. Finally some zealous opponent pulled out a little used law as a last resort. Was the Carp River navigable? If so, it could not be disturbed. The construction of the massive parking lot in Kanata for the arena was precariously close to this "navigable" river which was at least a foot deep and six feet wide at that point.

The authorities were forced to fund an engineering inspection to determine the navigability of the Carp, but those who had ever taken a look at it, knew the result beforehand. Of course it was not navigable — even by canoe!

The Village of Carp's main claim to fame up to this point had been the "Diefenbunker", so named after Prime Minister John Diefenbaker who had it constructed at the start of the cold war.

It is a massive underground nuclear shelter, designed specifically as a retreat for senior government officials, as an alternative centre of government in a nuclear attack. It is nestled into the side of a ridge, massively constructed of reinforced concrete about 100 feet underground with all of the comforts of home — except wives! Absolutely no provision was made to shelter the poor wives! They'd never get away with that today!

Until about 4 years ago the Diefenbunker remained an active military post. When it closed, it was taken over by the Village of Carp, which then began guided tours (which I took). The interest was such that the proceeds paid for an expansion of the local library, and are now repeated every summer as a tourist attraction.

The other important attraction in Carp is its fairgrounds. Every September the Carp Fair draws thousands of people from miles around, for a real old fashioned country fair. We particularly found the pig races hilarious. We had no idea that pigs could run that fast.

As is the case with most rural villages in the Ottawa Valley, there are numerous churches in Carp which raise funds through a variety of events such as bazaars and bake sales. In early December some of the most mouth watering baking can be bought at these events and attending them can be an experience in itself. It is a wonderful (but very competitive) way to stock up your Christmas larder.

There is also one such event held in Kanata which stands alone in size, variety and imagination and that is the annual "cookie walk" held at the Glen Cairn United Church in Kanata. Thousands of beautiful and lovingly decorated Christmas cookies are displayed on a network of banquet tables laid out so that lines can access the cookies from both sides. Each customer buys a plastic container and is allowed to stuff as many cookies into the container as it will hold. There are cookies shaped as trees, balls, stars, Santas, round ones, square and rectangular ones, and many decorated with brightly coloured icing.

The doors open at 9 a.m. I was there at 8:50 and was already about 50th in line. They do a roaring trade!

But, Carp is not far behind.

This week, a major event took place at the Carp Fairgrounds. It was the world Clydesdale Horse Show and Trade. Over 360 horses from around the world were entered, with many events, culminating on Sunday with the crowning of the supreme world champion Clydesdale horse. A tremendously significant experience for anyone who earns a living in agriculture.

The Clydesdale is one of the largest horses in the world and is considered a draft horse. It can weigh up to 2000 pounds and stands at 16-17 hands (64-68 inches). Its origin has been traced to Lanarkshire, Scotland from where the first Clydesdales came to America in the 1840s. It is one of the handsomest draft breeds. Striking markings on its face and legs and long flowing hair beneath its knees, called "feathers", give it a distinctive look.

Draft horses have now largely been replaced by mechanical means, but Clydesdales, because of their good looks and high stepping gate, remain popular for use in parades and other show purposes.

We arrived at the Carp Airport on the last day of the show, where a huge parking facility had been laid out, with OC Transport providing bus connections to the Carp Fairgrounds and the Clydesdales.

We entered through the north gate where the major commercial displays were concentrated. Everything from small sawmills to the latest in highway tractors with comfortable sleep areas behind the cab. And of course anything imaginable related to horses from feed to fancy brasses.

The stabling barns were surrounded by beautifully designed and maintained carriages used in the multi horse team events. And then of course the Clydesdales themselves. Marvellous athletes, beautifully groomed and conditioned. Huge powerful animals being put through the motions, walking, jogging, then back to walking, their huge fluffy hoofs flexing loosely with every step. You would almost swear that as the teams pass by the grandstand, the horses seem to be glancing at the audience, as if to say, how am I doing?

We watched three of the events from the stands.

During the first, the ladies western pleasure riding event, a young woman rider lost control directly in front of us and fell from her horse. She was unconscious on the ground and after a fifteen minute examination, she was taken away by ambulance. We were assured that her injuries were not critical.

This was followed by an eight mule team handled by Dr. Hunt from Michigan who demonstrated amazing skill in making the team perform several difficult manoeuvres.

Next came the 6 team hitch event. Highly decorated harnesses and wagons. Twelve teams competed for this event, so that at one point there were 72 horses on the field.

We then toured some of the commercial booths and the crafts booth. As usual we ended up with fudge.

The highlight of the day was the crowning of the world champion Clydesdale which was won by a local Clydesdale, "Carsons Delight" owned by the Watson family, from Sarsfield, Ontario, 20 miles from Ottawa.

It was a highly successful event attended by over 80,000 people, which will be repeated in two years time.

As we had crossed over into September, the time was now appropriate for us to obtain visas for our trip to Egypt in nine weeks. The embassy and consulate are located on Laurier Street East, directly across from the now defunct Cercle Universitaire, which recently closed its doors after many years as a private dining club. I have eaten there several times in the past. The food and service were excellent, but the market must have headed off in a different direction. It just couldn't make the transition. I once took my son, Peter, to lunch there. We were seated next to a table of senior staff officers from National Defence and two tables away sat Kim Campbell, who was back in Ottawa after a brief stint as Prime Minister and a holiday at an American spa. She looked wonderful!

The Egyptian Embassy is nestled on Sandy Hill with several other embassies immediately nearby.

Visas are issued from a side door basement office. The clerk who handles the details speaks about as much English as I do Egyptian. He knew enough to supply us with an application form at the mention of the word visa. This was followed by a gesture and instructions to "sit", which we did. He also understood the meaning of the expression "no problem", which is how he answered every question we asked him. Finally we determined that the visas could be ready at 2 p.m. if we were willing to come back. We said "no problem."

It was shortly before noon so we headed over to the Byward Market for lunch and a chance to check out Eaton's going out of business sale. It isn't hard to understand how the family owned major retailer had blown its lead position in a short period of one generation. If it wasn't that they were the fourth generation you could argue that it was the classic example of "third generation damp rot", a banker's term for credit alert.

They were a part of every Canadian family's life and until twenty-five years ago an outstanding retailer. Some of the clues were evident earlier than that. We used to subscribe to American

Home magazine and were looking for colonial furniture at Eaton's just before it became so popular in Canada. "Colonial furniture! We don't carry that at all." So we ended up importing it from the States.

I wanted to see for myself what the last days of Eaton's felt like. 20% to 40% off most merchandise — which was already 30% above the market. The store in the Rideau Centre was unusually quiet. Muted conversations, no sound of busy cash registers, plenty of curious shoppers but probably only 1 in 20 coming out with a package. Joyce being among the minority! Even the piped in music sounded weary. The few clerks still around seemed reluctant to engage you. It is a sad chapter in Canadian business which will undoubtedly have other repercussions.

We grabbed a quick bite in the Byward Market and headed back to the embassy. Our visas were ready. The clerk asked us our names, reached for an envelope, handed it to us and said "no problem."

For over thirty years a group of enthusiastic and artistically gifted people from Kanata and a number of other nearby communities have been staging successful productions of little theatre four or five times a year in our town.

In the early years, productions were held in the auditorium of the Earl of March High School. The quality of theatre presented was such that support grew year after year. Unlike many theatrical companies, the Kanata Theatre was not only artistically successful but very well managed, and as a non profit organization was able to reinvest proceeds until a sizeable "building fund" had been accumulated.

One of the leaders during the early years was Ron Maslin, who by his initiative and creative abilities drove the growth and support of the theatrical company. By the early 90s the group was not only filling each evening's production to virtual capacity, but had accumulated a building fund of $250,000! This was a phenomenal achievement, particularly when weighed against other artistic companies which often operate at a loss.

In the early 90s the decision was made to go for it. A campaign was begun to enlist the support of the community, with the objective of constructing a town theatre devoted to the production of little theatre and other related artistic presentations.

The City of Kanata agreed to contribute the land in Walter Baker Park. The theatrical company undertook to raise $700,000 (including the $250,000) by public subscription and other clever initiatives such as naming a seat after contributors of $1000 or more (which we did) and by listing the names of all contributors who bought 1 square foot or more for $150 a foot in each production flyer for a period of up to seven years.

During the recession of the early 90s, the federal government established initiatives to create employment. The proposed theatre qualified for this and a federal grant of one million dollars was committed. Construction began in the summer of 1995.

In the spring of 1996, the Ron Maslin Playhouse opened its doors for the first time, with a production of Oscar Wilde's "The Importance of Being Earnest". It is a beautiful little theatre with an unobstructed view of the stage, a capacity of 350 seats, and ample parking on the site.

They have never looked back! Support for the group has continued to grow to the point where many productions are sold out. Four performances of each play are presented each week for two weeks.

When you drive up to the main door to drop your lady off while you park, you are met by a volunteer member of the company dressed in black tie, who escorts her inside (under an umbrella if necessary).

The lobby becomes a meeting place for friends and neighbours to gather, before or during intermission, when coffee and sweets are sold by more volunteer members of the company. The walls of the lobby are hung with works of local artists which are for sale.

It has been so successful that by 1998 the Kanata Theatre Company managed to pay off the balance of their financial commitment to the City of Kanata. It is now debt free! It is a wonderful example of dedication and true entrepreneurial spirit.

The first production of the 1999-2000 season, their 31st year, was a presentation of Ed Graszyk's comedy "Come Back to the Five and Dime, Jimmy Dean, Jimmy Dean".

Having been directly involved in both production and performing many years ago, I can appreciate the fun, excitement and hard work associated with little theatre. It is a vital and important part of our culture and should be supported. How much easier it is to do when the productions are excellent!

Chapter Twenty-two

C.P.B.M.A.

Whenever I open up a magazine or book, fresh from the printer, I am immediately captured by the smell of printing inks, which I associate with my first job in the paper industry. At age 22, I became a sales representative for the E.B. Eddy Co., Hull, Quebec, working out of the Montreal office.

I had been assigned responsibility for paperboard sales to the paper box trade in and around Montreal. I thus began a career which would take me into very large and sometimes small converters of "boxboard" as it was referred to in the trade. I did not know it at the time but, after I officially retired from CIP (later CP Forest Products), the company that I ended up spending most of my career with, I would return to the paper box industry as an agent for Baldwin Paper supplying boxboard, while I operated my own company.

So, from the beginning to the end of a career encompassing nearly forty years, I had a close association with those who produced paperboard boxes and containers. Everything from common suit boxes to high quality packaging for cosmetics, pharmaceuticals, milk cartons and other highly sophisticated printing, and in later years, highly automated converting systems. Like the friendly smell of fresh cut lumber, printing is something I have memories of, and through it, a number of associates in the trade whom I count among respected friends.

When I opened my mail this morning, there was an invitation to come to Toronto on the occasion of the Canadian Paper Box Manufacturers Quarter Century Club's 50th anniversary. It really took me back. Over a period of forty years I had many learning experiences, both of a business as well as of a personal nature.

I learned how to listen for the clues and opportunities that come from being informed. I learned when to keep my mouth shut, when silence can be a better ally than a loose tongue. I learned that behind every decision maker that I dealt with, there was usually someone coming up behind him, who would probably assume that position in due course, and should therefore be treated with respect and not ignored, a fatal mistake made sometimes by those who "only want to deal with the top man", and find themselves on the outside looking in when a promotion occurs.

I learned to be persistent, in spite of rejection which was sometimes justified. In one case early in the game we had supplied a shipment which was marginal. Unfortunately, it was to be used for packaging steel bolts and some of the packages just didn't stand up. Although we did make a concession to enable the boxes to be used, the converter felt we hadn't stood behind the product. We were cut off. Nevertheless, I continued to call on the account, always getting the same negative response. The thaw came 3 or 4 years later when the gentleman I was dealing with, looked at me and said, "Mr.Garred, you have a lot of guts. I'm going to give you an order," which he did.

Perhaps he had mellowed, perhaps supply had tightened. Perhaps he had had a similar experience with another supplier. Perhaps I was just too naive to give up. Whatever the reason we began doing business again.

When I was first interviewed for this job, I went through a couple of meetings. On the third and final one I met the general manager of sales. He asked me many questions. I had spent a couple of years in banking and didn't particularly like it. "What

The CPBMA 25 year club dinner

The surprising thing about attending a 50th anniversary dinner of a trade association is not so much the shock of hearing who has died since you last saw the group, but even more so the shock of seeing people still alive that you thought should have been dead years ago!

There are other ironies. The pompous blowhards of yesteryear, stripped of their expense accounts and other perks of office, are now just one of the boys. Somehow they now look pathetic, like overweight out of shape lumps of anatomy parading around in a men's locker room with a drink in their hand and a towel around their middle. Gone are the symbols of power. Gone is the respectful obeisance they demanded, and in its place is plain disinterest. In the eyes of their peers they have come full circle.

The fun part of such a reunion is to discover that some likeable, hard working stiff has suddenly made it big, and is able to laugh off the pretensions that the others still hang on to.

At this stage of life it is sometimes much easier to be magnanimous, setting aside those issues that one might have fought over tenaciously. We do indeed learn from growing older.

It seemed to me that there was a stronger desire to reach out for camaraderie. Simply to have survived the bloodbaths, was in itself an achievement.

It wasn't a night for long speeches. It was more of an evening of reflection. So many changes. Takeovers, acquisitions, and examples of mismanagement in some cases, all having played their part.

In the end, time once again proved to be the great leveller.

In my father's day, an evening such as this might have been referred to as a "smoker". But even that is passé. Among about 60 men present, I didn't see one cigarette lit up — let alone a stinking cigar. We are finally winning that one.

Unlike the manoeuvering which used to accompany dinners of this type twenty years ago, where some people, engaged in conversation, would look surreptitiously over their shoulders, in case someone of greater importance to them walked by, most seemed content to seek out long standing associates who had travelled similar career paths.

It was significant that four of the sixty men present began their careers in the same company. I was one of them. Each of us went off in different directions, succeeding to a greater or lesser degree, as fate dealt us our hand. Some had endured periods of severe hardship. Others had simply taken their share of knocks and gone on from there.

It was the kind of event that was worth attending not for the contacts that might be developed — it was far too late for that — but perhaps as an opportunity to put one's own life in perspective. It had been a pretty good one, and all these people had been a part of it.

Chapter Twenty-three

Shirley, Gretchen, and Max

It seems that among many of our friends of long standing, dogs always play an important part.

Yesterday we received a call from Shirley McKnight whom we have known for over twenty-five years. Probably going back to tennis, which she plays often and very well.

We haven't seen her for about 6 months. She called to say that she intended to come out to Kanata for a visit, and also to give the dogs a run.

She owns a pair of dachshunds, Gretchen, an affectionate little lady dog, which she has had for about 5 years, and Max, a fine looking fellow which Shirley picked up along the way. For the first year or so it was evident that Max must have been mistreated. He was wary of men, but quickly bonded with Shirley and will stare adoringly at her for hours.

It is interesting to see the dogs side by side. Gretchen is clearly the lady, with a pretty feminine face and demeanour. Max looks the part of a male with features that are more characteristic of a tough guy. It is quite hilarious to watch the two of them chasing one another in and around the tables and chairs, going full speed, seemingly in all directions.

But don't let this playful manner deceive you. On occasion Shirley will leave them in her car (with the windows open) guarding it while she visits. I came home one afternoon under such circumstances and as I walked up the driveway, the two of them cut up a storm. There was no compromise. Without Shirley present, there was going to be no trespassing.

Two years ago, Joyce and I visited Shirley at her friend David's house, on Cudjoe Key, Florida. Shirley had established a routine each evening whereby about 9 p.m. she would go to bed and watch television with Gretchen at her feet. She might have become a victim of habit because one evening while we were there, Shirley sat up on the sofa later than normal, reviewing instructions for an appliance she had just bought, Gretchen patiently sitting beside her. Finally, about 9:30 Gretchen became restless, sat up and began making dog noises at her. Getting no response she then put her long nose in Shirley's face and still got no response. She sat back staring at Shirley impatiently and then, got up on her hind legs and pushed Shirley's shoulder with all her little might with her front paws. Shirley got the message, trotted off to bed, with Gretchen following behind her. That was all she wanted!

David's house on Cudjoe Key was in a community called "Venture Out". I am certain that the height of land on this and many other of the keys couldn't have been more than 4 feet above sea level. So we were amazed to learn about a year later that his house survived after a tidal surge from a hurricane scored a direct hit on Cudjoe. Mind you, every house is anchored to a concrete slab with steel cable and the surge hit the opposite side of the key, so he was fortunate.

David is an avid boatsman and fisherman and has a fishing boat equipped with twin 90 HP outboards, sonar depth sounding equipment, and radio communication. He tends to pilot it as though he was riding a horse, on the full gallop.

While we were visiting, a Cuban vessel, over 600 feet long, grounded about 15 miles offshore on the American shoal. It was hung up there for several days and was finally freed at high tide after a substantial volume of bunker oil had been taken off by salvage vessels.

Before it was freed, David and I took a ride out to sea in his boat and circled around it. It was interesting to see from David's depth sounding equipment that it was in only 19 feet of water. As we circled it we could see the shoal clearly in the water. Parts of it measuring only 8 to 9 feet deep — and this fifteen miles away from the keys!

Key West is only 30 miles from Cudjoe. It is a fascinating city, quite unique, and more like a town in the British West Indies than a Florida settlement. It was the home of the southern White House during the Truman presidency.

Less than 10 miles north across the highway over the keys to Miami is Marathon Key. It is one of the larger keys on which is found a variety of miniature deer not much bigger than a medium sized dog. The key is a sanctuary, and the deer will come to the side of your car without fear.

It is a region of Florida which is entirely different in nature from the rest of the state and worth the extra miles to visit.

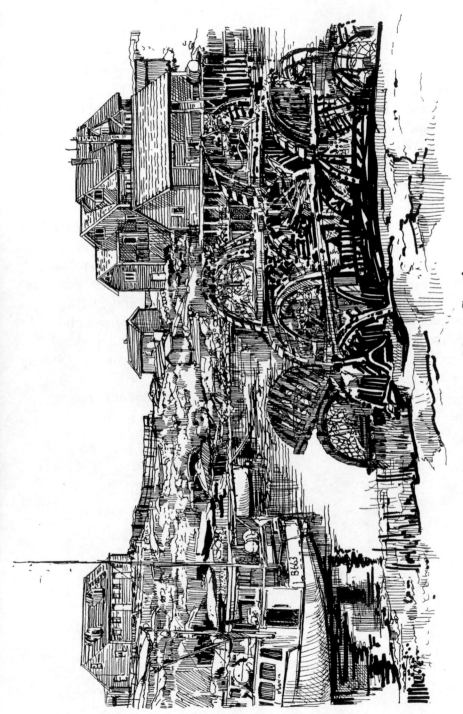

Peggy's Cove, Nova Scotia

Chapter Twenty-four

Dick and Maureen

For most of the twelve years that we owned our home in Quechee, Vermont, Dick and Maureen Mehrman were our immediate neighbours to the south. They lived in New Jersey and Dick worked as a consulting engineer in New York city. His experience lay in infrastructure with emphasis on the hugely complicated sewer systems found in the Big Apple.

His interest was such that when he visited Paris, his priority was not the Champs Elysée, nor Montmartre, nor the Eiffel Tower, but the intricate sewer system of Paris! Parisiens are sufficiently proud of their sewer systems that one may take a guided tour of them — which he did!

Typical of people who live in Jersey, Dick quickly learned to steer his car on the way to work with his knees, while he balanced a takeout cup of "cawfee" in one hand and a doughnut in the other. We found this out, to our chagrin, when we took a trip through Canada's Maritimes with them in a rented van. It took some getting used to!

We met them in Halifax and took off on a circuitous route around Nova Scotia, stopping first at Grand Pré, the land of Evangeline, made famous by Longfellow. It was July 1st, Canada Day, and inside the chapel a suitably decorated red and white cake was displayed with the red maple leaf in icing. Visitors were offered a slice to share, which we did, although it looked so nice it seemed a shame to cut into it.

We spent the first night at the Digby Pines, which for years had been a famous railway hotel on Digby Harbour, the connecting point for the ocean going ferry which crosses the Bay of Fundy to Saint John, N.B. It didn't take long to assimilate our American friends into the Canadian pastime of coffee and donuts at Tim Horton's, which became a ritual as we toured from place to place.

The following day we cut back to Annapolis Royal, one of the earliest French fortifications established in the 1630s, then on to Lunenburg on the Atlantic coast. Lunenburg was settled by German and Swiss immigrants. The Kaulbach House near where we stayed is an historic house originally owned by ancestors of a good friend and neighbour, Judy Schlieman. We were fortunate that the Bluenose II was in port. We showed it to our friends with pride. The original famous racing schooner is portrayed on the back of a Canadian dime.

We continued eastward through Mahone Bay, Chester, and stopped at Peggy's Cove. It truly is an awe inspiring work of nature; every rock on the point juts out from the bay, washed and worn smooth by thousands of years of pounding surf. Later and sadly, it gained world prominence as the site of the Swissair disaster which took so many lives. It remains a place of stark natural beauty contrasted with the colourful fishing vessels and shanties which line its tiny harbour.

Then on to Halifax, the place of my birth, which has undergone such change in the harbour front area, with historic building renewal and many new and imaginatively designed structures along the shore, including the casino, as to be unrecognizable from the post World War II era.

We paid a brief visit to the casino, where Dick showed his Big Apple savvy by cleaning out the numerous unclaimed credits in the slot machines which many gamblers don't realise they are leaving behind. Maureen then promptly gave it all back at the blackjack table in a matter of minutes!

I was curious to visit Point Pleasant Park where, as a young boy of eleven, I had discovered the Martello Tower with another young friend. We toured the Citadel and its museum and had a great dinner on the harbour front at Salty's from which we watched a marvellous fireworks display set off from barges positioned in the harbour in front of us. It was July 4th and this was no doubt for the benefit of visiting Americans.

The following day we set out along a route that I had never before taken, on the eastern shore north east of Halifax. We were aiming for Liscomb Lodge, a rustic retreat on a relatively unpopulated stretch of coastline. En route we passed near Sheet Harbour and found a lovely rest area by the road set beside a rushing freshwater brook, where we lay out our picnic. There is nothing that can equal the natural beauty, peace and isolation of a spot like that. It has all of the four star restaurants beaten by a mile.

Our target for the next day was to cross over the Canso Causeway to Cape Breton. This was a mammoth engineering feat which linked the island of Cape Breton to the Nova Scotia mainland. We stopped on the Cape side for lunch in the marvellous open air. A young girl, suitably dressed in the tartan of her ancestors, played 2 or 3 traditional tunes for us on the bagpipes. Then on to Cheticamp, a small fishing community on the west coast just before you enter Cape Breton Highlands National Park and the Cabot Trail.

Entering Cheticamp, there is a zany display of scarecrows operated by an enterprising individual named Joe who picks up the passing trade in ice cream. Many of the mannequins are quite clever and masked with faces of prominent Canadians (mostly politicians).

Finally we hit the Cabot Trail which circles the northern tip of the coastline over spectacular terrain which rises to 1750 feet and strikingly resembles Scotland's coastal regions. The trees are stunted and windswept, with much of the upper plateau resembling an Arctic bog. There are dozens of unusual wildflower varieties, most of which must be viewed up close to be appreciated. Along the walking trails there is much evidence of moose being present. Heading around the tip toward the east, the descent seems much steeper. All through this first week we had been blessed with brilliant sunshine. There is always a breeze, the air is wonderfully clear and somehow the blue of both the sea and the sky seems more intense.

We continued southeast and stopped at Ingonish to have a look at Keltic Lodge, a first rate hotel and golf course set on a narrow point jutting out to sea. Then on towards St. Ann's en route to Baddeck, the summer home of Alexander Graham Bell. All along this section of road there is a profusion of colourful wild lupines bordering it. Every colour imaginable, with stands of these lovely flowers sometimes stretching for hundreds of yards.

The Baddeck Museum is large and fascinating. Bell didn't confine his talents to the telephone, but conducted many experiments in aeronautics and marine engineering. It is an outstanding museum. Baddeck itself is situated on the Bras d'Or Lake, an enormous saltwater lagoon over 60 miles long.

We then retraced our steps back over the Canso Causeway, turning west to Antigonish en route through Pictou to Cariboo, and the ferry to Prince Edward Island. Of course a visit to Green Gables was a must, and then over to the north coast to Cavendish Beach. There we engaged in a conversation with a family which included a very old man who took much pleasure in singing several old folk songs of the island. He was probably in his 90s and was fascinating to listen to. The beach itself seems endless and unspoiled with little evidence of commercial development. The sands of the dunes show off a pristine hue of salmon pink which contrasts gently with the lush dune grasses. There is no litter and no ghetto blasters to shatter the sounds of the steady breeze and breaking waves. The ocean is shallow and in summer is as warm as one would find as far south as Virginia.

We enjoyed a performance of the musical "Anne of Green Gables" which seems firmly ensconced as a perennial production. It follows Lucy Maude Montgomery's story quite faithfully. The characters are old fashioned down-to-earth people, experiencing the joys and struggles of growing up in a different and simpler time.

Contrast that with modern entertainment which would never sell without guns, violence and explosions in your face.

We stayed overnight in Charlottetown at the Prince Edward Hotel. Tired, we asked for a quiet room. About 10 p.m., all hell broke loose. We had been sandwiched between several rooms of a wedding party which went on until about 3 a.m. In the morning Joyce protested vigorously and to the credit of the hotel the room charges were waived.

At this point our good luck with the weather had run out and a real maritime deluge set in. However the weather cleared on our way back to the mainland and Halifax, where we boarded our flight to St. John's, Newfoundland.

I had been to Newfoundland many times on business and had always been very hospitably received. The province is finally entering a period of prosperity as a result of the Hibernia oilfields and, more recently, the enormous nickel discovery at Voisey Bay, Labrador. Hopefully it can wean itself from its dependency on fishing and the outrageously unfair contract it is locked into with Quebec which gives Newfoundland about 1/100th of the hydro revenues generated at Churchill Falls. Although it is still one of the poorest provinces in Canada, Newfoundlanders are among the most generous supporters of charities per capita in the country, reflecting the historic philosophy of helping one another.

We arrived in St. John's in mid afternoon and checked in to the Hotel Newfoundland, a first rate modern facility. We then toured the immediate area including Quidi Vidi, a quaint fishing village and Signal Hill where, in 1901, Marconi received the first transatlantic wireless message. The hill, at 525 feet high, offers a commanding view of the harbour and the sea. On one business trip about twenty years ago I brought my son Peter with me to go fishing on Newfoundland's west coast for salmon. It was the end of June. When we drove to the top of the hill there was a huge iceberg just outside the harbour entrance and literally dozens more as far as the eye could see. Some of them must have been over 200 yards in length. Shades of the Titanic!

When we and the Mehrmans looked down from the Cabot Tower on top of the hill, we could see 2 or 3 small whale watching boats circling around a quarter of a mile out to sea. Even from our height we could spot the whales "blowing" down below. Although we had booked a whale watching trip for the next day out of Bay Bulls, some 40 miles south of St. John's, we would not find out until then that we would have seen more whales right there at our home base than we eventually did at Bay Bulls.

It is rare to see a huge cruise ship tied up in St. John's Harbour. But the Europa was in port that day. We could hear its orchestra playing so we walked down alongside. It is a very large ship and was about to sail. All the passengers lined the railings facing the dock. I saw no sign of tugboats and wondered how on earth they were going to get the ship turned around. Then the ship's foghorn blasted and we witnessed a strange custom. Every automobile and truck in St. John's replied with a long blast of their own horns!

The ship released its moorings and slowly began moving sideways away from the dock. It was equipped with a thrusting system on its sides as well as propellers in the rear. In a matter of minutes it had swung completely around and set sail for the open water, to the tunes of "Auf Wiedersehen", "Anchors Away" and all the traditional songs associated with departures.

The following day we headed for Bay Bulls and the whales. Part of the experience was to pass very close by the Witless Bay Ecological Reserve, the largest sea bird colony in North America. We saw thousands of puffins, murres and kittiwakes in their natural habitat. Unfortunately the whales, which normally put on a spectacular show as they cavort around the boat, weren't cooperating. We did get within 200 yards of a humpback but that was just a teaser.

We were coming near the end of our trip and had just one leg left, which was to Cornerbrook and Gros Morne. We would be only 200 miles from St. Anthony and L'Anse-aux-Meadows, of great historical importance as the site of the first landing by Vikings in North America. Ever since I was a schoolboy I have always been fascinated with its story, but unfortunately I got outvoted and we didn't take the side trip to see it.

Nonetheless, the weather remained fair, and Cornerbrook, which has a picturesque harbour at the innermost part of the Bay of Islands, looked great as we approached it from Deer Lake. Off in the distance there was still snow visible on the peaks of the "Blow Me Down" Provincial Park. The Glynmill Inn was, as always, a warm and friendly place to stay, with a very good dining room which serves, in season, Newfoundland specialties such as cod tongues, seal flippers, cod au gratin and partridgeberry pie.

As usual I was up early the next morning. When I got down to the lobby a group of folk singers called the Sharecroppers had set up to play their own songs and other traditional Newfoundland music for a tour that had stopped overnight at the hotel. It was a rousing awakening for Joyce and the Merhmans! Later I talked to the Sharecroppers at breakfast and bought a tape recording of their own songs including their hit, "The Little Red Schoolhouse".

We had determined earlier that in order to time our entry into Gros Morne, we would have to stay the following night at Rocky Harbour Hotel, where we were served, without doubt, the finest lobster dinner I have ever eaten. This is a tiny settlement not far from Gros Morne. There is a superb crafts shop in the town, called Heritage Crafts and Bake, which has wonderful hand knitted pure wool sweaters at prices about one third of comparable quality on the mainland. As in Hong Kong, they can knit you a special order overnight! We bought about 7 sweaters between us and they are beautiful.

Gros Morne is the main attraction on Newfoundland's west coast, rising to 2644 feet with cliffs dropping 2500 feet to Western Brook Pond. It was proclaimed a world heritage site in 1987.

There are two ways of accessing the park. The first and more challenging is to climb it. We chose the other alternative which is to walk into the fiord like lake, a distance of about 3 miles over a bog, from which point a tour boat sails into the lake with sheer cliffs on both sides. There are several spectacular waterfalls. We got close enough to one to feel the spray. The longest drop we saw, which starts on the upper plateau, was the "Pissing Horse Falls"!

Most of the promotional photos are taken from the summit of Gros Morne which offers a spectacular view to the lake below. During our visit we saw moose grazing at lakeside and wonderful examples of flora on the 3 mile walk through the bog.

We had reached the end of our itinery and a great experience shared with the Mehrman's. We headed for home the next morning with a lot of good memories.

Chapter Twenty-five

Florida

For several years Joyce and I had gone south to Florida for a month or two, until the strength of the US dollar became such that we were faced with a premium in excess of 50% by late 1998. This was the principal reason we began to explore other winter holiday options and how we came to choose the south of France in 99.

Now, being realistic, there are few, if any, places on the north shore of the Mediterranean which get as warm as southern Florida. The temperature in the south of France in March ranges from 60 degrees F. to 70 degrees F., cooler by 10-15 degrees than Florida, but very acceptable when compared with 20 degrees F. in Ottawa. Besides, the net cost to us was very favourable in France against Florida. We will probably try Portugal on the Algarve next.

Notwithstanding all of this we have had some great holiday experiences in Florida and have established friendships which we continue to value.

Our exposure to Florida ranged from Clearwater and Sarasota on the upper gulf coast which were short but good holidays, to a two month stay in Venice which was less than good. I swore after that experience that I would never book a condo through an agent again, and would only deal direct.

We were staying at the Plantation in Venice which is an excellent, well managed facility with 36 holes of very challenging golf, plus numerous tennis courts and swimming pools. The problem is that there is very little control over the rental condos as they are privately owned. Ours was a disaster. The carpet smelled so badly they agreed to replace it. The microwave door radiation screen had a hole in it. They had to provide us with a new set of dishes and the sofa was full of snack foods behind the cushions. On top of all this, Joyce was bitten in bed by a brown recluse spider.

The agent would not refund our prepaid rental, so we were just stuck with it. By comparison we visited the condo owned by Canadian friends in the same complex and it was spotless and beautifully furnished, but never rented out by them.

The one good memory we have of Venice (besides great golf) was hunting for fossilized shark teeth on the beach. We came home with about 30 shiny black ones about three quarters of an inch in size. A serious collector can purchase shark teeth up to about two and a half inches in size from specialty shops, which also sell the rakes and wire trays that so many collectors use on the beach. It is a very popular pastime.

In the year of El Nino we again booked in Florida, but this time in New Smyrna Beach, about 20 miles south of Daytona. The beach is among the cleanest found on the Florida coast. The weather is generally 5-10 degrees cooler than Miami but normally from February through March well into the 70s and 80s.

In the year of El Nino, the weather played all kinds of tricks and Florida was not left out. Smyrna temperature ranged from 60 degrees to 70 degrees and the breeze was cooler than normal.

Tornadoes were being spun off right and left and a tremendous amount of devastation occurred throughout the state.

During our stay a wild weather system was developing on the gulf coast and was predicted to cross the state through the Orlando area exiting land at Daytona. Tornado warnings were up.

What in fact happened, was that the storm hit us with a two pronged attack passing within 5 miles to the south and about 12 miles to the north with about 9 tornado touch downs and vast destruction of anything in its path. Over 40 lives were lost.

The peak of the system passed through Smyrna about 9 or 10 p.m. from west to northeast as predicted. For a period of about one hour there were lightning flashes every 20 or 30 seconds. The rain was being driven under the doorway thresholds. The television broadcasts were coloured red and everyone was urged to take cover — preferably in the middle of the apartment in the bathroom!

The following morning there was much evidence of the storm damage in neighbouring buildings close to our condo on the beach. When the damage and death toll reports of direct hits began to be published we realised how lucky we had been.

The unit we stayed in was directly on the beach, on the third floor. It had an unobstructed view in three directions from the large balcony looking out to sea.

The timing of our stay was lucky. While we were there, there was to be a launch of the space shuttle from Cape Canaveral some 30 miles south of Smyrna, and it was to be at night. I remember watching a daytime launch from Venice some 100 miles away and we could see the trail of spent fuel quite clearly.

Watching a launch close up at night is an experience not to be missed. We could see it from the balcony. At ground level it is as bright as the setting sun. As lift off is achieved, the whole sky is lit up around it and even at 30 miles away, the beach, which was full of people, was floodlit for miles. It is a spectacular sight and although commonplace to Floridians, it is an outstanding experience for visitors.

In the early morning there are numerous fishermen casting into the breakers and very good size fish are taken. It is amusing to watch the pelicans and egrets who will wait patiently beside the fisherman in the hope that fish too small for him might become great snacks for them. One morning we watched as a fisherman hooked something very big and was straining to bring it in. It took him about 30 minutes to finally get it to shore. What his hook had snared was a very large and very dead giant turtle about 5 feet in length. It became a major curiosity and the marine biologists took great interest in it.

There are hundreds of white egrets to be seen in and around the beach, in addition to little flights of pelicans who cruise along just above the buildings by the shore, taking advantage of the thermal currents to keep them aloft without too much effort.

There was one egret in particular who was nicknamed Freddie the freeloader. One of the residents on the first floor used to feed him hot dogs. The bird loved them. But the spices must have given him a terrible thirst because he would immediately go to the edge of the chlorinated swimming pool and gulp down gallons of water.

We made some very good friends at Smyrna, especially those with whom we golfed. We played many different courses and on one occasion, about 10 miles north of Daytona, Joyce, Bill Burgess and I were teamed with a fourth gentleman who appeared with a full set of clubs and only one arm! He had lost the other in a motorcycle accident. We were somewhat apprehensive at first, but by the time the day was over it had taken everything we had to barely beat him. He swung backhanded and hit the ball straight and about 200 yards!

On another occasion, with one of Bill's close friends from California, we were playing a hole about 350 yards long which had a small pond in front of the green. As he walked up to the green, Bill's friend was astounded to see dozens of balls in the bottom of the pond. He became very excited expecting to fill his pockets, ignoring what he thought was a log in the water. He jumped about 6 feet in the air when he realized that the balls were there because the resident alligator was also there — all eight feet of him! He was still talking to himself on the drive home.

The Daytona area is famous for auto racing, which originally was run on the beach. Today a huge stadium, which is visible from I-95, hosts the now famous race. It is big business. During and preceding race week there is an influx of thousands of racing enthusiasts. Every commercial enterprise in the region capitalizes on the market opportunities associated with it. Half the population sports the traditional black baseball cap embroidered with the Daytona 500 logo.

Sponsors of racing teams often have more than one car. The extra cars are placed around the area on display and arouse a great deal of interest. For a couple of days we had the Kodak car in our condo parking lot and residents had a great time having their photo taken beside the car or in some cases seated in it.

Another phenomenon which occurs is bike week. When this happens there are literally tens of thousands of motorcycles to be seen up and down the coast, some of which are the most elaborately chromed up machines imaginable. During that week the biker is king. They are generally well behaved, civilized people having a ball. You will find many professionals, physicians, lawyers, etc. who are into biking for the fun of it. Restaurants and bars are set up with a special welcome to bikers and it too has developed into a major commercial opportunity.

Daytona is also home to one of the largest flea markets I've ever seen. Normally I stay away from flea markets. Most of them are outlets for junk. But the Daytona Flea Market which is across I-95 from the raceway has some very good merchandise at excellent prices. There is one stand specializing in baseball hats of every colour and description. They must buy overruns or bankruptcy stock because you can buy excellent quality hats for as little as 2 or 3 dollars. There is a large display of watches at great prices. Excellent farm produce and citrus fruits are also available. They can handle thousands of cars in the well organized parking area. It can be a fun filled diversion when you've had enough of the beach.

Quechee, Vermont

Chapter Twenty-six

Quechee, Vermont

In 1978, a lead story in the travel section of The Montreal Gazette told of an utopian development in central Vermont, in a tiny former textile mill town named Quechee. It sounded interesting and the promoters offered a free weekend with unlimited use of the recreation facilities (which were already in place) provided that we agreed to take a tour of the project and what it had to offer. They didn't have to try very hard. The minute we saw it we loved it instantly.

Tucked in between Woodstock, Vt., a prosperous town which had somehow managed to dodge the wrecking balls and with the help of the Rockefellers had been restored to the way it was in the early 1800s, and Hanover, N.H., an ivy league town, home to Dartmouth University and equipped with a first rate hospital and a number of cultural attractions, Quechee was a natural fit.

We toured the facility, admired the ecological objectives of the covenants, virtually swooned over the thirty-six holes of magnificent golf with a great club house to match, a ski hill and enough tennis courts to keep us well occupied. We made the decision to buy a building lot on Royall Tyler Road, which automatically gave us access to all the facilities.

It called for a celebration.

We had noticed an interesting restaurant named "Philbin and Wife" in Hartland Four Corners, a small village a few miles south. We had a memorable evening.

Philbin was prominent in the bar area but wife was nowhere to be seen. Joyce saw this as an opportunity to open up a mischievous dialogue and demanded to know where wife was. Well we never did get to meet her. Wife was too busy slaving over a hot stove in the kitchen while Philbin socialized in the bar.

We then began a twelve year adventure with the Green Mountain boys and girls whom we found to be wonderful, honest and hard working people. We never encountered a native Vermonter we didn't like. The old values were everywhere. Business could and was done on a handshake. In time we came to know and admire many Vermonters with whom we came in contact.

In the summer of 1979 we were ready to build. The world was right in the thick of the energy crisis and every conceivable idea and gimmick was being touted for new home construction. We chose a timberpeg post and beam saltbox.

The house was to be constructed on a rock ledge which required part of it to be blasted away. Our contractor, Gordon Ware Jr., had chosen his subs carefully, based on each having a proven record.

By early October the site was cleared, after which we entered the deer season. In Vermont the deer hunt is a ritual which every able bodied man participates in until he bags "his" deer. And so we waited and waited for the dynamiter, a man appropriately named Harry Bumps, to prepare the site.

By late November the foundation crew arrived. It is no mean feat to lay footings on stepped ledge. They were enormous and our neighbours must have thought a high rise was going in. From that point on the project flew and with no snow the shell was closed in before it arrived.

We had provided for a Rumford fireplace in the living room, a wood stove in the basement and off peak electrical heating throughout the house. This meant that there was no electrical heat between 7 a.m. and 11 a.m. and again from 4:30 p.m. to 8:30 p.m. However if the wood stove was fired up an hour beforehand the well of heat thus created was enough to hold the comfort level.

The Rumford fireplace proved to be not only lovely to look at with its large high opening but also as efficient as it was possible for a fireplace to be. It was a beautiful and cosy year round home which provided us with many happy hours.

Once the house was completed, I embarked on the famous dry stone wall which supported the driveway and parking area. There were many flat rocks in the woods nearby but eventually we had to have them drawn in. There were over 120 tons of stone in that wall and it is as good today after twenty years as when I laid it.

I had always been fascinated with the way in which skilled stone masons could shape a stone. I began making various enquiries with various technical trade schools without success. Finally I determined that I could learn the trade in Montreal at the Parthenais Centre — a medium security prison! They laughed when I called, stating that I would find it easy to get into the program but a lot harder to get out! I declined with thanks.

Several large hemlock trees screened our home from the road. There was also a large limestone outcropping across from our driveway. I discovered that by raking the forest floor of debris that there was an extensive natural growth of lichen on it. By keeping it clear I was able to cultivate a marvellous moss lawn which followed the contours of the forest.

The bonus to all of this was that in springtime the moss bloomed with miniature red flowers called "American Soldiers". It was totally natural, never needed cutting and looked like a small waterfall as it grew over and down the rock face.

Over the twelve years that we owned it we met some interesting characters in the various service trades.

Roger Potvin who had supplied the rock for the stone wall was one of them. He could fell a tree within a foot of target in two or three minutes. He owned a small bulldozer and a backhoe, both of which he operated with an unlit cigar in his mouth.

We had an insurance agent from Woodstock who could quote Jefferson verbatim. He eagerly took part in any and all town meetings.

We hired a young fellow who was an expert at climbing and trimming trees, who in the true spirit of independence always charged $17.76 an hour for his work. He was a free living character who later became a candidate for governor on a platform of free marijuana for everyone. He didn't win!

Jim Phelan, a skilled carpenter and dry wall finisher, also did work for us. He played guitar and sang folk songs in a Woodstock bar. He had a very unusual message on his answering system. It would begin with a few guitar notes "Plunkety plunk!" Then he would sing "Hi this is Jim, and I ain't home. So please leave your number at the sound of the tone. Plunkety plunk."

There were many places to see and things to do nearby.

In Cornish, N.H., there was a wonderful old antique shop run by an elderly man named John Nichols. He had many rare period pieces of Americana. Once, I saw a fine old Windsor settee and asked him how much. "That'll be fifteen" he replied, meaning fifteen thousand! Nevertheless, all of the eight Hitchcock chairs that we own were bought from him for twenty-two dollars each. I of course had to clean them up.

The St. Gauden's Estate was nearby, now a museum with displays of sculptures and designs created by him, including large replicas of the American coins which were his design. On Sunday afternoons there were often classical musical performances offered which were enhanced by the beautiful natural setting.

We spent many hours at the club, golfing or playing tennis. When a new verandah bar was created, a contest to name it was called for. I submitted two names, "Casual Waters" and "The Last

Hazard". They chose a really original name — "The Nineteenth Hole"! I thought mine were better.

The club offered canoe "outing" trips which we participated in. We also experienced "tubing" on the Connecticut River. Whole families could be seen drifting for miles downstream, some times even with picnic hampers tied inside the huge truck tubes. It was a marvellous old fashioned way to spend an afternoon.

We often listened to the local news on radio. There were many stories of human interest emanating from the colorful small towns along the Connecticut River which separated Vermont from New Hampshire.

Most rural residents take advantage of their constitutional right to bear arms, by keeping a rifle at the ready. Usually it only came into use during the deer season, but our ears perked up one evening over a radio item in which a resident of West Lebanon, N.H. had been fined for firing his rifle within city limits.

It had been time to cut his grass, but his lawnmower stubbornly refused to start. So he shot it!

Our fondest memories are of the fun times we had with Zeb and Reedy Hastings, our neighbours to the north, and later with Dick and Maureen Mehrman, our neighbours to the south. They were golden years.

Footprints

Chapter Twenty-seven

George

"I am the resurrection and the life" -- so began the memorial service for George, a parishioner at St. John's Anglican Church for many years and a true gentlemen with whom I had worked when we were both sides persons. Father David Clunie continued on with the traditional Anglican, and indeed Christian readings, which we have come to expect at services dedicated to the passing of one of our brethren. David is always at his best on such occasions, bringing a warm and personal touch to his responsibilities as presider.

As one enters that period of life when the biblical definition of a lifetime of three score years and ten has been reached and the achievements of the deceased are extolled, it gives rise to personal self analysis. How did I do? What have I achieved? Did I measure up to the golden rule?

"Footprints in the Sand", the beautiful philosophical poem in which the subject follows God's steps, so that for most of life there are two sets of footprints, except during those periods of severe difficulty which most of us experience, when only one set of footprints is visible. "Where were you," asks the subject "when I needed you most?" "That was when I was carrying you," replied the Lord.

Up until two years ago George had been an active, spry, and bright eyed man whom I would have estimated to be in his mid seventies. He was 87, when he finally lost his battle with cancer.

By coincidence, sitting beside me in church was an elderly gentleman from Carleton Place. He had known George since the time when they were young spirited men full of adventure. He pulled out a small snapshot taken 61 years ago in 1938. It was a photo of his wedding at which George had been best man.

It was not long after that World War II began. George enlisted and served in the signal corps. The other gentleman served in the artillery. Both survived that horrible war and eventually drifted apart from regular contact.

But, here was this elderly gentleman sitting beside me with a newspaper clipping of George's obituary, which he stared at from time to time during the service. Looking at the wedding picture taken 61 years ago, I could only imagine what was running through his mind. He must surely have recognized that his own time could not be that far off.

And yet, those fresh young faces in that photo also told a story. The beginnings of a life together with his new bride. The invincible spirit of youth written all over their faces. I wish I had enough time to learn more about him and his life. 61 years. Time enough for a full plate of life's joys and triumphs, tempered by the trials faced by each of us as we trek along the paths that life has in store for us.

At the end of the memorial service we sang one of George's favourite hymns, "Onward Christian Soldiers". It had been a long time since I had sung or heard it. One of the great inspiring Christian hymns, it had fallen victim to political correctness.

Afterwards those who attended as supporters were able to express their condolences to his family. Once again the ladies of the church had sprung into action and produced a wonderful reception on short notice, as they always do.

Chapter Twenty-eight

The Pond

It was the end of the first week in October when Joyce and I drove up Highway 7 from Ottawa to Toronto. We hadn't planned it specifically to take in the fabulous display of colour that nature puts on in the fall, but we probably hit it at absolute peak.

This was especially the case as we drove through the western part of Lanark County, which has claimed for years that it is the maple sugar capital of Ontario.

We take so much for granted. This magnificent spectacle is all around us, and yet few venture beyond their own back yard to take it in. The State of Vermont has built an industry around the foliage season. It is virtually impossible to find accommodation during the 10 day period when it is at peak. Tour buses originating from the major cities of the Atlantic coast are seen all over the back roads looking for the perfect photo opportunity. There is even a special train excursion through the Green Mountains which is usually sold out.

If you are lucky, there will have been no major rains or wind storms in the days preceding peak, enabling the foliage to hang on just long enough for a spectacular display before "fall" begins in earnest.

And once it has happened, what an exhilarating experience it is, to tramp through the woods, ankle deep in fresh fallen leaves crunching with every step. With it comes the need to rake lawns and driveways clear, which creates a playful bonanza for kids who throw themselves into the spongy piles, something that seems to come naturally. They don't have to be taught. Those who try to make it on the land know the value of leaf compost as an organic additive. Others simply burn them, giving off a pleasing familiar aroma which permeates the surroundings.

When the life span of the leaves is complete, and the diminishing light of shorter fall days has robbed them of chlorophyll and its green opaque mask and then gives us the gifts of crimson, scarlet and yellow, we should stop for a moment and marvel at another example of natural evolution. As sure as the sun rises, the woods, having given us this marvellous show, in six months time will burst forth again with new life. That is the real meaning of the burgeoning of spring.

On and off over the past few weeks we have picked up the scent of a skunk outside. We dismissed it as another incident of road kill which is common at this time of year.

Yesterday while looking at our flower garden from our living room window, who trots by, totally unconcerned, but a scruffy looking skunk, who looked like he had been on an all night bender.

Well! We can do without that guy. Groundhogs are bad enough, but a skunk? I reflected on the problem. There is a large clearing project under way for new homes, about 80 acres on Campeau Drive, a quarter of a mile from us. Perhaps its habitat has been blasted away.

We have had direct personal experience with skunks and it isn't fun. Back in Montreal, when we lived in St-Lambert, the nearby golf course was expanded and dozens of small wild inhabitants had to look elsewhere for shelter. Unfortunately a skunk decided that life under the cement pad near our front door, looked like it might be pretty good, so the games began.

I first noticed a sizeable hole dug in the front flower garden leading to the pad. I simply filled it in, only to find it newly excavated the following morning. This went on for about a week. Finally I contacted the humane department of the city and found that I was one of many residents with the problem, which was related to the turmoil on the golf course.

The solution was to place a "have-a-heart" cage trap near the hole with a small dish with enticement such as bacon or peanut butter on it. The cage was wrapped, except for the door, with a plastic garbage bag (in case he sprayed). We set it out and waited.

The first morning I noticed the trap door had closed and sitting sheepishly inside the cage was a neighbour's cat. So much for that dish of bait. I released the cat and reset the trap. The following morning I checked again. The same damn cat was back in the cage! Before I was finished I had caught the numbskull five times! Eventually he got the message.

At last, after about a week, the cage door dropped and we had a skunk. The city was kind enough to remove it, but brought the cage back, in case he had set up house with his girlfriend.

Three or four days later — voilà! The second skunk was in the cage. At that time Peter was about 16 and his friend Yvan had just gotten his driver's licence. They spotted the skunk inside the cage and full of compassion, decided to place it in the back seat of Yvan's mother's car and drive it about 20 miles into the country, and release it, which they did. Fortunately the skunk cooperated — it must have enjoyed the ride — it was released without incident.

So, we are going to have to check out back to see what, if any, diggings have gone on. Hopefully what I saw was simply a skunk in transit. We can certainly do without the other alternative.

Montreal Harbour viewed from Habitat 67

Chapter Twenty-nine

Joyce's 40th Law Class Reunion

Joyce and I go to Montreal several times a year. Primarily, because my son and daughter live there with their respective families which are, at the moment, in an expansion mode for the fourth time. Sandy (Peter's wife) is expecting her third in December.

On this trip we have a twofold mission. First it is the 40th anniversary of Joyce's law class at McGill, and secondly, tomorrow we go on to Quebec City to help Joyce's Aunt Christine celebrate her ninetieth birthday!

The law class of 59 has provided Joyce with many happy memories. Always an excellent student Joyce was awarded the MacDonald travelling scholarship upon graduation, which is how she ended up in Paris at the Sorbonne.

The reunion was to be held at the University Club on Mansfield, a private club with an excellent reputation for fine cuisine.

We stayed at the Hotel Queen Elizabeth, still the "grande dame" of Montreal hotels. During my working career I spent many hours in the Queen E. The Beaver Club was, and probably still is, the leading restaurant and watering hole for the city's business elite. The Pulp and Paper convention has been held there for years. So it is with a sense of "coming home" that we checked in. After leaving Joyce at the University Club I visited with Peter,

Sandy, Julie, and Philip for the evening. The kids now 8 and 7 respectively are maturing beautifully, doing well at school and are fluently bilingual. Julie is artistic and Philip is the athlete. It is fascinating to see them develop. Once, when Philip was 4 years old we asked him why we should be careful of robbers. "Because they steal your milk," he replied.

The room we are staying in has a superb view across the plaza of Place Ville Marie, continuing up McGill College, now a wide boulevard which opens up the view to the Arts Building of McGill and the Royal Victoria Hospital, with Mount Royal in the background. It is exactly as it was envisaged years ago when the mayor at the time wanted a covered overpass to link the buildings on each side of the street which would have ruined the view. There was a great outcry by the business leaders against it and we can be grateful to them. The result is spectacular.

When she returned from the reunion, Joyce was all aglow. There were several people there whom she had not seen since graduation. It was great fun to discover what divergent paths had been taken by each of them. She was the only woman who had attended from four who had graduated. Joyce is one of a small group of twenty-six women who graduated from McGill Law School in the 40s and 50s. They are considered pioneers. A composite photo display of them now hangs in the law faculty at McGill to commemorate this fact. Today more than half of the students are women.

Like most women she wanted to look her best at the reunion. She needn't have worried. She looked absolutely lovely.

There are signs that the city is coming back to life. After many years of lying vacant, the former Simpson's department store building on prime land on Rue Ste-Catherine is being refurbished.

A large portion of the building is now occupied by Simons, a long standing Quebec City retailer.

Office space and occupancy rates show a marked improvement after a ten year drought. Housing values have firmed, although not near comparable levels in other major Canadian cities.

The professional CFL football team has been resurrected and is holding its own. Although attendance for the Expos major league baseball team would barely support a triple "A" franchise, there is talk of a new stadium in a downtown location.

Nevertheless the threat of separation still hangs in. New definitions of what constitutes a real "pure laine" Quebecer are proposed. The language police are still at it.

But with it all, it remains a beautiful city. In many ways a jaded lady, but still a lady. If the sabre rattling could ever be brought to a conclusion it might bloom again.There was so much promise.

True to form, our escape route from Montreal Island via the Victoria Bridge turned out to be closed for maintenance. With all of the rest of the downtown traffic we headed for the Champlain Bridge. Murphy's law prevailed. There had been a minor accident near the structural steel section and traffic ground to a halt. Half an hour later we had reached dry land and headed east on Riverside Drive to the south shore expressway which passes the old Expo grounds and continues east to the TransCanada highway connection at the Boucherville tunnel.

About 15 miles out on the TransCanada are two of the Monteregian Hills. Igneous intrusions known as Mt. Bruno and Mt. St-Hilaire. We turned off to Auclair's orchards to touch base with my old friend Peter Auclair from whom I had purchased several important Canadian antiques over 25 years ago.

It was the peak of the apple season and his business had grown immensely since I last saw him. He was now married with a fine young family. He always had an eye for commercial opportunity. Since I was last there he had added an area where one could buy and eat delicious home made apple pie. Like the true entrepreneur that he is, every square inch gives him a return.

We talked about the antique business which he had vacated years ago. He startled me by telling me what astronomical prices were now being realized for armoires that I had bought from him for $1-200. Pieces such as these were now going for $5-15,000 if you could find them at all. Frankly, I didn't believe it and it was not until later in the day when we arrived in Quebec City and dropped into a couple of shops on Rue St-Paul in lower town, that I realized that he wasn't kidding.

Armoires of good but not extraordinary quality had price tags on them ranging from 15 to $30,000! I asked a dealer in another shop if those prices were for real and he confirmed it.

If so, an investment in armoires made 25 years ago was probably better than any mutual fund over the same period. A gain of 50-100 times the original investment.

Of all the cities and towns that I have visited in eastern Canada, Quebec City is certainly among the most beautiful. Situated on a bend on the St. Lawrence River and strategically placed on rock face about 300 feet above the river, the upper town affords a spectacular view of Levis on the south shore and Isle d'Orléans to the east.

It is particularly striking in mid winter during the carnival, usually held in mid February, when the formidable ice floes add a new dimension to the view from Dufferin Terrace. It is there that the Château Frontenac sits, perched on top of the rock, dominating the surroundings within the walled section of the old city.

During the winter carnival there is an exciting race across the river among or over the ice floes in long wooden "bateaux" powered by oarsmen. It is fascinating to watch from the terrace, particularly if the ice is heavy and is carried out by the tide. When one of the boats becomes trapped in the ice the crew must jump out onto the ice and pull the boat over it to clear water. It takes enormous strength and skill, and quite often a crew will get hung up on the ice and find themselves a mile or two downstream.

Quebec City is also dear to us because it was the birthplace of Joyce's mother who was born and grew up on Rue Ste-Anne, which is inside the walled area and within two blocks of the Château. Her home was in a lovely old greystone near the Ursuline Convent, where Joyce's grandfather practised medicine. In the early years they had a cow in the backyard which supplied milk. It was a graceful old home which has since been converted into an upscale Mediterranean restaurant. After her mother died, I arranged through a Montreal art gallery to have an oil painting done of Rue Ste-Anne "autrefois" by John Little, a very prolific artist who gained prominence with his paintings of street scenes in Montreal and Quebec City. It is a very nice reminder of her origins.

Quebec was a natural stop in the years when the Manoir Richelieu was flourishing at La Malbaie (Murray Bay), some 90 miles downstream on the north shore. The Manoir was a wonderful convention hotel, first class in every respect and located on high terrain overlooking the St. Lawrence, which is about 15 miles wide at that point. There is a superb golf course located on the property with breathtaking views of the surrounding countryside and a turkey ranch across the road from the second hole. The gobbling birds reminded me of a ladies' bridge party between hands. One of my favourite restaurants in

Quebec was Le Vendôme, just down the hill from the Château. Very good food, nicely served, at reasonable prices.

Joyce and I first visited Quebec together the year we were married. As is our custom, we brought the ubiquitous picnic which we set up on the battlefield overlooking the river. There happened to be a large contingent of Americans dressed in battle gear from the 1700s who were there in a re-enactment of a raid made on Quebec prior to the conquest. It was a bit noisy for a picnic!

Two of her mother's sisters lived in Quebec for years and we managed to visit them on several occasions. Four years ago we were there, along with Joyce's sister Lois, on the occasion of a funeral. We were unable to book into the Château, but did manage to get accommodation (3 to a room) in a tiny hotel across the square from the Château and near the US consulate. I attempted to explain the "ménage à trois" to the desk clerk who simply brushed it aside saying, "We don't really care who you have up there with you." Oh, well.

———————————————

We were due to arrive at Christine's apartment about 4 p.m. Joyce wanted to buy her some flowers to go with the champagne we had brought. What a fool's errand we set out on. Where are the florists when you need them? Even the large supermarket couldn't help us. We ended up bringing her chocolates.

It was a wonderful nostalgic visit with someone who had always been one of Joyce's favourite aunts. We had lucked out. A mutual friend we had known at CIP lived in the same building. Marietta Freeland, a classmate of both of us at Harrington French courses, dropped in for a drink and some catching up. She had recently broken her ankle and was still using a walker. Marietta reminded us of the time at Harrington when our French professor was so pleased with our progress that he offered us all a "joint" to celebrate, which most of us refused.

Christine will be 90 in two weeks time. We will miss her real birthday because of our trip to Egypt and Israel. She is as sharp and witty as ever and runs around her apartment more like someone in middle age than old. After a delicious dinner she and Joyce delved into a scrapbook Christine had maintained from her early life. It was filled with historic and nostalgic gems about the family ancestry which was dear to both of them. We sat up far too late for our own good. Joyce was grateful that she had had the opportunity to learn many things about her family that she did not know.

Quebec City continues to have tremendous appeal. It is truly one of the wonderfully unique cities of North America and probably the only one of any size whose original fortification walls remain perfectly intact. The restoration of historic buildings is still being done with faithful attention to detail. The hotel and restaurant trade is having a very good year.

We spent Saturday morning with Christine and left for Montreal about noon. We were due to visit Vicky and Sarah later that afternoon. We had chosen the south shore autoroute en route to Quebec, so I elected to come back via the north shore. However, the old shore route on the north has some of the finest scenery in the province so we headed down 138 through Neuville, Cap Santé, Portneuf, and Deschambault. We stopped near Deschambault and found a beautifully carved decoy, reasonably priced, which we bought. We have two very good antique pieces which were found years ago in Deschambault. The elevation is fairly high all along this route until Deschambault, after which it begins to flatten out. There is a lovely view across the river to Lotbinière and its twin spired church which is a welcome landmark in the distance.

We then headed inland to pick up the north shore autoroute to Montreal.

Sarah, now 30 months, is growing by leaps and bounds and is an absolute delight. We spent a few hours with Vicky and her playing games that children of her age love. We then headed over the Mercier Bridge to Kathy and David's house on Westhill Ave.

We were somewhat apprehensive because our old friend Bagel would be there, with everything that that conjures up. Much to our surprise Kathy's daughter Juliet was there and with her was "Blitzen", a tiny white Jack Russell with enormous energy and enthusiasm. The big news is that Bagel was in love! Blitzen, an engaging female had swept him off his feet. Gone were the grumpy aggressive moods which made us nervous. In its place a never ending round of games and tail wagging with Blitzen which went on for hours. They are an absolute riot together and Bagel is a reformed individual.

The four of us went out to dinner at Restaurant "Sans Menu" on Notre Dame St. W., which has to be the best kept secret in town. We returned to find the two dogs itching to get into more games, particularly tug of war with a knotted rope. Bagel has learned that he can drive Blitzen nuts by taking a squeaky rubber toy in his mouth, making it squeak and flaunting it in front of Blitzen, who reacts as one might expect. Blitzen can't do it. Her mouth is not big enough. They are a real cartoon combination.

As we sometimes do, David and I relaxed after dinner and enjoyed a man's conversation. He is a great philosopher and very interesting to listen to when analysing a subject. He is scholarly, intelligent and logical and I find him easy to follow. He is a very caring person and deeply compassionate on the subject of his children. He worries about Bagel whose behaviour can be very erratic and unpredictable and of course Blitzen isn't around at all times to keep him balanced.

The following day, en route home, we passed several miles of spectacular autumn foliage near Hudson. There was still much of it to be seen.

As I write this I am sitting in our family room which is furnished with many of the Canadiana pieces that I have collected over the years all over eastern Canada since the mid 60s. We are very lucky to have them, particularly considering our startling discoveries over the past three days. The dark blue (original paint) armoire, with its rat tail hinges and cornice carved with dentils made with a curved chisel, looks far better than most of the old pieces we saw in Quebec. I will treat it with more respect from here on!

Puppy Love

Puppy Dreams

Chapter Thirty

The Pond

About 100 geese were on the pond this morning. We haven't seen them in any quantity for about six weeks. This is probably due to the feeding opportunities in nearby corn fields where we have seen hundreds of them making the most of the left over food following the harvest.

I watched them for a few minutes floating on the water. A second flight of about sixty flew over at about 3 or 400 feet some of whom dropped down and joined the locals. There must have been quite a debate going on up there because the rest circled around for about ten minutes, honking and squawking, with small groups of four or five landing. The rest kept flying around and eventually took off for some other location. There hasn't been any snow as yet so there are still many sources of food nearby.

I refilled the bird feeder a few days ago, but up to this point we haven't had any visitors. For that matter, except for a couple of blue jays over in the trees to the left, we haven't seen any local small birds anywhere within sighting range out back.

Shortly after I wrote this I went to the back of the house to see if there was any activity. The Colorado spruce which is now about eighteen feet high provides a great and secure observation post for all of the small birds. It is about fifteen feet from the feeder which is on a pole.

I could see some movement among the branches of the spruce. A small wood sparrow emerged, flew up onto our deck then back to the spruce from which he considered the feeder and then flew off. With that, the two blue jays surfaced from the inner branches of the spruce and flew over to the feeder. Our first customers!

The sparrows usually come in numbers, so this one may have gone off to find the rest of his family. Once the first bird shows up, the others follow quickly.

The blue jays tend to cast seeds around, waving their beaks from side to side. It doesn't take long for the squirrels to spot this activity and scoop up those seeds which have fallen to the ground. The pole has an inverted baffle mounted on it specifically to prevent squirrels from reaching the feeder. It is effective and frustrates the squirrels in their attempt to get to it. This way they all get fed.

Joyce and I always have a bet on as to what species of bird will be the first to discover the feeder refilled. We both lost. I bet on a chickadee and she chose a sparrow. We will continue to see finches and the occasional woodpecker. For the next six months at least, we don't get grackles, which would otherwise dominate the feeder.

The geese hung around for about 4 hours. Around 3 p.m. they began honking noisily and lined up in the water facing west. I said to Joyce that it sounded like they were about to take off. And with that, one final command and the entire flock rose together without hesitation.

In the six weeks that they had been absent they had all gained strength and developed new skills so that the lift off seemed effortless and closely coordinated. Where they go we do not know. Perhaps to one of the dozens of corn fields around us. After which they would probably head for the Ottawa River 3 or 4 miles away where they could safely spend the night on the water. Migration is now only 3 or 4 weeks away. Sooner, if we get an early snowfall.

Chapter Thirty-one

Montreal

On October 28 we were back in Montreal for the annual party for those people who managed to complete or exceed 25 years with CIP, now Bowater's. Many there were 40 year veterans.

It is always a warm and friendly occasion. Rank somehow seems less important and familiar faces are as refreshing as the excellent buffet and victuals.

The numbers are beginning to dwindle, since the original company was split up and sold about five years ago. Many who had lived and worked in Montreal most of their lives are now in some other part of the country.

We wonder who will show up. We speculate whether the same characters will be asking pointed questions of the host. This is the second year that Bowater's have very graciously given the party, with, I might add, a more positive outlook toward the future, in contrast with an extended period of difficult times for all those who were there when the old company finally broke up. And so, we look forward once again to being elbow to elbow with many old friends and associates.

"*Comme d'habitude*" as the French say, Joyce headed straight for the hairdressers. I took the opportunity to shop around old Montreal which was always one of our favourite haunts. It has become quite trendy. There are several warehouses and office buildings which have now been converted into condominiums.

I drove along Rue St-Paul, entering it beside the old Bonsecours church and market.

There are dozens of souvenir shops of every description and an even greater number of restaurants and bars.

One shop caught my eye with a very interesting display of "coq" sculptures. It was called "Tant qu'il y aura des Fleurs". Two excellent reproductions of "coqs" from the Quebec museum, one in carved wood and the other in sheet metal in particular. Both very reasonably priced. I considered them. A weathervane for the pole outback? Or perhaps an eye catching work of art for the top of one of the armoires?

I thought seriously about it and then, probably wisely, put it off until Joyce had her say.

I walked past Place Jacques Cartier, now all dressed up with quarried stone lanes and barriers to vehicular traffic. The Nelson Hotel is still there. It was the centre of activity for the separatists during the October Crisis of 1970. It must be a popular watering hole. It has expanded its bar and restaurant facilities into a courtyard which angles down behind it to Rue St-Paul.

I passed the artist displays on Rue St-Amable, where the wonderful little restaurant Le St-Amable is located. It has special meaning for Joyce and me. It was where I took her on our first date. Afterward we had gone to le Baldequin, an interesting intimate disco which took its name from an old four poster bed displayed near the entry. Later that evening we walked back to the car east of the Bonsecours market. It was past midnight although safe to walk around at that time of night (it still is). We turned a corner and came across a vagrant sleeping in a doorway. It was then that I saw for the first time how truly compassionate Joyce is. She felt genuinely sorry for him and wanted to help him.

In time, we would spend many memorable evenings together in old Montreal.

I continued over to Rue St-Laurent and grabbed a quick lunch at a restaurant at the corner of Notre Dame. Across the street was the Court House where I had the one and only experience in my life of facing a judge (when the clerk had reminded me not to read from the pocket book with the tranquilizer taped inside the cover, which Joyce had given me).

Then down Rue St-Vincent past what for years was the city morgue, now a trendy restaurant. During the sixties there was an outstanding antique shop called La Pigeonaire located there. They were experts in restoration. It was forced to close down because the restoration work they did fell outside of the zoning regulations for old Montreal.

Farther west on Rue St-Paul was the building where Theo Lubbers had his stained glass studio. It was always fun to do business there. He employed several talented stained glass artisans who were accompanied by taped classical music while they worked.

When we lived at Habitat 67 we had a great view across the harbour of old Montreal and the twin spires of Notre Dame Cathedral in particular.

We saw the beauty of the cathedral inside from two different experiences. Once, while attending a superb M.S.O. performance of "The Messiah". The other more disquieting time was at a midnight mass at Christmas where the tourists or revellers were more than a bit irreverent.

We still remember another more heartwarming experience at midnight Christmas mass at St. Patrick's, a moving homily, inspiring music, and some extraordinary readings by someone who we thought must have been a nun straight off the boat from Ireland.

We were so taken by the beauty of the readings that we casually mentioned it to a co-worker the following Monday. "That was my daughter," he said. She certainly had us fooled!

The extent of renovations along Common Street facing the waterfront has accelerated immensely.

My roots go back quite far in this part of the city. My father worked most of his life on Hospital St. for Cable and Wireless Limited. At that time the Montreal stock exchange operated across from the office. The Centaur Theatre now occupies it.

There were indeed fewer of us around to celebrate another year together. Bowater's once again a generous and gracious host. There were no unpleasant surprises. Just a collection of old friends glad to have made it through another year and still able to enjoy it.

After a leisurely breakfast we took a walk up Peel St. The old M.A.A.A. no longer exists as we knew it, and is being converted to a commercial health club. The Cantlie House is an apartment hotel. Two tour buses were loading as we passed. We continued west on Sherbrooke to Mountain. Holt Renfrew is featuring black for the fall/winter season. Then down to Ste-Catherine past Ogilvy's. Joyce tells me that many of the shoppers there yesterday were sporting the kimono like wraps that made such a statement at the Governor General's speech from the throne. Ste-Catherine is looking more upbeat particularly as you head east to McGill College. So there is certainly evidence of a comeback.

Joyce liked the large wooden "coq" I had seen yesterday so we packed it into the car and away we went.

En route to Ottawa we took a short detour via the Hudson/Rigaud shore road and ended up having lunch in a delightful little restaurant on Rue St-Jean Baptiste in Rigaud called "Soleil le Vent". Very good food, nicely presented, at reasonable prices. The owner told us they had only been open one month. She also told us about Rigaud's claim to fame — the sanctuary. Early on, when the area was settled, a farmer worked his fields on a Sunday. According to legend God punished him by turning all his potatoes to stone. The stone filled field is testimony to the story.

We'll check it out on another trip. God willing!

Chapter Thirty-two

The Pond

Halloween has gone high tech! Now we have witches who respond to voices or a hand clap with a sinister cackle and a scary message which says, "I'm going to get you."

We don't have a lot of small kids in our immediate area. Most of us are empty nesters. There are however a few grandchildren.

There were two waves of the trick or treat mob. About 6 p.m. the little geezers were first, under the ever watchful eye of their parents who are never far away. The youngest was one month old, dressed as a Teletubby and asleep in her grandfather's arms. Her older sister (21/2) was also a Teletubby, and really curious, she wanted to explore our house (with grandmother close behind).

The main group of 4 - 8 year olds hit us like a tidal wave about 6:45. At one point there must have been 40 -50 kids roaring about with pillowcases half full.

Fewer and fewer were carrying UNICEF boxes. Either they and their parents have lost interest, or it isn't being properly promoted in the schools.

By 7:30 we were down to the stragglers in the 8 -10 year age group. They don't even bother to dress up. Some carry a mask which they bring out if you ask them where their costume is.

At 8 p.m. I checked the street. No one in sight. I assumed it was over, shut off the front lights and closed her down for the night.

Five minutes later the doorbell rang. We didn't answer it. Then the phone rang. It was our neighbour, Win. His 14 month old grandson Matthew was dressed up as a dragon and he wanted to bring him over. Naturally we agreed. Matthew took one look at us and promptly fell asleep. But Win was not going to be denied the fun of Matthew's first Halloween.

It has become a major commercial event which is being promoted by everyone concerned with it, from the mini chocolate bars to the elaborate decorating and costume kits. There is a lot of money being made on the back of Halloween. Fortunately, the kids are still having a ball with it as they always have.

For the past week, about 150 of the extended family of geese have been spending 2 -3 hours a day at the pond and on the 9th fairway. Many simply sunning themselves as the occasional diehard golfer passes by. Looking more like a cross country skier than a golfer. The local songbirds have stopped sulking after I changed the seed mix in the feeder and are finally showing up at the feeder in numbers. Mostly purple finches and wood sparrows.

The trees have now shed their leaves which the very strong winds of the past week have scattered toward the bushes. Very few remain on the lawn out back. The shrubs have been wrapped with burlap and the snow fencing around the perennial garden is in place.

We have pretty well seen the last of Indian summer. I had to reinforce the burlap wrapping which the wind had blown partly off. It was cold on the bare hands doing so, with the occasional flurry, but we are now as ready for winter as we ever get.

Today in church was Remembrance Sunday. It was quite moving as it always is. We sang the sailor's hymn. Then the prayers of the people were led by a veteran of WW II, now a gentleman in his late 70s. He is a wonderful reader with a north country accent who adds a personal touch to his reading. When he began prayers for those who had died, he broke down when he prayed for those lost in the war. All of us in the church could not help but feel the moment more deeply.

Afterwards at coffee, I spoke with him about it. He had been a pilot with the R.A.F. He chuckled when he told me that his wife, who was with us at coffee, had been a W.A.A.F., although he met her much later.

Over my lifetime I have watched or participated in memorial services, but it was only in Ottawa at the National Cenotaph on Elgin Street where the meaning hit home. Perhaps that was because the surviving veterans had grown older and showed their emotions more readily during the ceremony. The parade up Elgin Street to the Cenotaph is always a stirring one. There are usually several thousand people in attendance and as the old vets march by, trying to look as proud and vigorous as they were 50 years ago, spontaneous applause breaks out, which still sends a shiver up my spine. Many of the ordinary people become teary eyed and some weep openly.

For many years an attempt has been made to recognize those who served in the Merchant Marine, many who gave their lives, by allowing them benefits similar to other veterans. This has been a political football which the federal government has been dodging for years. There is hope that 1999 will be the year that recognition will be forthcoming.

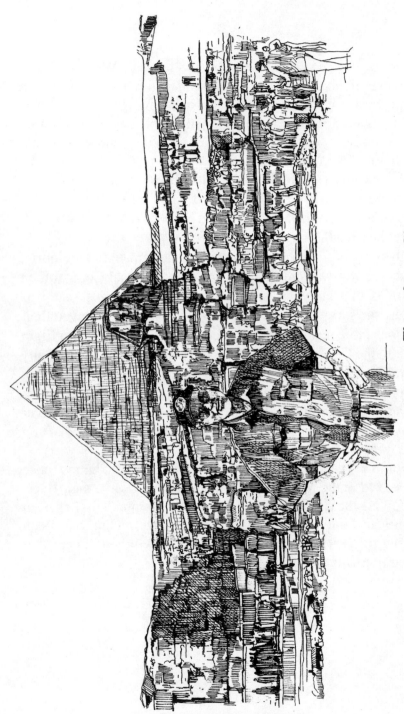

The author at Giza

Chapter Thirty-three

Egypt

Unlike the freedom and adventure of exploring a foreign country in a rental car, a tour, by its very nature, is limiting. On the plus side, everything is done for you. You don't usually get lost, the guides know the best way around and which destinations have the greatest appeal. On the down side, you sacrifice flexibility, often not staying long enough in places you are interested in, and sometimes visiting destinations such as commercial stops, in which you have no interest at all.

There is also a tendency to cram as much in as time allows, so that in retrospect the experience seems hurried. This was certainly the case in both Egypt and Israel. The alternative would have required considerably more time and money, perhaps putting it out of reach to many of us.

There is also the question of security in a region historically associated with conflict. There are always incidents of unrest occurring for political, ethnic, or religious reasons which professional tour operators know how to avoid.

We thus embarked on an eighteen day adventure which found us rising at dawn, tearing around from place to place and competing for space with hundreds of other tourists with the same objective. Some negatives, but overall a wonderful but exhausting experience which made it possible for us to see for ourselves some of the spectacular wonders of the ancient world, which were legendary in our early years of schooling.

We arrived at Cairo at 2 a.m. in the morning and proceeded directly to the Ramses Hilton, a first class hotel directly across from the Cairo Museum. The desk clerk was a dead ringer for Peter Lorrie in looks and in manner. I can just imagine him instructing an associate to round up the usual suspects!

Because the hotel was overbooked, we were given a junior suite on the eleventh floor of the hotel, with a view of the Nile, the museum, and what appeared to be a bus/taxi terminal on the street below. The atmosphere like many other Mediterranean cities was extremely polluted, in part because of the incredible number of vehicles racing along the streets, but also because this city of sixteen million people has an annual rainfall of only one inch!

About 5 a.m. I was awakened by the sound of a cantor in a nearby mosque calling the faithful to prayer. It was very compelling and would be hard to ignore by even the sleepiest Muslims. It was an eerie, mysterious sound which we would become used to hearing as we travelled through Egypt where prayers are offered five times a day.

About mid morning we accepted the challenge which Cairo offers to those interested in crossing a street. It proved to be formidable. We got about two thirds of the way to the museum, which was only a quarter of a mile from our hotel, but got hung up with the heavy traffic pouring off the 6th of October bridge. Finally the traffic light turned in our favour, A policeman stepped off the curb waving his baton for the speeding vehicles to stop. We followed him. The only problem was that all the cars and trucks ignored him and continued racing through a red light! We and others jumped back until finally they got the message. We circled around to the front of the museum past several armed soldiers, paid our fees and entered.

Later that afternoon we watched the pedestrians playing a kind of traffic roulette from our balcony. It was simply unbelievable. Dozens of them nonchalantly weaving their way across 3 and 4 lanes of fast moving traffic like bullfighters, the cars missing them by inches.

The museum is stacked to the rooftops with phenomenal treasures. The large or important items set up in place. Wooden cases containing more, lying carelessly alongside priceless artifacts. We did our own quick run through which we would follow with a guided tour in about a week.

Hatshepsut was prominently displayed so I took a couple of photos of her with Joyce alongside. Joyce is doing a book review of Pauline Gedges' "Child of the Morning" — the story of Hatshepsut, the only woman pharaoh in Egypt's history.

Ramses II was also dominant as might be expected. The whole world is familiar with Tutankhamen's treasures, and they are indeed fabulous. We were fascinated with the tomb within a tomb within a tomb display in gilded wood. The concept much like the popular Russian wooden toy dolls where each time you take the top off you find another inside in a seemingly never ending process. The Tut jewelry is exquisite in design and ornamentation. Gold earrings the size of one's hand. Beautiful breast plate necklaces in cleverly blended semi-precious stones of subtle colour variations. There are hundreds and hundreds of sarcophagi with elaborate carving depicting the life and greatness of its intended inhabitant. A 5000 year old barge recently discovered and in the process of restoration not far from the main entrance, which National Geographic deemed of such importance that a feature article was recently published on it. There is just no end to it.

We came back to the hotel, had an early dinner, and then strolled around the shops in the hotel. It is a very nice facility and probably because it contains a casino, is strongly guarded at the main entry with an electronic gate such as found in airports.

Not surprisingly when we passed through, the alarm went off but the guard simply waved us on. I guess we don't look sinister.

A hotel such as this has seen a lot of history and international dignitaries in its time. Many hotels of this type in exotic locations are often central points in mystery novels.

One such hotel which shows up in this manner is the Grande Bretagne in Athens. Some international spy is always cooking up some deal in the lobby bar. When we went to Greece we stayed at this fabulous old hotel hoping to have a drink at the bar and see for ourselves what a real spy looks like. All we saw were more idiots like us also looking for spies.

It was 5 a.m. the following morning and I had been unable to sleep. Perhaps it was the anticipation of our flight that morning to Luxor and the mad rush of checking out and moving on to the next tour destination.

Anytime now, my friend in the minaret will again be calling the faithful to prayer. There is no missing it. You have to admire them for their disciplined adherence, especially during a time of upheaval in traditional thinking in the Christian church. The rules are revised even as I write. It is a troubling period for anyone who believes in the status quo. There must be something to be said for the established traditions, otherwise why are we making a huge happening out of the millennium? We must have been doing something right for 2000 years.

The night plays strange tricks on the way we think. You find your mind wandering down some dark and puzzling trails. Little problems loom larger and only begin to clarify when you get yourself upright. Back home we have had a lot to think about. Joyce's niece facing a difficult period of chemotherapy. Vicky my daughter fighting to regain her strength after two bouts of surgery.

And while this is happening, Sandy my daughter-in-law is only 5-6 weeks away from giving birth to her third child. And so, whether some of us agree with it or not, we are in God's hands.

The Egyptians believed that, and made elaborate preparations for the after life.

Within a distance of a few hundred miles we are within reach of the birthplace of some of the great world religions. Judaism, Christianity and Islam were seeded and flourished in this area and if you stretch the mileage a bit further many of the most important early civilizations. As the French Impressionists learned there is something about the Mediterranean light which raises the creative birthrate. The Egyptians saw that too, and their legacy is ours to marvel at.

We rushed to get our baggage out at 7:30 a.m. and raced to gobble down our breakfast so that we would be in good time for our 10:30 flight to Luxor. We needn't have. By the time we got to the airport the original plane was declared unserviceable and a different aircraft was designated with departure at 1 p.m. That would carve into our touring at Luxor.

The airline turned on drinks for all, but they turned out to be soft drinks only. Oh well. What could we do but wait. We met the people who got our beds last night. Doug and Margaret Shultis from St. Catherines. They had a great sleep.

We also met an American couple from Kentucky who were interested in horses and racing. We got into a discussion on horse racing.

I remembered a brief experience I had years ago at Blue Bonnets raceway in Montreal.

I had been dating a very sweet young lady for about a year when we decided to try our luck at the races. There were 8 races on the day's card. We pooled our money and I made the selections on the first 7 races. We lost every time. Finally she said, "I want to choose the horse on the last race." I agreed. She chose a horse called Brown Bantam. On the way to the wicket I bumped into a guy I knew who played the horses. I asked him what was good in the 8th. "Little Ginny can't miss," he replied. So I put the money on Ginny.

Brown Bantam won and I had to come clean. Shortly thereafter we broke up. I have avoided the track ever since!

We had to scramble to get back on track. Since Luxor is well lit after dark we had no difficulty appreciating it. The skies were clear and a new moon was shining overhead. The massive columns (pylons) with elaborately chiselled hieroglyphics and symbolic cartouches signifying that they had indeed not only been inspired by Ramses II but also subsidized by him took on an even more striking appearance.

At the main entrance, there is an immense obelisk covered with detailed carving. There were originally two of them but in 1831 Mohammed Ali, who had the winter garden constructed, gave the second obelisk to France, where it now stands in the Place de La Concorde.

Our guide "Ash" proved himself well up to the challenge of explaining to his audience, in fascinating detail, how the temple came about. He has a very professional, scholarly approach which he flavours with highly amusing asides which his audience ate up. It was a great place and way in which to begin our tour, particularly considering our late arrival. He proposed, and we agreed, that in order to catch up we would need an early start in the morning. So, even though we were all quite tired, wake up call was set for 5 a.m.

If Luxor got us interested, Karnak, the largest temple ever constructed in the world, really stepped it up a notch. Both Karnak and Luxor were in fact linked as part of a great complex which for 1400 years was Thebes. At one time they were connected by a wide, grand road over 3 kilometres long lined on both sides by statues in the form of sphinxes. At its peak Luxor and Karnak sustained over two and a half million people.

Across the river lies the Valley of the Kings, now accessible by a modern bridge linking these two major historical attractions. Some monuments found near the Valley of the Kings are clearly visible from the valley floor on the west side, particularly the Temple of Hatshepsut. The main body of the tombs are in fact hidden inside a valley of sandstone mountains a mile or two further in. The line of demarcation between the lush flood plain and the beginning of the Sahara Desert is clearly defined. In fact on the flight down from Cairo those who had window seats commented on the abrupt colour change from sand to green as the two converged.

We began with a stop at Hatshepsut's Temple which is actually a reconstruction done by Polish engineers in the 1950s. The original temple was destroyed after Hatshepsut had a falling out with her lover, the architect of the temple. The setting is magnificent. The main objective was to erect the temples so that they would catch the first morning light. Hatshepsut's Temple faces directly east and is wrapped inside a wide sweeping U shaped mountain which cradles it. The mountain itself is inspiring.

A few miles to the north is the Valley of the Kings. There are over 60 tombs to be found there. Some major, such as Ramses II and others minor, such as Tut's Tomb. The latter's claim to greatness was due to the fact that it was the only one found intact. All the rest had been plundered. We were able to get inside those of Ramses VII, Ramses IV and Ramses II, each of which had an impressive approach to its entrance. Tut's Tomb on the other hand looks almost like an afterthought, although it is closer to the main drive. Having seen the fabulous treasures from it in the museum we simply looked quickly at its entrance and then pressed on.

On our way back, we stopped at Habu to see the Temple of Ramses III. There are many columns and walls deeply chiselled with relief drawings many of which still retain their original colour. Because it was Friday, schools were closed and there were many classes of happy, bright eyed children being led through the temple. They are a delight. Many of them dressed to the nines. They seem to get a great kick out of sneaking a "hello" at you on their way by, which makes them all giggle.

We got back to the cruise boat, had lunch and headed for the top observation deck, where I wrote this. It is a beautiful way to unwind. The lush shore on either side is being farmed on every usable inch.

Our ship had been moored a bit upstream from Luxor, along with two or three sister ships. The narrow road leading down to the pier was lightly populated with quite decent housing. This was the first time that we had taken notice of an unusual Egyptian tradition in construction which provided for future generations of the family.

This was done by extending steel reinforced columns above the existing roof in anticipation of the next generation, the objective of which was to maintain a tightly knit family unit on an ongoing basis. When a son or daughter married, the next floor would be completed and when the new roof was laid, it too would have reinforced columns rising up to the next floor level for the grandchildren.

Obviously there must be a point after which it isn't economical to build higher but wherever we went from then on it was clear that this practice was widespread throughout Egypt.

As we sail by, the kids in the fields wave frantically trying to capture our attention. When they do, they break up in peals of laughter. If they can get us to wave at them they consider it a victory.

It is truly one of the most peaceful relaxing experiences I've ever had. (Joyce folded her tent early and went to bed for a power nap!)

One of the things that seem to go with a trip to this part of the world is the profusion of peddlers of every description from old men to small children selling all kinds of souvenirs, fake artifacts and touristy hats and clothes. They are everywhere. It is like running the gauntlet, when you emerge from one of the major tourist areas. The rule is if you take it in your hand to examine it, you've bought it. Sometimes they will follow a tour bus from one destination to another, even to the point of racing on ahead of you so that when you arrive at the next destination the same guy is waiting for you with the same stuff you said no to at the last stop.

A Nile cruise offers a new wrinkle. We had no sooner dropped anchor at the Esna lock when the ship was surrounded by about 18 small boats each with 2 or 3 young travelling salesmen peddling their wares. They try everything. If you happen to be on deck they will throw an article up at you in the hope that local custom — if you touch you've bought it — will translate into a sale. On this ship the dining room is on the lower level. These clever entrepreneurs row their small boats alongside the dining room windows and begin showing everything from dresses to scarves through the windows. It was extremely entertaining.

When we got off the ship we were given an identity card which had to be presented on return. That way they know how many people got off and if they all returned.

Out of the 48 people on our tour, 8 were honeymooners. Trafalgar makes a big deal out of it, and along with a lot of good natured kidding, the kitchen staff presented them with a beautiful honeymoon cake accompanied by a wild Upper Nile dance which they all had to participate in, which would certainly have lubricated their joints — if they still had them at the end of all the gyrations.

Of the four couples, one was a golden age pairing. Both, after 6 days together, had the radiant glow of love written all over them. Another pair were middle aged, both doctors, who combined for a ready made family of 6 children. A third couple, the man an Australian and the woman from New Delhi, were having a great time even though one suitcase had been stolen and the second badly damaged by the airline. While we were at Karnak they pranced around the Scarab Statue the required 7 times in order to be blessed with fertility. The fourth couple were middle aged from California.

It was a happy occasion for all of us.

The cabin steward who looked after our room was very creative. Each night when he turned down our beds, we returned to our room to find clever artistic creations done with our bath towels carefully placed on our bed. The first night they were formed in the shape of a swan, the second they were in the shape of a sphinx.

The ship was moored, along with about 5 others, at the downstream side of the Esna lock. It is quite an elaborate system of engineering. It is closed for a week or two each year for maintenance so travel plans should be made which allow you to avoid this period. We entered the lock around 4 a.m.

With all of the power systems normally used to bring the ship through, winches, reverse, side thrusters etc., it is a noisy process with the result that it would be hard to sleep through it. Convinced that — if you can't beat them join them — was a more practical approach, I got out of bed and watched some of the process from our large cabin window. The general impression I got was positive. The surrounding buildings looked fairly new and well maintained. Delivery trucks were clipping along beside us on a parallel service road. I was thinking to myself that this area is quite progressive when along comes a donkey pulling a load of produce! I hope he got extra rations for being on the night shift.

By 5 a.m. we had cleared the locks and were on our way again, destined for Edfu and Kom Ombo.

The Nile appears to be wider upstream of Esna. Probably because the flow is partly restricted because of the lock. There were quite a few small fishing boats out early. Mostly perch is caught but I don't think I'd eat it. The shoreline continued to look lush but the impression is that the area was newer. About a mile in from the shore we passed a fairly new 3 building mid rise apartment complex. There was quite a bit of floating vegetation flowing along with the current.

One of the tour members who happened to be an avid boats man commented on the absence of navigational buoys. On our way upstream yesterday there were numerous cruise ships on the river in each direction. When they pass they kick up a storm with their musical horns. Not just one blast but almost a song, which is then outdone by the responding ship. It is much like the sound of Cairo traffic where the drivers' first instinct is to sound their horn rather than hit their brakes with the not surprising cacophonous result. Our tour member boats man didn't approve. "Once is enough," he commented dryly.

Edfu! What a cultural shock as we rounded the corner to the main street and bazaar. Not the slightest hint of anything western — except for bottled water. Transportation from the ship to the Temple of Horus was by horse and carriage. But not before we had to walk the gang plank — literally! In order to get on land we had to handle a makeshift disembarking plank with no handrails on either side and a 15 foot drop for the unsteady. Some elderly women balked at it.

Then, total immersion. People, animals, milling around or competing for space with small trucks. A street cleaner's paradise. Droppings everywhere. Then into the Temple of Horus, largely intact, but with stone carvings distinct from what we had seen yesterday. For the first time the symbol of Moses, the two ended crook, one to hook the ears of sheep or goats and the other to break the neck of cobras. The Temple of Horus is not a tomb. It is a place of worship — Horus the falcon. Part of its survival may be due to its time of construction — between 300 and 57 B.C. The only significant damage was done by the Romans.

Back on the ship we ran into a problem with Joyce's new suitcase. The combination lock would not open and we had to force it. It was the first time it had ever been used. (Later when we got home we were shown a simple way to discover any combination!)

I had complimented our cabin steward on his creative talents with our towels. On our return from Kom Ombo we discovered that he had a hilarious sense of humour. This time he had created a scarecrow. He had stuffed Joyce's towel inside her windbreaker, put her sun visor and sun glasses on the fake head made from the towel and left it sitting up in bed. We all had a good laugh including the steward. Later he helped me wind the desert headdress around my head in preparation for the Egyptian party. Joyce thought that I looked as though I had just had a brain operation. The party proved to be a lot of fun.

They are a friendly, fun loving people and we are appreciating them more and more. They are exuberant and remind me very much of the happy go lucky West Indians we have met.

When we say we are Canadians they respond with "Oh, Canada Dry!"

During the tour we have gotten to know Doug and Margaret Shultis quite well. At the party last night we found out that we are closer to them than we thought. Doug is the brother of Kay Cloutier who is married to Remi, with whom Joyce and I worked for many years. Kay and Remi also live at Habitat 67 and were there during the 8 years we lived there. What a small world.

Our destination today was Aswan, where the giant dam constructed by the Russians is located. It has served two purposes. Flood control, which has changed forever what is and isn't possible in the downstream agricultural valley, and hydro power generation, which has made possible the development of heavy industries in the area. This has resulted in major environmental adjustments, some clearly negative, but on balance it is felt that the benefits outweigh the disadvantages. There was an opportunity to take a one day side trip farther south to Abu Simbal to see the enormous statues of Ramses II, but the cost was excessive, so we found other avenues to explore. At Aswan we were not far from the Sudan, as the crow flies only about 100 miles. Looking out our cabin window to the west bank, the terrain becomes less lush and more desert. The sand now comes within 100 yards of the Nile. It is abruptly hilly as you move away from the river. A fairly large bridge was under construction connecting to what appears to be a major highway on the west side. On the west shore, there is much less emphasis on agriculture. Large power transmission lines were visible which no doubt are a direct result of Aswan.

The desert look on the west is probably due to the fact that the ground is too high to have ever been flooded. The east shore on the other hand is flatter, easier to irrigate, and this is where the agricultural concentration was. While waiting for Joyce to get dressed for breakfast I went up on the top deck. From there I was able to see over the first ridge of sandstone to the next ridge. It is certainly the Sahara.

The city of Aswan has 500,000 inhabitants. Much of it is modern and prosperous. This is related to its appeal as a resort destination as well as the development of industry made possible by the Aswan dam which is 600 feet high! There is a very fine school of hotel administration located here. Kitchener's villa is now the beautiful botanical gardens.

We toured the harbour in a felucca named Titanic. It was a relaxing fun filled experience. We passed the mausoleum of the Aga Khan, and Elephantine Island, so named because of interesting rock formations at river's edge which resemble elephants. This was near the former home of Kitchener.

We drove up to the unfinished obelisk, a monstrous slab of granite rock weighing 1168 tons which is 35 metres long. The obelisk was commissioned by Hatshepsut who wanted to have the largest obelisk in the world as a personal memorial. Unfortunately the rock cracked in two when it was about 75% completed and was abandoned in place.

We then went to the high dam and Lake Nasser. This is a mammoth piece of engineering which has resulted in major environmental ramifications. No longer is the precious silt being deposited downstream during the floods. The bright side of this is a project aimed for completion in about 20 years which will permit recovery of the silt above the dam and a tripling of arable land in Egypt. There is a huge modernistic symbol of the high dam designed in the image of the lotus flower.

We visited Ani Papyrus, a dealer in high quality papyrus art, where we saw a demonstration of how papyrus is made into a parchment like paper. We bought two hand painted papyrus paintings which we will hang at home.

In the afternoon we went out on Lake Nasser to see the Temple of Philae dedicated to the goddess Isis. As the high damn filled, Philae was threatened with inundation and as a UNESCO project the temple was moved to higher ground about one half mile away. The 200 B.C. temple shows Greco Roman influence and later the cross of the crusaders has been cut into the entry area on each side. The wall drawings are in high relief and depict in greater detail those events which had illustrated the cultural advancement made to that point.

The surrounding landscape and islands created by the flooding were extremely eerie in the sense that hundreds of huge boulders are scattered across the top almost as though each one had been deliberately placed in its position. There was evidence of a high water mark some 30 feet above the current water level.

We were now getting close to winding up the cruise part of the tour. Tomorrow we visit a Nubian village and in the afternoon return to Cairo for 2 days. Among other things, we will do another tour of the museum, this time guided by Ash, and make a trip out to Giza to check out the pyramids and Sphinx.

Some observations about the Egyptian people we have encountered on this trip. Ash, our principal guide and overall leader of the tour, is an exceptional young man, an M.A. in Egyptology and working towards his Ph.D He had an extraordinary memory, an inexhaustible well of facts, a great sense of humour, and he obviously loves what he does. He has made a huge difference in making this trip truly enjoyable.

Mahmoud, our cabin steward on the ship was efficient, friendly, unbelievably creative and genuinely interested in making our trip enjoyable. His sense of humour and playful creations each night with our fresh supply of towels added greatly to our pleasure.

In general the officials in the streets and major archaeological sites have been courteous and relaxed in their dealings with us. The extensive security everywhere is comforting.

The street merchants will go to any length to make a sale. But they were not as aggressive as some we have encountered elsewhere.

The children, especially those we saw at the various temples on field trips with their class mates, are healthy, clean, very well dressed, and fun loving. Even the urchins in homemade boats in the Aswan Harbour had a sense of humour, singing "Row, Row, Row Your Boat" as they came alongside to beg.

The country is on the right track. It has the human resources and the interest of the western world to bring it around again to greatness. There is no question that there are areas of poverty and squalor. But there is a spirit of equality and the facilities to educate those who have the desire to make it. Aswan seems to be a very progressive upbeat city with a great future. There is evidence of modern efficient techniques.

I had a good feeling about all of it.

We set out after breakfast to see the Nubian Village near the dam on the other side of the river. About 10 of us had decided to do this side trip so we did so in a small power boat with a fixed roof. The unexpected bonus was that we toured the nature reserve in and amongst the dozens of small islands. This was originally the sight of the first cataract.

We had wonderful close up views of wild birds. Herons, egrets, kingfishers and dozens of others. We saw water buffalo close up, and on the shore, teams of men using what looked like fish nets on a huge racquet like frame to trap birds in flight. I watched them for a few minutes. Three men with nets hide behind large rocks along the shore, along with a fourth man who is the spotter who alerts the netters to an oncoming flight by the shore at low level. At the key moment they raise the nets suddenly and the birds are trapped. On one pass I saw 15 or 20 birds taken.

The Nubian Village is about a mile upstream from the Ali Khan Mausoleum. We beached the boat and headed up to visit one of the houses. It is basically a mud brick structure with sand floors. The sitting room is walled 3 sides with an arched roof. We were served mint tea while the ladies considered purchasing trinkets. The open play area has a small fish tank open on top in which 4 or 5 baby crocodiles are kept as pets. Our guide picked them up and Joyce reluctantly patted them while I took their picture.

Then the ladies went on a camel ride. It was hilarious. Two of the girls from Atlanta got on a camel which immediately began to head for a cliff and the Nile. They really panicked, but

Baby Crocodiles

Feluccas on the Nile

just in time the camel tender steered it back on track. There was a mini caravan heading downstream to the huge sand hill just south of the mausoleum. I was cruising along in the boat.

When we docked the small craft back near our ship we noticed a felucca all dressed up with bright red floral chaise lounges each with a woman lounging in it. The dock workers tending it said that the group was heading out for a two night sleep over on the Nile. This would have been much like the trip our friend Kathy took where they also prepared meals on board. Unfortunately the boats are not equipped with plumbing. So.....

The river cruise ships are becoming so common that multiple stack docking has become a necessity. If one of the boats on the inside has to get going, all the rest must move out of the way. It ends up looking like taxis at an airport jostling for space.

There are always many interesting and diverse groups of people on a tour such as this one. Two teachers from Castlegar, B.C. were in the first phase of a year long sabbatical which will take them completely around the world — even to Antarctica.

An Australian couple currently living in Thailand while he is consulting on an industrial chemical complex. A retired US Navy commander who had enlisted late in WW2, weighing in at 125 pounds but at the top of his class in physical fitness.

Four lovely black girls from Atlanta, who kept the cash registers humming every time we passed a shop! Two of them were particularly attractive. When we visited the Nubian Village we came face to face with a Nubian lady equally beautiful who was a look alike for one of the girls. The two of them stared at each other for a brief moment. Then the Nubian lady excitedly broke into a smile gesturing excitedly back and forth, as if to say, my God maybe somewhere from long ago we may be related. It would be interesting to see what a DNA test would reveal. It must have been an emotional moment for the American. Could this possibly have been the source of her ancestry?

Another of the girls was also very interesting. Back in America she was a 911 operator. Although she was very pretty, she was also quite overweight. During one of the fun nights, a crew member who was also part of the entertainment, coaxed her out onto the dance floor to demonstrate some exotic new dance step. She slipped right into the groove with it and seemed to sense the movement immediately. She was fascinating to watch and was quite seductive in a very low key way.

At Cairo, we had to take an early wake up call in order to get to the pyramids as soon as they open. The number of people allowed in is limited, to reduce the humidity level inside the pyramid. Our leader wanted to be first at the gate. On our flight from Aswan yesterday we were fortunate to have been sitting on the west side flying in, so we caught a glimpse of the pyramids and Sphinx from the air. Even from 5000 feet they look pretty big.

As planned, we tore out to Giza, got there at 8 a.m., the targeted time, only to find about 4 busloads ahead of us. For those who wanted to actually enter Cheops, this was cutting it fine. However we did manage to get tickets to enter and after a brief explanation by Ash climbed in.

It is a claustrophobic, exhausting experience. Cheops is about 450 feet high and the Kings's Tomb is about half way up. The climb is at an angle of 30 degrees, much of it in a narrow tunnel about three and a half feet high. As a consequence several of us gave a good workout to thigh and buttock muscles that hadn't been in the game for years.

After about 75 feet Joyce packed it in. I was determined, having gotten that far, to make it to the King's Tomb. It has been a long time since I expended so much effort. The tunnel has little or no ventilation so the oxygen supply wasn't the best. I found myself gasping for wind and stopped a couple of times to reduce the stress. When I finally got there both our friends, Doug and Margaret, were at the top gasping for air — and they swim every day of their lives!

Reaching the tomb proved to be a bit of an anticlimax. The only article in it was a stone sarcophagus. There were no etchings on the walls to extol his virtues and no painted areas. We took a few photos and then headed down which was almost as difficult as climbing up.

The size of Cheops was totally beyond anything I could have imagined. As high and larger than just about any building in our major cities at home.

We circled around behind Cheops to the pyramid of Khafre. Some also entered this one. I chose to shoot photos outside of it. The pyramids are positioned so that they lead to the west, the setting sun, symbol of death. Once again I took some wonderful shots with camels and people dwarfed by the pyramids. We then drove down the hill to the Sphinx, quite a bit smaller than I thought it would be, especially when viewed beside the pyramids, but nevertheless enormous by North American standards.

We next set out to Sakara where we viewed a rug making school and showroom. I was particularly taken with the pure silk carpets hand woven from silk cocoons that are grown in the Nile delta.

We then visited the stepped pyramid at Sakara, erected about 2800 years B.C. It was the first of the large pyramids, and is considerably cruder than those at Giza.

Finally we stopped at Memphis to see a giant statue of Ramses II which had fallen during an earthquake. It weighed over 700 tons. He must have had quite an ego. We also fed the tiny dogs until they began fighting over the pickings. We returned to Cairo to prepare for tomorrow's departure.

Cairo and its environs are distressingly dirty. There is absolutely no concept of putting garbage in a designated place. They just dump it anywhere. There is virtually a complete absence of refuse containers even at the historic sites. The ditches are littered with plastic water bottles, construction rubble and anything that falls in between.

It is absolutely mystifying to look down on the rooftops of otherwise decent buildings. Roofs seem to be a depositary for old bricks, cement blocks, steel bars, boards and anything else they might pile there. At first we thought that the collection of debris seen on most of the roofs in a given area might have been a leftover from a previous war. It certainly looks like it.

It has only been in the last few days that we have begun to hear the infamous word "baksheesh". Once at Philae where a beggar had staked his claim to one part of the temple and demanded money from you if you photographed the temple.

In Khan el Khalili, the Cairo bazaar, young boys bug you until you give in. Pull out a wallet to pay for a purchase and it will draw them like flies. Zigging and zagging in the narrow dark lanes of the bazaar, black cats darting across your path, then hearing the word "baksheesh" on top of it can be unnerving. I suppose we need to see this side of life to appreciate our own. But it is a far cry from the luxurious isolation of a Nile cruise, where you rarely see it, except when you get off the beaten path.

Early on in our marriage Joyce and I took a trip to St. Lucia, one of the lesser known islands about 50 miles from Guadaloupe in the Carribean. It is quite primitive.

It originally did have some strategic significance which the French saw fit to recognize with fortifications near Soufrière.

The dormant volcano above the town still provides a source of hot springs, and was destined to have an impact on our stay.

The major landmarks on the island are of course the two tetons which rise abruptly on either side of a lovely bay to a height of 1800 ft.

There is a spectacular view from the hill looking down between the tetons. When we were there some enterprising developer had constructed condominiums which looked much like early native construction with a completely open side facing the bay.

The unit we looked at was owned by a couple from New York City. The gentleman always kept a pair of binoculars handy. At least once a week the large pleasure craft "Vendredi 13" would anchor in the bay with a full load of nude sunbathers from the Club Med.

Farther up the hill at the centre were the remains of Mt. Soufrière and the dormant volcanic crater. At one time there must have been a huge volcanic explosion which blew away the side of the mountain.

Although it is dormant, it still causes the surface water in the shallow crater to bubble. In fact it is possible to boil an egg in it.

Because it is a tourist site there are young boys around who beg very aggressively. Joyce was standing at the edge of the crater with her back to it when these kids began pressing for charity.

She was looking in her purse for change as they came closer and closer, causing her to back up. One step too many unfortunately, because she fell into the shallow volcanic crater, luckily landing on rock and not in the hot water.

She was not injured, but certainly shaken up. I handed the kids some money and told them to back off. How many people do you suppose have fallen into a volcanic crater and lived to talk about it. Joyce had survived another amazing experience.

The day of departure was as usual hectic. Because we were leaving for Tel Aviv that afternoon we had to have our baggage outside of our rooms by 7 a.m.

We loaded up at breakfast to carry us through to early afternoon. Then we headed out to the Sultan Hassan Mosque, a beautiful structure with elaborate decoration on the carved dome. Then on to the Mosque of Mohammed Ali (the Alabaster Mosque). Behind it, there is a fabulous view of Cairo including, in the distance, the pyramids.

Our final stop was a guided tour of the Cairo Museum. Although we had been through it on our own a week earlier Ash, our scholarly guide, selected a number of special exhibits, for which he gave an in depth explanation, and put a whole new perspective on the significance of each. He is preparing for his doctorate on Egyptology. He will concentrate on the everyday life of the early Egyptian people. He has been an outstanding guide who has protected our interests and on occasion driven us a bit in order to ensure that we see and appreciate the really important sites. At the same time he has managed to keep a watchful eye on the welfare of each, especially one or two of the older participants. He has been a very good shepherd!

When the tour ended, we exchanged good wishes with each other, especially with those whom we had come to know quite well, and had in fact bonded with. After a week together, a group such as this becomes "our" group, in effect a team for which we feel pride, affection and genuine interest. The Indian honeymooners now heading off for the other side of the world to begin life together. The Australian couple who have a daughter facing major surgery with whom they have had difficulty in making telephone contact. Their concern became shared by all of us.

In the final analysis we were now down to eight people heading off to Israel, everyone else scattering off to distant places.

Our final "internal" flight via Air Sinai, a subsidiary of Egypt Air, was scheduled out of Cairo at 6:40 p.m. When we reached the airport it was shown as delayed to 7:30 p.m.

The whole process of leaving Egypt was confusing. From seat selection to tagging baggage there is no logic to it. The eight suitcases were tagged in succession and the bags put on the conveyer. The clerk simply stuck the receipts on his free arm one on top of the other and then handed them all to one of the passengers. I would have hated to be faced with a problem of missing baggage. The master departure electronic sign showed us out at 7:30 through gate 9. The electronic sign at gate 9 showed another flight going to Beirut at the same time. We sat outside of gate 9 having a coffee and became a bit puzzled why nothing about our flight was indicated.

I walked back to the information stand just in time to hear a boarding announcement for our flight through gate 9. I shot back to our table. The others hadn't even heard it. We moved immediately into the boarding line all mixed in with Beirut passengers. "Is this Tel Aviv?" I asked. The agent said "yes." All of us, passengers for Tel Aviv and Beirut milling around in the same departure area. It didn't instill much confidence.

There were two buses waiting to take us out to the plane. Most of us got on the first one, but two of our members boarded the second one. We would hear later of an incident on the second involving a woman being dragged off the second bus screaming hysterically. Something definitely wasn't quite right.

Our bus got to the plane first, but it stopped on the opposite side from the passenger entry. Our bags were laid out on the ground and we were asked to identify them. When I did, one of the baggage handlers immediately asked me for tips — bloody baksheesh! On an airport tarmac in the dark! I had no more Egyptian money and told him so. He threw my bags carelessly onto a cart and we walked behind the tail of the plane to the side where we could board. There was one employee waving us on. Pretty loose security in my opinion.

The boarding passes we were given were a complete jumble. Husbands in one row, wives somewhere else. Fifteen minutes later we had that sorted out. We could see some kind of heated discussion going on about 10 rows ahead between 4 men. That got resolved.

The flight was finally underway and took about 45 minutes to get within descent range. We began our approach, then levelled off and started circling. One of the crew came walking hurriedly down the aisle muttering something about a problem. Three rows behind us they began frantically pulling up the carpet looking for something. Still no calming announcement from the cabin. The crew member kept pulling up carpet and in frustration blurted out an expletive.

Joyce was beginning to panic (as was everyone else). Finally he went running (not walking) back to the cabin and after another circle we began our descent. There was an eerie silence among the passengers. I'm sure that each of us had the recent experience out of New York on our mind.

A few minutes later the plane touched down and the entire group of passengers let out a cheer. And I'm sure — a few thankful prayers. It was a very unnerving experience.

When we collected our luggage it was covered in mud. I don't know what on earth they managed to do to it.

Joyce on a camel

A point of law

Chapter Thirty-four

Israel

One way or another we had made it to Israel. Tel Aviv is a clean, colourful airport. We piled everything into the transport and headed off to Jerusalem. The highways were well marked and clearly lit. Much like we would expect in North America. We arrived at the Dan Panorama hotel and immediately sensed that we were in an organized, competent environment. No confusion. No shouting. Very little horn honking. And above all squeaky clean!

We climbed into bed exhausted and thankful that we had come through the Egyptian experience, which was a wonderful one, albeit somewhat hairy in places. I would certainly recommend it as something that makes a memorable adventure to be tried at least once.

With all the early rising for early morning deadlines Joyce managed to stab herself in the ear lobe trying in a rush to put her earrings in and missing. It became infected. We had brought some cipro antibiotics for diarrhea caused by bacteria so she took a few of these which didn't help.

She felt she should see a doctor in Jerusalem which we did in the morning.

Dr. Lipman! What a fascinating character. Born in Argentina, he had lived briefly in Buffalo, N.Y. and studied and settled in Israel.

He has a craggy face reminiscent of Abraham Lincoln. Street artists love to draw him and his office is filled with caricatures done of him all over Europe. He himself is a talented artist who learned to create silver jewelled necklaces as occupational therapy while he was in a hospital years ago. He has sold them successfully through jewelry stores. He examined Joyce, gave his opinion and prescribed antibiotics.

He still makes house calls, and is happy to give you his paging number to call in the middle of the night if you need it. He is certainly of the old school.

Joyce's parents were also of the old school and believed in traditional values. In late spring of 1976 Joyce and I had decided that we would marry. Up to that point I had not met her parents who were living in Westmount.

We thought it would be fun for me to ask their permission to marry Joyce — even though she was well over twenty-one at the time.

Her father was an honours graduate in engineering and had been an outstanding athlete in his youth, winning dozens of medals in track and field, and having been a member of Toronto Varsity's 1920 Grey Cup team.

Her mother was a lovely, vivacious woman, daughter of a physician in Quebec City and on her mother's side from a prominent Quebec family.

Although highly intelligent, Joyce's father was beginning to become a bit forgetful. Her mother on the other hand was sharp until the day she died some years later.

We went through the normal formalities of introduction and getting to know one another, with the usual cup of coffee and sweets.

After about an hour I made the announcement and popped the question. Neither of them said a word.

We continued talking socially for another hour or so until it was time to leave. At the door I mischievously said "You didn't answer my question."

Joyce's mother looked at me quizzically and said "what was the question." At which point her father jumped in quickly with a resounding yes!!

We all had a chuckle and went on our way.

After freshening up we set out again with the objective of doing the Ben Yehuda Walking Mall. En route along King George St. we bumped into the couple from South Africa who were in the seats in front of us on the Air Sinai flight last night. We commiserated together thankful that we were lucky enough to be walking the street.

The Ben Yehuda Walking Mall is a fun street appealing to tourists and others. We found a tiny vegetarian restaurant at No. 10 Ben Yehuda. The food was very good. We continued down the street to Yafo Street and turned down into the Solomon/Rivlin Walking Mall. There were several excellent art shops which we explored.

Then we got adventurous and took a different route back to the hotel via Schlomtzion and King David Roads turning right at Karen Havesod and the hotel — overall, not too difficult and a good workout for those who had been spending too much time sitting.

After a brief orientation meeting with Trafalgar we headed out to Luigi's Restaurant on Yoel Salomon Mall, with Doug and Margaret. It is a very popular restaurant recommended to us by several people. It is located in a trendy section along with many restaurants and boutiques. The constant parade of humanity is fascinating to watch. Most of them are young, good looking kids, obviously from well to do families. You get the feeling that this could be any resort town in California. It is very upbeat, lots of lights, lots of life. Good food amid prosperity. What we have seen of the city so far has made a very positive impression.

At the end of the Nile cruise when we returned to our hotel in Cairo, I had the sensation that the 30 storey building was rocking slightly. I noticed it in bed, when I was standing, and also when sitting. The building is within a 100 yards of the river and probably built on the old flood plain.

I reasoned that over hundreds of thousands of years the build up of silt deposits during the annual floods must have been substantial and even with deep pile foundations, vibrations caused by heavy traffic close by would radiate through the silt which creates a jelly effect.

One tour member suggested that it was more likely to be a function of the middle ear sending the wrong signals to the body. 6 flights, 4 days on a cruise ship, numerous bus rides and sleep deprivation probably added to it.

Nevertheless, by the 3rd or 4th day I had several members of the tour absolutely convinced that the earth was indeed moving! When we got to Jerusalem which is built on solid rock the sensation persisted. So I reluctantly concluded that it was me and not the earth who had the problem.

Last night sitting at Luigi's for dinner I could still sense it and mentioned it at the table. Immediately Marg and Joyce said, "So do we!" The power of suggestion! It can play strange tricks on us.

My son Peter is a very good golfer who usually shoots in the low 80s. One of his best friends, Martin, used to drive Peter crazy on the golf course because he had a terrible slice. They were spending more time in the woods than on the fairway.

One day Peter made a decision. They would bring a video camera out with them the next time they played, capture Martin's swing on film and then sit down, replay it and analyse the problem, which they did.

The following weekend they returned to the links to see what effect it had had. Peter sliced on every shot!

We began our Israel tour with a visit to the Hadassah Medical Centre famous not only for its medical excellence but for the Chagall stained glass windows. It is set high on a hilltop with a huge view of the new part of West Jerusalem. A tremendous amount of reforestation (over 2 million trees) has been done on the neighbouring hills.

We followed this with a stop at Vad Yashim, the memorial to the 6 million victims of the Holocaust. The display analyses the development which took place in Nazi Germany in the 1930s leading up to the second world war. The documentation, which is excellent, includes newspaper stories and public notices from the era. As the story progresses, shocking photographs of the incredibly brutal treatment of the Jews vividly illustrate just how horrendous this sad period in western history really was.

The driveway leading to the memorial is lined with carob trees dedicated to those righteous persons who aided the desperate Jews, often at the risk of their own lives.

One cannot help but wonder what kind of reaction anyone viewing this shocking exhibit, might have, especially the younger Jews who see it. They are now 3 generations removed from it and in most cases never knew their ancestors who died in the Holocaust. I discussed this with our tour guide, Eiton, who reflected for a moment and then replied that it was a deeply personal issue for each individual, but that they needed to be told about it and reminded of it to truly understand its significance.

We moved on to the national museum to see the beautiful structure that houses the Dead Sea Scrolls, written and hidden in caves at Qumran by the Essenes almost 2000 years ago.

After a quick lunch at the museum we headed out to Bethlehem only four miles from Jerusalem. It is in territory now controlled by the Palestinians.

The Church of The Nativity which has a crypt under the altar showing the location of Jesus' birth was absolutely swamped with tourists. For the briefest of moments I stood before the silver star on what is believed to be the manger floor, trying to grasp the significance of where we were, before being caught up in the flow of humanity once more. It was very difficult to be reverent under the circumstances. Nevertheless, Joyce lit a candle for her niece, and said a prayer for her as well, at a side altar of the church.

Next to it is the Church of St. Catherine the Virgin which was undergoing frantic renovations in time for the millennium. There was also a great deal of construction going on in the immediate area, much of it financed by Belgium.

Bethlehem is also the home of Rachel's Tomb, a heavily guarded Jewish Memorial where it was found necessary to erect a wall to defend it and visitors against vandalism.

Not far from our hotel is the YMCA. It is a magnificent building which must have been a legacy from some very wealthy estate. Because today was the Sabbath, restaurants were closed, except for the YMCA and a very limited menu at the hotel. We thought we would try the "Y". When we looked in, it seemed fancy enough to rate with any French restaurant. However it was priced accordingly. We regret to confess that we could not have afforded to eat at the "Y". We turned around and ended up having a beer and a tuna sandwich at the hotel.

Friday night is of course the beginning of the Sabbath for Jews. There were several families with young children taking part in a special Sabbath dinner in one of the dining rooms. Many couples observing it were dressed in their finery. I happened to be sitting near the doorway to the dining room and within sight a very religious couple was standing before dinner reading Sabbath prayers and exchanging blessings. It was much like the Christian grace except that it was extended further by the blessings.

At the far end of the lobby a meeting room had been given over to Sabbath observances with many of the guests participating in prayers prior to dinner.

The following day was spent inside the old walled city. We visited the west wall, one of the oldest and holiest sites in Jerusalem. Several hundred of the devout were deeply involved in prayer. Our guide explained to me that the rocking motion that is commonly seen during Jewish prayers is a form of concentration which ties in with the rhythm of the prayers.

Non Jews are welcomed at the west wall. Christians include readings and psalms from the old Hebrew bible every Sunday. The wall itself is probably much the way it was 2000 years ago. I therefore had a compelling desire to pray at the west wall.

Because it was the Sabbath there were already many at prayer. I waited respectfully until there was an opening and then took a position and placed my hand on the wall. I gave thanks for being lucky enough to be there. I gave thanks for the love of Joyce my wonderful wife. For all the blessings that have been bestowed on us, my wonderful children, Vicky and Peter, grandchildren Julie, Philip and Sarah, and Frank and Sandy, my son and daughter-in-laws. I prayed for the blessing of the baby due to Sandy in December and for the recovery of Joyce's niece who is battling cancer. And I prayed for peace for all of the people in this part of the world, which seems to exist on a powder keg.

It was a moving emotional experience for me which I shall always remember.

Directly behind the wall is the Dome of the Rock and the El Aksa Mosque. Both exquisite examples of Moslem architecture.

Then on to the Via Dolorosa and the Church of the Holy Sepulchre positioned where the crucifixion of Christ occurred. We saw the pink granite stone on which the body of Jesus had lain.

During the time that we followed the stations and arrived at the Holy Sepulchre, there were literally hundreds, perhaps even thousands of tourists and pilgrims which made it extremely difficult to relate reverently to this holy place. Nevertheless we both placed our hand on the stone and said a brief prayer. Joyce then lit a candle and offered another prayer.

Further along in the old city we came to King David's Tomb and the site of the last Supper which is in the same building.

By then we had seen most of what was possible under the circumstances, so we headed for the kibbutz Rachel for lunch, one of the few places where it is possible to get a meal on the Sabbath. We ate in the very large cafeteria. While we were in line a large group of Africans from 15 different countries were in it with us. They were there to learn about agricultural techniques in an arid environment.

Finally we headed up to the Mount of Olives which offers a spectacular view of Jerusalem, the Dome of the Rock and the gold topped Russian Basilica. Some of our group tried their luck on a camel, which was quite hilarious.

It had been a big day. We got back to the hotel and locked the door. We hit the sheets early.

After a leisurely breakfast we walked up King George to Ben Yehuda. It isn't really much of a climb but the old legs were squeaking a bit. Marg had told us of a good store for tee shirts which we found and bought one with a little duck saying "shalom".

Jerusalem in the Souk

When we reached Zion Square at the bottom of Ben Yahuda we sat on a stone bench to watch the world go by. The Africans in fancy purple floor length kaftans. Modern young Israeli women strolling by in bare midriff outfits and nicely tanned tummies. A young moustached man passing by was stopped by two soldiers and had to produce his papers. A Ben & Jerry's ice cream truck drove up. We asked the driver if he had come all the way from Vermont — he said no.

We decided to move on to the old city entering through the Jaffa Gate. The souk was much less crowded as church was still not out. We stopped at a shop on the edge of the Armenian quarter where we bought tiny stone boxes with inlaid floral designs and with tiny lattice carved windows on all four sides.

We took a turn to the left and found ourselves in the middle of humongous pedestrian traffic on the Via Dolorosa. So jammed that we had no choice other than to go with the flow of traffic. At the first opportunity we ducked out a side lane and tried to make our way back to Jaffa Gate. One enterprising merchant in a tiny shop along the way had a hand-made sign hanging outside which advertised a blue light special 50% off. We asked him where the blue light was, he said "Upstairs!"

We exited from the Jaffa Gate and headed back towards Ben Yahuda. On the way we stopped in a gift shop on Rivlin where a CD of a really great Israeli singer caught my ear. His name is Schlomo Artzi.

By then we were ready to pack it in, so we took the route via King David to the hotel. We were meeting Marg and Doug at 6 p.m. for dinner. So we took a power nap in the interim.

Around 4 p.m. Joyce was beginning to feel a bit squeamish. She ordered room service of hot soup and dry rolls. It arrived within five minutes. Then a follow up came to ensure that everything was ok. Pretty good service I'd say. The relatively small order she had placed was accompanied by a pretty vase containing 3 pink roses. A very classy touch.

Later while waiting for Doug and Marg, I had a drink at the lobby bar. A very accomplished pianist was playing a grand piano nearby. Outside it was almost a full moon. I thought again to myself how lucky I was to be here experiencing all of this. Joyce stayed in our room and the three of us set out once more for Ben Yahuda. It is absolutely alive. Filled with bright lights and excellent street musicians. Outdoor sidewalk cafés everywhere and the smell of delicious foods permeating the air. Life and laughter. "Lochiem!"

The next day was a very long one, beginning with an earlier than normal wake up call. We then set out to do a major portion of Israel's eastern borders from Masadda to the Golan Heights with several stops in between.

When leaving Jerusalem we passed Maaleh Aduma a major Israeli settlement. Set high on a hill, the community is surrounded by desert. It is a classic example of what can be done with planning and engineering. It is literally a man-made oasis.

We continued on the highway which eventually leads to Amman, Jordan. In the distance to the north we could see the city of Jericho, the oldest city known to man, dating back 9000 years.

We turned south on the road which parallels the west side of the Dead Sea, stopping at Mipeh Shalem to allow those wanting to to experience floating in the Dead Sea, continuing southward past the Ein Gedi oasis, lush with date palms.

Our goal to the south was Massada. Totally beyond our expectations in terms of size and scope. Massada is positioned on the top of a mountain some 1400 feet up an almost vertical face. It is reached by a cable tram which carries 80 people to the top in two and a half minutes.

Once there you have an unbelievable view of the Dead Sea and the mountains of Jordan. It was the site of a siege by the Romans in the year 37 A.D. It is difficult to believe that 967 zealots actually lived on top of this mountain. It is even more difficult to understand how they survived. Where did they get the required water and food? The area is totally barren. The legend tells us that after a prolonged siege by 15,000 Romans the zealots committed suicide rather than live under the Romans as slaves.

It was one of the most memorable stops on our tour of Israel.

We then backtracked north, stopping briefly at Jericho, which shows little evidence of its age. The Palestinians have built a casino here which attracts Israeli gamblers, much to the chagrin of the Israeli government.

We had many kilometres still to cover so we pressed on to the Sea of Galilee. We stopped briefly at Yardenit where John the Baptist baptised Jesus. The Jordan River is a narrow creek about 50 feet wide at this point. An extensive facility for baptisms has been constructed here. While we were there several adults immersed themselves.

We circled around the east side of the sea. It was evening and the lights of Caesarea looked quite lovely from the opposite shore.

We continued climbing up near the Golan Heights finally reaching our destination and home for the next two days at Kibbutz Ayelet Hashabar. Within it is our hotel which offers comfortable rooms and a very good dining room. We would use this as our base for the next 2 days.

En route we passed 3 tractor trailers each carrying an Israeli armoured tank. Having listened to our guide's litany of all the wars fought since 1948, Joyce hoped we weren't about to see the next one!

There has been a serious drought in the region and as a result, the Sea of Galilee was well below its normal level. Below Galilee, the River Jordan was hardly discernable. They are desperately in need of a major rain. Looking at the erosion on the hillsides of the Dead Sea, when a rain does come it must come in spades. There were many examples of dry creeks running to the sea.

The next day our first stop was at Tzat where we visited a typical Sephardic Synagogue which was located in the old Jewish quarter. Nearby was the Judith Art Gallery where we saw more of the work of Sholom Moscovitch. This is the artist whose work we bought at the Hadassah Hospital. He signs "Sholom of Safed".

Our tour director talked about the history of the Israeli kibbutz. At one time the kibbutz population accounted for 40% of the Jews in Israel. Today it is 3%. Some 500,000 have emigrated to America. The typical Jewish family has 2.9 children. The typical Arab family has 5-6 children. So there is a growing demographic problem.

While we were at Tzat I got into a conversation with Debbie, wife of Pastor Mike White from Florida. She told me that about 6 weeks prior to leaving on this trip their pure bred cocker spaniel had given birth to 6 puppies. After they were weaned the pups were given away to neighbours.

The mother dog wasn't about to accept this, so she calmly went out and brought them back home one by one, with the exception of one which hasn't shown up yet. Strong is the maternal instinct!

The pastor has also talked to the people of his church by phone from Jerusalem describing experiences. He is now being called by parish members every day offering him good wishes.

We then drove to Akko (Acre) and saw the remarkable Roman fort and crusader ruins which are in excellent condition. Akko was at one time the leading port. The Source, Michener's book about an archeological dig, was based on a nearby tell, the Tell Makor, about a mile inland.

We moved on to Megiddo which existed for 6000 years. It was conquered by Egypt's Thutmosis III in 1479 B.C. It is where the apocalypse (armageddon) is predicted to happen in The Book of Revelations. It is directly on the Via Maré, the road used by the Romans to enter this part of Israel. The Tell is about 80 feet high. Once inside it we were able to enter a steep passage down about 70 -80 feet which led us to a secret water supply inside the fort.

From the top we could see across the valley to Nazareth — about 5-6 miles away — which we would visit the following day.

Our kibbutz was well north and only 15 - 20 miles from the Golan Heights. We headed for them, first crossing the Jordan river, the major source of water for most of Israel. Incredibly, at that point the river is no more than 25 -30 feet across. It continues to astound me how the country can survive from this source of water. While the river is small, the surrounding terrain slopes steeply to the river bed. As a result, when the rains do come, the river must swell enormously creating a flood plain on its way.

The Golan Heights are just a few miles from the river. Vehicles are required to stick to the road as every field surrounding the road is mined, with warnings clearly posted.

We arrived at a vantage point from which we could look back to the Jordan Valley in one direction, see the hills of Lebanon about 10 miles to the north west and Mount Herman to the north which is right on the Syrian border. The lookout is placed on what had been an artillery position for the Syrians. The hill is dotted with bunkers and surrounded by mine fields. I took a photo of the view to Lebanon which would be of interest to Sandy and her family. I also picked up a small stone from Golan for Vicky's collection.

We then moved on to Capernaum where Jesus performed many of his miracles. There are the ruins of a 4th century synagogue and a modernistic church erected so that it is literally suspended over the ruins of an early church which is clearly visible from the outside. It is called St. Peter's House. The mature flowering bougainvillea shrubbery leading up to it was in full bloom and was spectacular.

Not far away was the Mount of the Beatitudes set a bit farther up where the Sermon on the Mount took place. There are several outdoor chapels on the grounds, one of which we used to hear a reading of the Beatitudes as well as its counterpart in the old testament in Deuteronomy. Our tour leader stressed the similarity in philosophy between the Judaic reading and the Christian reading, expressed in the two scriptures.

It was a beautiful setting in which to hear a reading from the scriptures and I thought to myself how much it added to our memories of the place and moment. I wished we had done more of it as we visited each historic site. It would have enabled us to instill a sense of being there when we heard them read once more in our own church.

We then took a boat ride in a wooden vessel very similar to the "Jesus" boat of old. We sailed for about 30 minutes to Tiberius on the western shore of Galilee. It is now a resort town with summer hotels dotting the hills leading down to the sea.

Tiberius also is home to Caprice Diamonds where we were shown how the stones were polished and set. This has become a major source of revenue for Israel.

In Nazareth where Jesus spent a great deal of his life, we got to see the Church of the Annunciation erected where the angel Gabriel first told Mary the good news. This has been the subject of much controversy ever since the Muslims were granted permission to erect a mosque directly in front of the church. To protest, the church has declared that all Christian sites in Israel will shut down 2 days a week until this issue is resolved. We had to reschedule our tour to work around this shutdown.

The church itself is very modern in design, but contrary to what we had been led to believe, it is not cold. Rather the contrary. The huge murals which line the outer walls and which were contributed by Christians of many different countries are quite beautiful. This huge church has also been constructed directly over the early Christian foundations which are visible under the main floor of the church. This was one of the few places where it was possible to quietly meditate and get some sense of the huge religious significance of this holy site.

It was getting quite late as we headed for Haifa, but once there the view from Mount Carmel is lovely, especially at night. We stopped at the lookout directly above the Bahai Temple and the Persian Gardens. We could see for miles.

Finally we arrived at our hotel in Tel Aviv about 7:30 p.m. Our tour was over and we began preparing for our return flight home Friday morning.

Some observations about Israel. Being here, where so much of modern religious philosophy started, I am more aware of the roots that Christians and Jews share. One cannot help but admire the determination and courage, and indeed the enormous human sacrifice that went into the development and realization that is Israel today. They are surrounded by forces in the Arab world which have never accepted the creation of the State of Israel by the United Nations following World War II and the Holocaust. It is equally understandable that the Arab people who existed prior to the partition of Palestine would harbour resentment against what some might consider an arbitrary decision by a world organization which had no direct involvement in the lands. There had of course always been a strategic involvement in the Middle East by England and France for years, so that one way or the other the Arab people have never been masters of their own destiny. That began to change in the early 70s after OPEC was formed.

Whereas in Egypt "baksheesh" is a way of life for many and extends even to those working, we did not run into this at all in Israel, particularly in the kibbutzes.

There is so much of major historical significance that one cannot possibly take it all in on a short trip. New discoveries are happening all the time. At home in North America we get excited if we come across ruins 200-300 years old. Here we were looking at discoveries thousands of years old.

I have always been fascinated with old things especially artifacts which have survived at home in the face of progress or ignorance of their value. At the Kibbutz Ayelet Hashabar there is a very high quality gift shop. The shop is an authorized dealer in authentic artifacts offered on behalf of the Israeli Government Department of Antiquities. Each item is sold with a certificate of authenticity.

In the sealed display I was looking at small items of pottery that dated back 3500-5000 years! Talk about survival.

Security is everywhere, both in the cities and in the countryside, more so as one nears the border to the north. I did not at any time feel threatened. We were able to completely relax at dinner among the numerous sidewalk cafés. During the entire trip both in Israel and Egypt we were blessed with excellent weather. Only on the last day when our tour was virtually over did we receive some badly needed rain.

For Joyce who had hitchhiked through the Middle East forty years ago, many of the tiny towns of that time were now unrecognizable because there had been so much development.

It becomes a game to beat the other tour buses to the sites, but even if you do, it isn't for long, and the sacred places which are best seen and felt in quiet meditation, are often difficult to appreciate, with literally hundreds of tourists and pilgrims competing for space.

After breakfast we met Marg and Doug and began a walk of about 3 miles over to Jaffa. The sidewalk paths along the beach are wide and attractively laid with pebble mosaic in geometric patterns. There was a strong wind from the west and 3 metre surf rolling in the full length of the beach. Although there were signs posted all along, prohibiting swimming, we did see several young men surfing. It took us about an hour to reach Jaffa. When we got there we walked up the slope to St. Peter's Church. There were several Israeli school children there on a field trip. We got into a very animated conversation with them which was a lot of fun.

There is a sizeable flea market in old Jaffa with a wide variety of merchants. Joyce found a very nice hammered copper pot which she will use as a planter back home. We had originally intended to take a taxi back but by the time we found an appealing restaurant we were three quarters of the way back to the hotel, so we simply walked it.

On our last night in Tel Aviv we and the Shultis' had dinner together in a small seaside restaurant near the hotel. One of the benefits of being on this kind of adventure is making new friends whose interests, sense of humour and background is similar to your own. We thoroughly enjoyed their company and will see more of them in the future. We exchanged addresses and phone numbers and it was only at that moment that I realized we had been spelling their name incorrectly for 3 weeks. Joyce recounted a favourite example used by law students regarding names. In a petition to the court a woman by the name of Ruth Lipshitz decided she did not like her name, so she changed it to Mary Lipshitz!

Then, we all split up and prepared for that early morning (3:30 a.m.) wake up call that signals to us that it is time to get moving. A quick room service breakfast, then off to the airport.

I have never, in all my travels seen security to equal it. We must have gone through four or five electronic gates. Every individual had his/her baggage examined in detail. We were all questioned inside out, and then finally admitted into the departure area. What a contrast with Cairo!

By the time we had completed 5 hours to London, 8 hours to Toronto, and a short haul to Ottawa, including the waiting time for connections, we were in transit for 26 hours. Both of us were basket cases.

Home on the pond never looked or felt better.

Is it really fresh?

Chapter Thirty-five

The Pond

I remember the first time I dated her. She was tall and shapely and very long limbed. She walked with a confident stride and a gentle sway. In a sense there was a touch of the awkwardness and innocence of a child which added immensely to her appeal. She was wide eyed and very believable and when she spoke to me it was in truth, with no attempt to hide her lovely eyes or to disguise her feelings.

Her laugh came from deep down within her and was contagious. She was a joy to be with and and made friends easily. Someone once said to me — everybody loves her. Much later I thought to myself, so do I! Yes, she was all of those things and it was a gift.

She was also a paradox. On the one hand she was inwardly insecure, although heaven only knows why. On the other she was confident, adventurous, and game for almost anything. Above all she had a twinkle in her eye and was not immune to mischief, which added to her charm.

She had a warm and compassionate heart which reached out unselfishly to anyone who needed it. Especially the ordinary people whom she was quick and assertive to defend.

She was strong and athletic and eager to participate. She had a mind blessed with a tremendous capacity and I sometimes stood in awe of her.

I remember a very special moment when I held her in my arms for the first time. Both of us trembling with emotion upon the discovery of mutual love. Almost as though we had found something never before known between two people. We seemed to be electrified with emotion, afraid to let go, afraid that it was all a dream, too good to be possible. And when I kissed her sweet lips and saw her misty eyed, my eyes as well began to swell and our tears combined. Tears of joy, tears of peace, which told us both that here and now at last, we had found one another. And all of the pain and hurt that life can deal to every one of us was washed away by our tears.

A gentle calm came over us, and we were at peace. That was the way it all began.

Sometimes in early morning while I am still lying in bed my mind races over all the thoughts of the preceeding days. I had been wrestling with the question of the major theme or themes within this story.

Initially I had felt that the emphasis should be on my travels with Joyce, but as the story developed, other themes beside travel became important. In fact I found myself writing compulsively in defense of the Canada geese which I marvelled at. I also became increasingly aware of the power and beauty of other examples of wildlife around us.

I began to take notice of the habits and activities of the songbirds who visited our feeder, and I found myself watching their performance from our rear upper deck. I began asking questions of friends from the Ottawa Valley about the behaviour of many of the colourful birds who visit and gradually widened my own knowledge of their habits. I became increasingly aware of the hazards and difficulty to survive that all of these creatures contend with.

I also began to sense something spiritual about my thoughts and writings, particularly in light of what has been driving me on and more so as we widened our exposure to first hand knowledge of ancient civilizations. This was especially so when we toured Egypt and the Holy Land which from a religious and cultural standpoint has shaped our lives and beliefs immensely.

I particularly became fascinated by one of the male geese who appears to have shown up on the pond for several years, has fathered dozens of offspring and who is clearly a leader among the flock. He is recognizable by virtue of a scar just above his beak which was pointed out to me three or four years ago when he was only six or seven feet away while we fed his family bread crumbs.

As we ventured out to all of the wonderful places we have been, we inevitably came home to the pond. Watching each phase of the development of the goslings and their interaction with other goose families as they also came home to the pond, the stature and importance of the leader goose continued to grow. It became clear that his role as leader was respected by all including the other mature geese who chose and were allowed by him to reside here.

I was fascinated by the personal self sacrifice he appeared to make in support and defense of his family. I rarely saw him eating. He was always in the sentry position as all the others, including mother, ate voraciously. Even when the mother was resting with the goslings tucked in around her he remained on the alert.

He was courageous, ready to fend off intruders which he would attack at full speed, head and neck extended forward. Even the osprey respected him. His major concern was, and would continue to be, the aggressive behaviour of golf club employees who repeatedly attacked the flock in golf carts.

By early December about 300 Canada geese had gathered on the pond and on the 9th fairway. We could see their markings clearly as they flew past our 2nd floor bedroom window on the way in, barely 50 yards away at eye level.

As they got ready to leave, about 4 p.m., I was mystified by a new pattern.

They lined up on the 9th fairway but took off in individual flights of 5 or 6 geese. After a pause of about 30 seconds the next small flight would take off, repeating this process until all of them had left, but only in small groups.

I am convinced that the origin of Canada geese must have been British. From the day they are born they immediately know enough to form a queue which they continue doing automatically for the rest of their lives.

The pond is now frozen over with a light coating of ice. Near the inlet it is still possible for them to break the ice and bathe their feathers. For many it was their first exposure to ice. There were some hilarious landings as their feet slipped out from under them. We haven't had more than a dusting of snow so there is still grass for them to munch on. Very shortly we will have seen the last of them for this year as they head out, probably for Chesapeake Bay, for the winter. By then, all of the local dogs who are forbidden on the golf course during summer, have a field day, with the links all to themselves. So even once the snow flies, we will still have a source of animal entertainment to amuse us.

In December I had an appointment with Dr. Finkelstein, my dermatologist. This was the fourth quarterly examination since he discovered the melanoma cancer on my temple which he removed a year ago.

I have been blessed with good health and have passed through each quarterly examination without incident. He is very thorough and I am fortunate to have found him in time.

We now move into the second phase where I will be examined every six months.

There is little doubt that the wake up call I received a year ago has stimulated a desire to get moving to see and do things. Joyce has been game for each proposal I have made, and a tremendously compassionate and enthusiastic companion for all we have seen and done together this year.

We are still unwinding from our pressure packed tour of the Middle East, so any thought of major long distance travel is not met with enthusiasm by either of us. Our friends are hot to trot to China, but we will settle for postcards from them.

In March we are booked to Portugal for a month on the Algarve, but we intend to use that more as an opportunity for R & R than touring. We will fly out of Montreal via KLM which affords us the opportunity of a 3 or 4 day stopover in Amsterdam on the return flight.

In a phone call from Peter last night he tells me that they have received an offer on their house in Montreal which he will probably accept. They can then begin looking in earnest for larger quarters which they will need as their family increases.

Sandy is now expected to give birth about December 6th, so all of us including Julie and Philip, our grandchildren, are anticipating this blessed event with great excitement. Our travels in December will no doubt be centred around the new arrival!

My role as a grandfather is coming into play for my daughter Vicky as well. They do not receive T.V. Ontario in the Montreal area. TVO runs a very good children's program called "Elliot Moose" weekdays at 8:30 a.m. My mission, if I choose to accept it, is to tape record 5 or 6 telecasts of "Elliot Moose" for the benefit of my 3 year old granddaughter Sarah. By the time I am finished I will no doubt have become an authority on the moose called Elliot!

It has been a wonderful year of adventure for both of us, capped off with the birth of a new grandson on December 6th. He will be named David.

I was moved to commemorate this event and indeed all of Peter and Sandy's children, with the following poem dedicated to her, and to her family.

And It Was Good

In the beginning there were two, named Julie and Philip.
And it was good.
They grew strong, and handsome, and learned quickly,
And brought great happiness to those around them.
And their father learned his role with diligence,
And did it well.
And their mother made a home for them,
In which there was much love.
Which was reflected in their eyes.
Bright shining eyes, happy eyes,
Eager, energetic eyes.
And it was good.
And it came to pass that they were blessed with a third,
Who came into the world quite tiny,
But strong, alert, and powerful of frame,
And it was good.
And the father was both wise and forthright,
In his role as defender and protector.
And the mother nurtured the child,
With love, tenderness, and goodness.
And it was good.
And the firstborn spoke proudly
Of their new brother.
Who was named David.
And all of them were thankful
For this wonderful gift from God.
And it was good.

Acknowledgements

I thank my daughter Victoria for proposing the idea of recording my observations in the first place. David Waters, whose journalistic expertise and critical suggestions have guided me wisely. My wife Joyce who is my most supportive critic. Daphne Dain who has illustrated my writings so cleverly. I also thank Rev. David Clunie, Katherine Waters and Margaret Shultis for reading the manuscript and offering constructive criticism. Martha Prince who has edited the book with skill and diligence.

David Garred was born in Halifax, Nova Scotia, raised in Montreal and was educated at McGill University, where he studied commerce. His career in the paper industry covered many facets as marketing and general sales manager of important divisions of a major North American producer. Following retirement, he operated his own company as President of D. H. Garred International Inc. His personal interests include the restoration of early Canadian furniture and collecting Canadian art. He makes his home in Kanata, Ontario, overlooking the pond described in the book. This is his first book.

Daphne Dain, who illustrated the book, is both a teacher and artist who runs her own business. She attended London Central School of Design, England. She holds a National Diploma in Design and studied under some of the most prominent artists of the later sixties, such as Victor Passmore and Keith Vaughan. More importantly she was influenced by the genius of Mervyn Peake who became both friend and teacher. Dr. Peake wrote and illustrated the celebrated Gormanghast series which was recently presented on British television and aired in Canada. She resides in Ottawa.